Little Apples Will Grow Again

Ramon Towers

RobRay Publishing

First published in the UK in 2009 by RobRay Publishing

A CIP catalogue record for this title is available from the British Library

ISBN: 978-0-9564036-0-5

Typeset by Andrew Searle

Cover design: RobRay Publishing

Printed and bound in the UK by CPI Anthony Rowe

ROBRAY PUBLISHING
3 Devonshire Street East,
Failsworth, Manchester, M35 0TE
Tel: 0161 683 5446
Email: ramon_towers@yahoo.co.uk

After millions had been killed and maimed in the First World War, King George V was asked in 1919 whether he thought a day of remembrance should be set aside to honour the sacrifice of his subjects. The King dismissed the notion as sentimental nonsense!

Contents

Acknowledgments

Thanks to my niece Marion Hanvey, who was always ready to help in any way; to my sister Jacqueline Towers, who unfortunately died just before the book was published, and especially to Sylvia Barnes, whose typing and patience in changing text to accommodate newly discovered facts was 'beyond the pale'.

Finally, my thanks go to the members of the Queen's Own Highlanders, who allowed me access to the 1st Battalion Seaforth Highlanders' First World War diaries in the Cameron Barracks, Inverness.

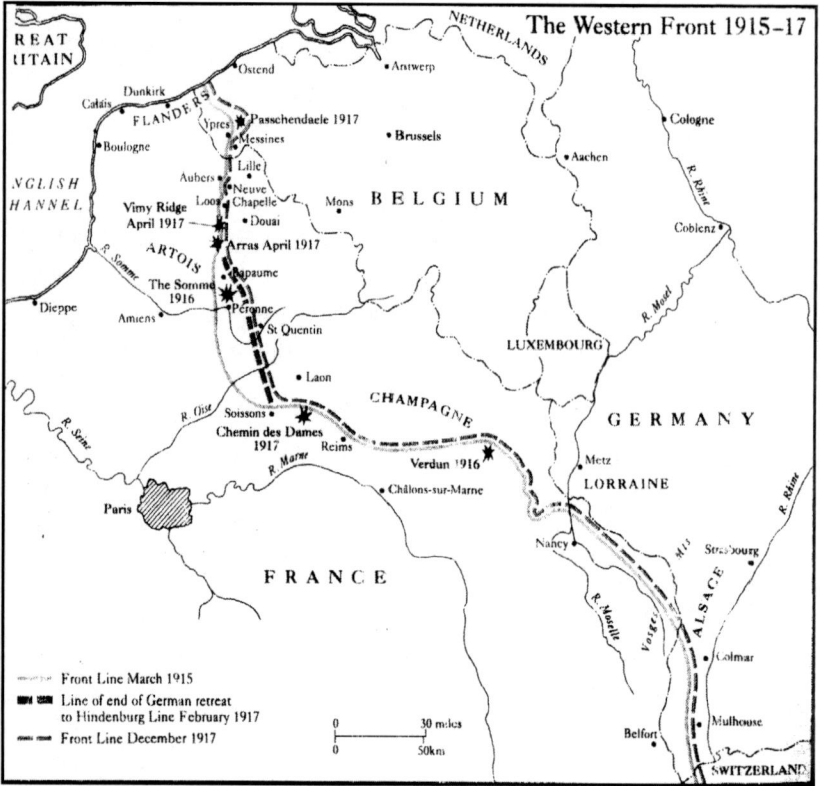

The Western Front 1915–17

GREAT BRITAIN

ENGLISH CHANNEL

NETHERLANDS

Ostend
• Antwerp

Dunkirk
Calais
FLANDERS
Boulogne
Ypres ★ Passchendaele 1917
Messines
Lille
Aubers
Loos Neuve
Chapelle
• Douai
Vimy Ridge
April 1917
★ Arras April 1917
Bapaume ★
The Somme
1916 ★
Péronne
• St Quentin
ARTOIS
• Dieppe
Amiens
R. Somme

• Brussels
Aachen •
BELGIUM
• Mons

Cologne
• Coblenz
R. Rhine

LUXEMBOURG

GERMANY

R. Seine
R. Oise
Soissons •
Chemin des Dames
1917
Reims •
R. Marne
• Laon
CHAMPAGNE
Verdun 1916 ★
• Châlons-sur-Marne

Metz •
LORRAINE
R. Meuse
R. Rhine

Paris
FRANCE

Nancy •
R. Moselle
Strasbourg
Vosges Mts
ALSACE
Colmar •

⎯ Front Line March 1915
▬ Line of end of German retreat
to Hindenburg Line February 1917
▬ Front Line December 1917

0   30 miles
0   50km

Belfort •
Mulhouse •

SWITZERLAND

ONE

Origins

Monday, 12th October 1914, the lights of the port of Marseilles twinkled in the early dawn. The convoy of ships stood off at the harbour mouth awaiting the French tugs to shepherd them into port. The flotilla's escorts, R.I.M.S. Hardinge, Minto and H.M.S. Dartmouth, together with the French battleship 'The Jacques Berry' stood further off from the harbour and signalled with flashing lights to one another. Their charges consisted of 18 transport ships brought from Bombay and Karachi. On Board were the 19th Dehra Dun Brigade, the 7th Meerot Division and soldiers of the 1st Seaforth Highlanders Battalion, who, together with five hundred men of the 1st Leicester Regiment, crammed into one ship, the H.T. Devanha, went to make up the 1st Indian Army.

On the Devanha the men were preparing to disembark. They had breakfasted early, rolled and secured hammocks. With the equipment packed, the men stood above and below decks watching the harbour come to life before them. In the growing light they could make out the rows of tied-up fishing boats, high dock cranes and two tall sailing ships with their furled canvas sails. James Donna, a private in the 1st Seaforth Highlanders, viewed the scene from a cramped lower deck. Donna, a Mancunian, was of average height with brown hair and small facial features, giving him a boyish appearance younger than that of his 23 years. He was a quiet man but by no means timid, although he disliked violence he could 'take care of himself' in a fist fight.

He was born in the Irk Valley, Collyhurst, in 1891 in the Star Inn in Keats Street, just a few yards from the polluted fast-flowing River Irk. In Neolithic times the vale where Donna was born had been covered in dense forests. Centuries later Roman feet had trodden on the beaten meandering track of the Irk. The Danes had foraged up the Irk from the River Irwell a mile to the east. In more recent times Dick Turpin is said to have used the valley road in his dash to York because of its few inhabitants. Not until 1870, when a road was laid and Jones and Pilkington had built cotton mills by the Irk, did the area become populous.

This district attracted mainly Irish migrant workers, who had come inland from Liverpool looking for work; some had followed the railways constructing the huge viaducts that straddled the hills of Collyhurst. One astute man called Higgins had set up a brickworks in the Vale. He supplied bricks to the railway, the mills and later the two-up, two-down houses. There was Fitzgeorge Street, a row of terraced houses which stood beneath the huge viaducts that carried the main Manchester to Leeds railway line. Three rows of houses stood alongside Jones' Mill: Bratt, Bebbington and Appleton Streets. More houses lined the Collyhust Road, and two pubs - the Grapes and the Star Inn - all built from Higgins bricks.

The settlers were poor and hard-working people whose minimum working day was 12 hours. For many the only release was the pub. In Collyhurst there was a tendency towards large families, the reason being that the mortality rate for children under five in the area was over 50%. The new Collyhurst 'ikes' were a bright and talented montage of souls. The people of the area were tough and they brought their own customs, philosophies and religions with them. Catholics and Protestants lived together in the community, yet there was no sectarianism. Grievances were settled not by bottle or club, but with fist fights on Sunday mornings. The venue was always on a spare piece of flat land behind the Grapes public house known as the croft. The croft was where the young boys of the village played football using a pig's bladder as a ball. The land between the Grapes and a huge hill named the 'tip' (due to contractors' habits of discarding refuse on its slopes) witnessed many battles royal, yet afterwards, though bruised and bloodied, they usually shook hands. If a fight was not resolved at the first meeting then the combatants arranged to meet again the following Sunday. Two men once fought on four consecutive Sundays before honour was satisfied and the following morning the victor called at his opponent's house at 5am to make sure he wasn't late for work, such was the spirit of this hard Collyhurst Valley community.

James Donna's father came to live in Collyhurst soon after the death of his first wife. He brought his two small children with him, Joe aged five and his sister Jane, aged four. He moved into number 69 Fitzgeorge Street, next door to a widow, Mrs. Chadd, who also had two small children. James Donna senior was born on a farm near the village of Lymm, Cheshire. He had nine brothers and one sister, all strikingly tall, six feet or over. Even his sister was five feet ten inches tall. They were a resigned, hard-working family, obedient to their parents and hoping one day to run their own farms. All that is except James, who had little time for the rigours of ploughing, planting and harvesting. Every opportunity he got he would be off, 'wasting his time' as his father called it, into the lush Cheshire countryside or getting into scrapes in the village. He endured more than one strapping from his father because of this. The reason for James' lack of interest in life on the land was because from being a small boy he had dreamed of the romance of life at sea and the places to be visited. He learned of the sea from books which painted a rosy picture of the life, omitting the details of how low the pay was, the poor conditions, the diseases etc. The authors of such books no doubt had never been in a wooden ship in a gale.

His father, realising that his son had been lost to the land, had him apprenticed to a shoemaker when he was ten. James, being good with his hands, enjoyed the work and learned the trade quickly. Another crisis occurred when he was 14; he had a minor argument with his father and the young giant left home and decided to make his way to Liverpool, where he planned to sign on a ship. By the time he got to Chester the impetuous lad had a change of mind and decided to enlist in the Grenadier Guards by giving his age as 16 years. In the same year war broke out between Turkey and Russia and he was sent with his regiment to suffer the appalling conditions of the Crimea. After the war ended he was sent to China. When his regiment eventually returned to England and he to Lymm, he met a woman older than himself whose husband had recently died. They married and had two children. His wife, never a strong woman, died when Jane was three years old.

The restlessness stirred in him again and he decided to take his family to Manchester. Once there he left the army after securing a job as a stevedore on the docks, a job for which his credentials could not have been better, an ex-guardsman and a former army heavyweight boxing champion. To work six days a week and raise two small children would have been impossible for James Donna senior had not Mrs. Chadd, the red-haired widow who lived next door, agreed to look after his two children as well as her own. A gentle woman, she not only minded his children but also kept his house clean and had a meal ready for him when he came home at night. Mrs. Chadd became a second mother to his children, so much so that at school other children referred to Donna's children as Joe and Jane Chadd. In return for her devotion to his children and house cleaning, Donna paid her a weekly wage and brought foodstuffs and other merchandise home from the docks.

This arrangement with Mrs. Chadd lasted for about five years. Then he met Mrs. Mary Higgins, an Irish woman born in the Dublin army barracks. Her husband treated her badly and James first showed her kindness when her alcoholic husband threw Mary out of the house late one night after coming home from one of his binges. James gave her shelter for the night and the next morning she returned to her husband, mainly for the sake of the three boys the couple had, but after many months of abuse and ill-treatment she left and moved in with James. Things were peaceful in Fitzgeorge Street until late one night Mr. Higgins came hammering at James' front door demanding his wife back and threatening violence, claiming James had enticed her away. Mary refused to return to her husband and after much arguing the two men decided to meet at the 'croft' on Sunday morning.

At the appointed time, the two combatants left their houses and, coatless, wearing collarless shirts, they made the short journey to the spare piece of land behind the Grapes. The men did not have seconds, but word had got around and more than one door opened at the appointed time and several men in flat caps began to drift towards the croft.

The fight did not last very long. James, though taller than Higgins, was not as stocky and compact. James met Higgins's rushes with hard left and right hooks, knocking him to the ground, where he lay holding his head. James stood glaring down at Higgins for a while, but seeing that he was reluctant to carry on, turned and without a word to the spectators made his way home.

Higgins never bothered James or Mary again. Six months after this incident, it was discovered that Mr. Higgins had emigrated to Canada, taking his three sons and leaving Mary with Donna. As time passed news filtered back to Collyhurst (through a relative) of how the Higgins family had fared in the New World. Their fortunes were certainly mixed. It appears that one of the Higgins sons had been hanged for horse stealing, whilst another son had become champion jockey of Canada.

Mary Higgins, unable to get a divorce, lived with James and became his common law wife. She bore James four children, Richard, Daniel, Elizabeth and James Junior. With his children Joe and Jane from his first wife, the family numbered eight.

Mr. Donna married Mary (twenty-one years his junior) in the autumn of 1876. He was in his early fifties when James Junior was born. James Junior's earliest recollection of his father was of a grey-haired, grey-moustached giant of a man who no one in the family dared to answer back. He was a stern man who socialised little, spending most of his evenings reading or smoking his clay pipe by the fire. Even in the summer, when people in the street sat at their front doors talking well into the warm nights, James Senior either sat on the back yard steps or strolled along Collyhurst Road, crossing the small bridge spanning the Irk. He then climbed the fifty-three stone steps over the railway lines, from where he could gaze down on the valley where he lived. He'd sit alone smoking his pipe, content while thinking his own thoughts. The view from here was reminiscent of where he was born above Lymm village. On his way home he occasionally called into the Star Inn for a pint. No great drinker, he was home and in bed by 11.00pm in preparation for the 6.00am start at Pomona Docks in Old Trafford.

A tough, hard man, he loved his children. Yet he was of a generation that didn't show it openly. Although money was scarce he insisted the best food be bought for the family. To supplement this he brought home from the dockyards chicken and fruit and vegetables when he could. He instilled in his children from an early age the importance of 'looking after your body'. He bought boxing gloves for the boys and taught them in the summer how to defend themselves. In the back yard, sessions of swinging Indian clubs to develop shoulder and arm muscles had to be gone through before the lads were allowed to play outdoors. These sessions usually took place two or three times a week, with Joe, the oldest lad, taking charge if their father was too tired or not at home to oversee the exercises. Joe was 18 years old, tall and serious like his father. He had been thinking of joining the army; he was at the stage of his life when he wanted more than the mill. He wanted adventure, to travel, and joining the army was the way he thought he could achieve this just as his father had done before him.

"Come on you lot, let's get some training done, the skills you lean now will insure you for later life," Joe would say, echoing his father's words.

Richard used to play Joe up, pretending he had hurt his arm or had a stomach ache. The two younger lads used to do the same when they were fed up with all the exercising. They knew that Joe was more easy going than 'the old man'. How different it was when their father was at home, no one dared to raise their voice, let alone refuse to do an errand. The 'old man' only needed to look at the offender over his glasses and his stare caused any dissent to flee. As the years passed, James senior became stern, even with Mary, and more than once she had felt the back of his hand.

Jane was like Joe in appearance, tall with the same dark colouring but a year younger. She helped run the house and look after the four younger children. This was when she wasn't earning money by collecting scrap iron and old clothing for re-cycling. Her hired handcart covered quite a few miles when the weather permitted, helping to supplement the family income.

Richard at last left St. Oswald's School in Forest Street and took a job at the Collyhurst Finishing Company. His headmaster told his mother that he was the only pupil to stay in Standard Four for three years. Far from being a dullard Richard was a bright child and certainly on a par with the rest of the class. The teachers were at a loss to explain why Richard always failed the end of term Standard Five examination. He took quite a bit of ribbing from his parents and schoolmates for this, but it did not seem to bother him. The truth of the matter was that, as young as he was, he had fallen in love with his teacher, Miss Shaw. She was a pretty girl of 20 years and Richard couldn't bear to leave her class.

There were few flush toilets in Collyhurst at the time, and out of school Richard's favourite source of amusement, like some of the other lads at the time, was 'lighting up middens'. The midden was the name given to the latrine each house had in the yard. Situated in a small brick outhouse, it consisted of a tin commode toilet which had a small wooden door set into the yard wall just behind it. It was through this door that the council 'muck men' emptied the contents, usually once a week, as they moved from house to house along the entries behind the rows of dwellings. The young miscreants used to wait quietly by the midden door until they heard the occupant of the house come into the yard and enter the toilet. The lads would then light a piece of newspaper, open the wooden door and thrust the torch onto the bare behind of the sitter before racing off down the alleyway bursting with howls of laughter.

Richard loved a joke. He also loved sugar, three and some times four spoonfuls to a cup of tea. His father was forever lecturing him for his excess because when he finished his tea there would be a quarter to a half-inch of undissolved sugar in the bottom of his cup. Dick looked attentive enough when his father pointed out the waste in the bottom of his cup and how unnecessary it was. He had heard the same dialogue scores of times, but it made little impression, he still shovelled the sugar into his tea.

Daniel, meanwhile, was 12 years old, a big strong boy for his age, one his father often predicted would be the tallest in the family. Daniel, with his mass of brown hair often falling into his eyes, was sometimes clumsy about the house. Dan was often grumbled at for knocking ornaments from the mantelpiece, or for upending utensils on the dining table. In the kitchen there was a medicine shelf where the family stored their remedies: bottles of linctus, febrifuge, toothache tincture and so on. It would be a safe bet to the rest of the family in the living room that if Dan was quiet he'd be in the kitchen stood on a chair at the medicine shelf, drinking from a large bottle of cod liver oil as though it was lemonade.

Daniel would often bring home injured animals of some type, a half-starved dog or a pigeon unable to fly. He was allowed to keep them in a wooden box he kept in the yard where he tended them until they either died or got back to good health and scampered off. Once he brought home a black and white kitten which had been mauled by a dog and had an eye hanging out, resting on the animal's cheek. On the kitchen table covered with newspaper, Daniel held the kitten while his father cleaned the wound and carefully pushed the eye back into the socket. Then he fixed a lint and bandage dressing over the orb and a cardboard collar was fastened around the kitten's neck to prevent it from pulling the dressing off. For three weeks the little invalid was allowed to stay indoors, where Dan looked after it religiously, even giving it a few drops of the precious cod liver oil every day. In time the wounds healed and the animal recovered, but the retina of the eye must have been damaged because when the cat leaped from one level to another it either overshot or fell short, until it learned to angle the good eye forward to improve its judgement. It acquired the name 'Isiah' or 'eyes higher'. Isiah stayed with the Donnas for a couple of months, until one morning when Dan went into the back yard to feed it before going to school and discovered it had left.

Elizabeth Donna was a round-faced pretty girl or ten with her mother's features in miniature. She had red hair done in plaits, the only member of the family to possess that hair colour, a throwback to the women of her father's family. She was a helpful and hard-working girl, usually busy with housework or assisting her mother with the cooking. When she wasn't helping around the house with the chores she would play whip and top in the street, or play 'house' on the croft. On Fridays after the evening meal she liked to curl and set her mother's hair in the kitchen; her mother with a towel around her shoulders often dozed in her chair as the little fingers gently combed and curled the greying locks with setting lotion. Elizabeth, or 'Tizzie' as her father called her, slept with Jane and her mother in the back bedroom whilst the males in the family had the front bedroom of the small two-bedroomed house.

James Donna was four years younger than Tizzie, and like the youngest of many families his parents indulged him more than the rest. He, unlike Elizabeth, Richard and Daniel, had been born in the pub in Keats Street. James Donna senior, aware that another child was on the way and hoping to improve his circumstances, had applied to the Cornbrook Brewery for the post of Landlord. His subsequent letters and interviews with the brewery had impressed the owners and he was granted a licence to manage the inn.

However, it was not long before the family found they had swapped one verminous dwelling for another just as bad. The cellar was overrun with shiny blackjack beetles. Most of the houses in the vale had bed bugs and the Star was no exception. Regardless of how much effort was put into scrubbing and cleaning with disinfectant, washing and changing the bedding, the parasites were never completely vanquished. Indeed, most people in Collyhurst welcomed the winter months, when the bed bugs had hibernated, giving their hosts a few months of undisturbed sleep.

In the Star, Donna senior did his best to relieve the situation by sealing all holes and chinks in the floorboards and skirting, but the beetles still managed to invade the lower floors during the hours of darkness. These verminous conditions were typical, though it varied in the degree of infestation. When tenants complained to their landlords the complainants were accused of not being clean in their habits. Another favourite explanation given was that the flour and water solution most poor people used to save money to stick the wallpaper on the walls was the cause of the bugs. In later years this was proved to be pure fabrication designed by the landlords to divert blame onto the tenants. Untreated foreign timber and hurried foundations were the real reason for the parasites.

James junior was born in June when the bugs were at their most active. It was December three years later that the family moved back to Fitzgeorge Street, to No. 36 this time. There was, however, one dubious advantage that came out of his time spent in the Star. It was from his perch at the counter that he learned to play cribbage by watching the men playing card games in the vault.

Young James slept in a big bedroom at the front of the house with Daniel and Richard. Bedtime usually meant a few tears for James, not that he was afraid of the dark because he had his brothers upstairs to accompany him. The reason for the tears was that once settled in bed with his brother, Daniel would pinch him on the arms and legs with his fingernails, the result being that James would cry himself to sleep. It was a couple of years later that James learned the reason for Daniel's strange behaviour at bedtime. Daniel could always get around his mother and he had an agreement with her which was that, providing he could get young James off to sleep, he could go back downstairs for an hour or so.

Collyhurst, like other poor communities, had its share of characters. There was Tom McCarthy, a textile worker whose clogged feet could be heard every morning at 4.00am as he clip-clopped down Bebbington Street as he walked to work in Irlam, Salford. Tom, a short square man who had been a good boxer in his time, walked the eight miles to work and eight miles back at the end of his shift at the mill every day, summer and winter.

Wicked Walter Jones lived in a house near the Irkdale Dyeing and Bleaching Company, and a more genial, smiling villain you couldn't wish to meet. He did no work yet he always had money. Women found him irresistible and every week it seemed he would be seen stomping down Collyhurst Road with a different female on his arm. Yet his behaviour with them was far from gentle. A few sported cut lips or black eyes. Jones had a gang of about half a dozen reprobates who used to meet in a public house in Angel Meadow, a rough district about half a mile from his home. It was in the back room of the pub that Jones used to gather information and plan the various illegal ventures that he and the gang were continuously involved in.

However, justice finally caught up with him. He was charged and convicted of the murder of a nightwatchman who was guarding road diggings near to the pub where he and the gang met. The newspapers reported the case for the Crown, which was that while passing by late one night Jones observed the nightwatchman asleep in his small wooden hut in front of the large coke fire. In an act of malice he tipped the hut and the man inside onto the white hot coals, resulting in the poor man's death. Walter Jones was sentenced to death, later changed to life imprisonment. His gang got various terms of hard labour. The remarkable thing about Jones was that although he led such an active life in crime and in the bedroom, he was disabled and needed a crutch to get about.

There was also 'Pigeon Billy', who neglected his wife and spent every moment in his back yard coop with his birds. Billy devoted his life to the pigeons while his wife came a poor second.

Mr and Mrs Stringer were another family of local interest. George, the husband, was a Protestant from Ulster and his wife, Margaret, was a Catholic from Southern Ireland. The Stringers had five children, Sarah, Catherine, Margaret, William and John. They had lost their youngest son, George, who died aged nine months. The Stringers were typical of a Collyhurst family, seven or eight people living in a two-bedroomed house.

Irish Molly was an exception. She lived alone, an eccentric woman whose family had either died or left her. She had a mania for scrubbing and cleaning. Her day started at 6.00am with a bucket of warm water and a cloth. She would donkey stone the pavement at her front door, sweep and donkey stone the slabs at her back door whilst continually talking to herself, after which she would start on her house. She scrubbed the floors and cleaned the walls from top to bottom with the occasional break for a cup of tea. She never drank or used tobacco and went to bed early to save gaslight. In her mental condition she could not work and she eked out an existence with the help of neighbours, who brought her small basins of potato hash or whatever they could spare. Once a week a charitable body called 'the Board of Guardians' visited her in their long dark coats and tall hats. The Guardians' visits were to ascertain Molly's means, questioning her to see if she had worked or come by any money that week. They usually stayed for half an hour and before leaving they'd put a few shillings on the mantelpiece for rent and a pittance for food.

In common with other poor and exploited communities, the people were taught to fear the Almighty; the Catholics of Collyhurst all went to church on Sunday whether they wanted to or not. Woe betide any person, child or adult, who was absent from worship without good reason. The priest or nuns soon sought out the offenders at school or in the home, where they were subjected to ecclesiastical bullying.

For Protestants religion was easier, though the Reverend, like his Catholic counterpart, visited the homes of some of his absentee flock. His manner was more persuasive and conciliatory, so for a lot of Protestants Sunday was a day to catch up on sleep and rest after the week's toil. The Protestant Church was never as full as the Catholic Church, but both were influenced by the Good Book, as illustrated by the names they gave their children. There was Aaron Mills, Abel Roberts, Zachariah and Adam Perslow, Luke Murphy, Jeremiah Murphy and others.

It was common, especially in summer, to go to school and play in the streets in bare feet, the idea being that they should save the footwear for bad weather, especially rain and the winter conditions. Nevertheless, the sight of shoeless urchins sometimes wearing only socks picking their way through the snow on their way to school was far from an uncommon sight. Once at school the children without clogs were allowed to dry their socks in readiness for the return journey home through the bad weather.

To the authorities and the religious zealots of the church, spiritual help seemed far more important than bodily need. To Donna senior, like a few free thinkers in Collyhurst, the sight of children unshod in the bitter conditions caused within him a cold fury, especially when the ecclesiastical preached about the meek and the poor inheriting the earth.

'Only fucking six feet of it,' he would grunt to himself.

TWO

Fucking good oranges

It was just after 10.00am when the Devanha dropped anchor, the gangplank went down and the Seaforths began disembarking. All along the seafront other ships of the convoy were doing likewise. Lines of Sepoy and Gurkha troops, burdened with rifles and kit bags, were streaming onto the dockside and lining up into companies before being marched short distances to harbour buildings where they were to spend the next 24 hours.

'A' Company's billet for the night had once been a tea warehouse. Loose tea still lay between the cobbles of the floor. Now the building was filled with two-tiered bare wire bunks. Donna chose a bunk along one wall of the warehouse. He slumped down and was joined by George Campbell, a giant of a man, and James Robb. The three of them busied themselves unslinging packs and kit bags. The minimum of unpacking was done as this was only a temporary stay, tomorrow they would be moving off again.

"Why the stop here Jimmy?" asked Donna of Robb, who had just lit a cigarette.

"Well av heered we're to be issued with a new rifle," he replied. "A weapon that can fire o're hills," he added with a smile.

Robb was an inch or so taller than Donna, a slim dark man with a pencil moustache. From Sutherlandshire in the Scottish Highlands, he gave the impression that he was from a reasonably wealthy family. However, he spoke little of his past and it seemed that he was something of a black sheep. Despite this he was a popular man in 'A' Company and had befriended Donna a couple of years before when the Englishman was sent to Agra from England to make up battalion strength.

At the Seaforth barracks off the General Maguire Road in Agra, Donna was drafted into 'A' Company, whose whitewashed bungalows faced north to the hills of Kalanah. Donna, not by nature a man who made friends easily, found that the men in his bungalow were veteran soldiers who had served in India for years. Some had fought in South Africa and wore the Boer War medal ribbon. Donna didn't care for these Scots and felt alien amongst them so kept himself to himself.

At the end of the day's duties, when the men were not required for guard, they relaxed on their charpoys and talked or smoked pipes on the veranda. Donna preferred to change into a pair of shorts and a singlet and go running out into the Indian countryside at a steady pace. His run normally covered about five miles. He usually arrived back at camp by dusk, by which time the bungalow would be deserted save for a lone letter writer, most of the men by this time having gone to the nearby village or the canteen for a drink. This was more or less the pattern of his life for weeks, hardly speaking to anyone unless asked a direct question. He liked to keep his own company, finding some relief in the odd letter home, until one warm evening as he entered the bungalow and stepped past the old Indian punkah wallah asleep, still clutching the rope. He heard laughter and the clamour of voices. He was perspiring from his run, but now he grew tense, for grouped round his empty bed were half a dozen Jocks. To a soldier his bed and locker were personal, his only possessions in a regimented life, and were forbidden to others, except by invitation.

He felt his heart beat faster as he glided across the highly polished floor of the bungalow towards the group. The men noticed him and grew silent as he drew near. Donna deliberately brushed against the man nearest his locker. From the top of the cabinet he took a towel and draped it across his shoulders. His stomach was tight; he trembled a little, not with fear, but with adrenaline. His face was drained of colour as he looked into the semi-circle of bronzed faces, all with close-cropped hair, some with moustaches. He was ready for action, but realistically he realised that there were too many of them to take on by himself. Donna thought that if only he could wallop a couple of these Scots bastards before they got him he would be satisfied.

He stood, hands on hips, facing the men, expecting some snide remark about his family or his nationality. He measured the jaw of the man nearest to him, then a voice cut in.

"What's yer name?"

There was a pause and he replied, "Donna." Then he said testily, "Have you never seen a bed before?"

There was another moment of silence, then the first voice cut in again.

"Thank God fe' that. We all thought that ye' had ne' spoken to us these last few weeks because ye' wer' dumb."

There was a roar of good-natured laughter.

Donna looked at each one in turn and saw there was no malice in their eyes. He felt the tension leaving him and smiled, 'These men have a point,' he thought to himself.

Another man with black hair and a thin moustache spoke.

"Do yer' run every night Donna because ye've nay money for a dram?"

Donna shook his head. "No, I run to keep healthy. I've been doing it for so long now I suppose it's become a habit."

"Och well, anyway I've put a few rupees under yer pillow in case ye' fancy a dram later," said the man as he and his companions began to drift away from the Englishman's bed.

Later, having showered and changed, Donna found ten rupees under his pillow, left by James Robb. After that night Donna felt less isolated amongst these men.

In the afternoon the warehouse bustled with activity. The men, having been issued with the new Lee Enfield Mark 3 rifle, sat about on packs and bunks cleaning away the preservative grease and getting used to the feel of the new weapon. Donna laid the new rifle aside and started scratching his calf just below the hose top.

"This place is lousy," he said.

Campbell was rubbing his back against a wooden upright, one or two others were fidgeting also.

"What do ye' think of the new rifle?" Robb asked of Campbell, who had fought in the Boer War.

"Well, feels lighter and I'd say quite a wee bit shorter than the Mark 2 but ahm no sure it'll be able to shoot roon hills," he replied dryly. He shouldered the gun and, squinting down the barrel, took aim at the rafters in the warehouse roof. "Ye' ken during the South African War we had the old Martini Enfield rifles. They were heavier and not as accurate as the Mark 2," he continued, breaking off to scratch his back again.

It was then that Lieutenant Roylance entered the building. He started calling for attention and silence.

"I wonder what that twat's after," murmured Donna.

Roylance was a short, dark-haired Scot whose red and white glengarry always looked too small for his head. He had small piggy eyes set into a fat pasty face. Accompanying him was the tall gloomy-looking Sergeant Cooper, carrying a thick bundle of typewritten paper under one arm. Most of the men in the company had little time for the officer. In any fighting force a soldier needs and has to earn the respect of his comrades. An officer, together with other aspects, is judged by the men he leads by his integrity and example. Roylance drank too much and was petty and vindictive.

During his time in Agra, Donna had suffered his displeasure on numerous occasions. On the Battalion's shooting range, where twice a year each man had to 'shoot for his pay' in a test of rapid fire and accuracy with the rifle, the Englishman had scored highly on the former, but with the maxim machine gun he recorded 580 hits out of a possible 600 score on his first sweep. An almost equally brilliant score of 570 on his second pass broke the regiment's record of 520, previously held by the lieutenant. However, Donna paid for his success on the range by being awarded extra duties courtesy of the lieutenant.

On the parade ground, on occasions he had previously been awarded the 'stick' for being deemed the smartest soldier. Because of this there were rumours originating from 'A' Company's office of a stripe for Donna. Instead, Littler, another man from the Company, got it, but Donna didn't mind. He liked Littler and anyway Littler had been in 'A' Company longer than the Englishman.

Donna enjoyed service life in India: the somewhat relaxed discipline, the native boot boys who cleaned your kit for a few annas, the colour and smells of the bazaars, the warm scented nights, the deep fire of the sun below the hills. Even the route marches up the Khuds and the singing of columns as they swung along the dusty roads with shouldered arms he enjoyed.

Lieutenant Roylance was speaking again.

"The battalion is to spend the night here. Reveille is at 6.00am, breakfast 6.30am. 'A' Company will be ready to move off at 8.00am."

"Where to sir?" someone added.

"Ye'll find out when we get there."

"What aboot leave sir?" another voice asked.

"I'm coming to that," Roylance barked impatiently. "The C.O. is allowing ye' a few hours to stretch yer legs, defaulters are ta' stay behind and guard. Remember," he continued, emphatically, "behave yer selves. Anyone rolling back drunk or late will be charged and dealt with at the next camp. That's all, carry on with whatever ye' were doing".

Before he left the billet, he ordered Corporal Cooper to issue each man with a copy of the typewritten bundle he was carrying.

The leaflet read:

MEN OF THE BRITISH ARMY

You are ordered abroad as a soldier of the King to help our French comrades against the invasion of a common enemy. You will have to perform a task that will need your courage, your energy, and your patience. Remember the honour of the British

Army depends on your individual conduct and perfect steadiness under fire but also to maintain a most friendly relation with those with whom you are helping in this struggle. The operations in which you are engaged will for the most part take place in a friendly country and you can do your country no better service than in showing yourself in France and in Belgium in the true character of a British soldier

Be invariably courteous and kind, never do anything likely to injure or destroy property and always look upon looting as a disgraceful act. You are sure to meet with a welcome and be trusted. Your conduct must justify that welcome and trust. Your duty cannot be done unless your health is sound so keep constantly on your guard against any excess. In this new experience you may find temptation in wine and women. You must entirely resist both temptations and while treating all women with perfect courtesy you should avoid any intimacy.

Do your duty bravely. Fear God. Honour the King

Kitchener, Field Marshal

****

The streets near the Marseilles waterfront were narrow and cobbled. They sloped upwards and were bordered by high terraced dwellings. Water ran slowly down the gutters and vanished into the sewer openings. A few negroes sat in doorways watching the soldiers with indifference. Black-headed seagulls wheeled and dived above or perched like masked robbers on the flat roofs. The area stank of fish; clouds of flies hovered above the piles of horse droppings on the broader thoroughfares.

Away from the dock area the town opened up into vistas of two and three-storied houses painted in bright shades of pink, blue and white. There were soldiers everywhere.

Donna and Robb, armed with a few francs issued aboard ship, wandered aimlessly, peering into shop windows and weaving in and out of other uniforms doing likewise. Initially, George Campbell had been with the two men but, characteristic of the big Highlander, something or someone had caught his interest and he had wandered off. The sound of a Lancashire accent made Donna turn and move nearer to a group of soldiers clustered round a fruit vendor. Their khaki uniforms bore the badge of The Manchester Regiment. It was a sublime pleasure for Donna to listen unobtrusively to his home town tongue being spoken after such a long time. He listened to one of the soldiers explaining to the street hawker in a mixture of pigeon French, Lancastrian and sign language.

"If you want to sell oranges, say 'fucking good oranges'. Parley? Understand?"

"Ah, oui," smiled the French barrow boy.

The sound of accordion music drew the two Seaforths into a café in one of the side streets. The tables around the door were filled with soldiers and one or two prostitutes with rouged faces. Inside there were more tables and uniforms. Just by the door a little old man of about 80 years sat perched on the top of a pair of step ladders playing the squeeze box; on his shoulder perched a small monkey wearing a collar and a red fez.

Robb nudged Donna and nodded to where Campbell and another man from 'A' Company were sitting at a table talking to two artillerymen. Cigarette smoke hung in a bank near the ceiling. The café buzzed with conversation.

"Vin monsieur?" asked the barman.

Robb shook his head and held up two fingers. "Two mugs of coffee with rum," he said.

The Frenchman looked puzzled, his appearance, or what was visible of him above the counter, was of a middle-aged man of about 50 years with straight grey hair brushed back and a black waxed moustache. He wore a blue striped collarless shirt and a dirty grey apron. Robb tried again, more slowly this time. Again the barman didn't understand, he held his head to one side and shrugged, lifting his hands in a gesture of hopelessness. Then Donna picked up an empty pot off the counter and with his finger indicated three quarters up the cup.

"Coffee," he said deliberately. Then he pointed to a bottle on the shelf behind the bartender. The bottle contained a dark brown liquid, but it was the label that attracted Donna's attention. It depicted a white sailing ship on a blue sea. He motioned the Frenchman to give him the bottle; one sniff was enough for Donna. It was rum all right. He indicated the last quarter of the pot mug, pointed to the bottle and said, slowly, "Rum."

For a moment the Frenchman looked mystified, then his face lit up with a sudden understanding. "Voilà, caffee crum," he shouted. "Voilà, caffee crum," he shouted again.

On a call from Campbell, the two men took their steaming mugs and threaded their way through the tables. By the time they got to where

Fucking good oranges

Campbell and his companion sat, the two artillerymen had left. Rabb Laidlaw, the other man from 'A' Company, made a space amongst the bottles for Robb and Donna to place their drinks.

"Ye know we could be hame for Hogmanay if, as everyone says, the war will be o'er by Christmas," said Robb as he sat down.

Campbell and Laidlaw looked at him with that rather bright-eyed look men get who are half drunk. Campbell shrugged and took a swig from his wine.

"Ah dinna ken, six month? It's hard ta' say."

"The two artillery men who jess left told us," said Laidlaw, indicating himself and Campbell. "Their C.O. had a signal saying the War Office estimate the war ta' be over by January at the latest."

"Ah, but January o' what fucking year?" asked Campbell. "How about yer'sel' Donna. What de ye' think?"

Donna shook his head. "I dinna know but I've heard ducks quack afore."

After three years with these Scotsmen his speech sometimes, not surprisingly, took on the cadence of the men around him. He nodded towards Campbell. "Ye' should know George, the war in South Africa was supposed to last but a month but those Boers could fight and the war lasted three years."

Campbell nodded in agreement. "Aye, they were brave men," he said quietly, "an' first class shots."

The table grew serious for a moment. Then little bow-legged Laidlaw got to his feet.

"Ah'm away," he slurped, "these square 'eds have ne' met the like of me yet."

He tapped his bayonet at his belt. "A year at the most an we'll all be gone awa' from France. Will ye' have a dram Jimmy? Donna?"

The two men shook their heads and without a word Laidlaw shuffled off to the counter for more drink.

It was then that the accordion player's monkey caused curses and laughter, flitting from table to table sneaking drinks and collecting coins in a brass cup.

"Aboot the size of yours?" asked Robb to Donna, indicating the animal. Donna looked at him and nodded.

The monkey to which Robb referred concerned an episode that happened back in India. One day the Englishman purchased a young monkey for a few annas in the bazaar. With its cheeky antics it was a source of amusement in the bungalow. One of its tricks was to pull the hair of anyone who happened to fall asleep. Another was to take items from Donna's tunic pockets and hide them amongst the folds

27

of his mosquito net. It was responsible for a few curses, but far more amusement, a welcome relief from bungalow life.

At night Donna had the animal tethered to a post a little way off the bungalows so as not to disturb his comrades' rest. It was an arrangement that seemed to work well. However, one morning he went as usual to feed and release the animal and found the monkey in a pathetic little heap. It had a bullet hole in the head; the rope was still attached to its collar. The night before Donna had not slept in the bungalows. He had been on guard duty on the camp's perimeter. Apparently everyone questioned seemed not to have seen or heard anything unusual. James Robb, who had been on guard duty with Donna, shed some light on the affair after he had a word with one of the char wallahs. It seemed Lieutenant Roylance was seen drunk at about 1.00am with a pistol in hand the night the monkey was shot.

Another aspect, which someone mentioned and Donna had not thought of, was that just ten days before the Englishman had bettered Roylance's score on the machine gun range. On reflection, it was the type of callous act that Roylance was capable of. Donna also remembered a bungalow kit inspection a few months before, when the Lieutenant had kicked the old white-bearded pankah wallah, who had fallen asleep still holding the rope, in the head to wake him from his doze. In the old man's moustached face he had seen something of his father's features, but he was powerless to act against the officer. It was only with a great effort that he remained at attention while the inspection went ahead.

****

Laidlaw came back to the table with four bottles of wine.

"Heer ye' go," he said, and placed a bottle each before Donna and Robb. The other two were for himself and Campbell. The little man dismissed a look of reproach with a wave. "Och away Jimmy, ah con spend ma' money on what ah wanta'. Ye live but once, drink up mon." He took a swig from the bottle, then dived his hand into his tunic pocket. "Did ah tell ye' ah had a letter from ma' sister Mary? She's a bonny lass so she is." He gazed at Donna with heavy drink-laden eyes taking in his youthful boyish appearance. "Ave ye' no' a lass back home Donna?" asked Laidlaw. Donna shook his head a little self-consciously. "Will ye no write to ma sister in Perth? Oh she's a bonny lass, lang broon hair, wee and slim, ah so bonny," he said reflectively.

Before Donna could reply, Campbell spoke. "Does she look a bit like yoursel'?"

"Och, no," replied Laidlaw. "Bonnier than me, but she does have ma bow legs, but that's a good thing in a woman, good for getting a grip when ye're abed," he said with a roar of laughter.

Laidlaw, who was five years older than Donna and more worldly, knew that talk of fornicating embarrassed the Manchester man. Although he had two sisters, Donna always felt awkward and tongue-tied when in the company of a pretty girl. He envied these men who were completely at ease and witty when dealing with the fair sex.

On his last leave home before sailing for India he had been secretly envious seeing lads and girls he had known from school walking hand in hand together down Collyhurst Road, laughing happily oblivious to everyone else.

On his last night of leave he had gone with his brother Richard to the 'Hedge' public house on Rochdale Road. Gedder Jones, a lad whose parents owned a second-hand shop, had gone with them. It being mid-week there were few other customers in the bar, so the three young men took their threepenny pints of Cornbrook mild ale into the small vault where a quartet of labourers, who were acquaintances of Richard, sat playing cards. After nodded greetings the three sat and talked. As time passed the men's room began to fill up with more drinkers. Someone invited Richard, who enjoyed a reputation for being a good darts thrower, to a game. After he had got up to take the challenge, Donna turned to Gedder.

"How's your Liza getting on these days?"

"Not bad," replied Gedder, taking a swig from his glass.

"Is she courting yet?"

Gedder shook his head.

Donna continued reflectively. "She was a belting girl. She was in my class at school yer know!"

"Yes, I know, she was allus talking about the mischief you an Bob Brady got up to at Oswald's."

Richard interrupted them. "Fancy a game, Jim?"

Donna, due in a few hours to leave for distant lands, was disinclined to waste precious time throwing darts and said, "No thanks, you play him Gedder!"

His embarkation for India not far from his thoughts, Donna watched his brother beat a succession of opponents. At 11.00pm the three left the pub. But not before Richard had bought two bottles of stout for his mother and Tizzie. At the end of the narrow entry leading from Rochdale Road to an area called 'Jane's Hole', where Gedder lived, the three stopped and Gedder held out his hand and said: "Have a good trip Jim and take care of yourself." His handshake was firm and sincere.

"Thanks Joe. Goodnight."

"Goodnight, God bless."

The brothers carried on down the steep Brydenvilla Street, which led to the crescent-shaped gas-lit Fitzgeorge Street. Though it was well past 11.00pm it was one of those warm summer evenings where the sky stays light almost until midnight. The street skirted the fields known as the Redhills, an area of about sixteen acres of rising grassland with a central hump of red sandstone; at it's northern edge was the Leeds railway embankment.

A sudden warm breeze carried the scents of grasses and wild flowers to the two quiet strollers, then on the air floated the soft music of a girl's laughter, its courting owner hidden amongst the purple shadows of the grassland. Donna, unable to explain why, sighed and felt very lonely at that moment. Dick, usually so cheerful, said very seriously: "India is a hell of a long way away Jim. Make sure you come back, for the family's sake."

Donna looked at him. "Come on," he said, slapping him on the shoulder, "I'll be all right."

****

The table was now full of empty bottles, Donna, Robb and Campbell each having taken turns to buy wine. It was noisier and smokier now in the café, the man with the accordion had gone and it was getting dark outside. Oil lamps were lit and the conversation ebbed and flowed, speculating on how long the war would last, where they were going and when they would get leave home. At another table a group of Leicesters suddenly began singing. Soon everyone in the place joined in. The songs they were singing were 'Mademoiselle From Armentiers', It's A Long Way To Tipperary' and 'There's A Long Long Trail A Winding'.

The noise and the cheap wine began to affect Donna and he felt he needed air. He got to his feet, fumbled with his rifle strap, slung the weapon clumsily over his shoulder, threw a few coins on the table for the next round of drinks and then, because of the noise, took leave of his comrades with just a wave of his hand.

He was thankful to be out of the café and out into the fresh air. Almost immediately his buzzing head began to clear. He felt the need to relieve himself and did so at the primitive public toilet, which stank. The ammonia smell helped to clear his senses. He made his way towards the waterfront, passing houses and shops lit by coloured lanterns. High above the town the medieval church he'd first noticed from the Devanha also showed a light. He left the side streets and took the broad cobbled waterfront road. En route back to the warehouse he heard the fruit vendor shouting, "Oranges, furking gud oranges".

THREE

Officers only

8.00am on an overcast morning found the Seaforth Highlanders First Battalion fell in in four ranks on a cobbled road before the warehouse where they had spent the previous night. They were lined up in companies with 'A' at the head and 'B', 'C' and 'D' companies lined up behind. At the rear came the regiment's support company, the cooks, storemen and drivers who managed the lines of transport wagons and teams of mules conveying the battalion's stores and equipment. Each soldier carried a F.S.M.O., which stood for 'Full Service Marching Order', together with other items consisting of a pack: rolled ground sheet, ammunition pouches slung across the chest, water bottle, bayonet and scabbard hung from the webbing waist belt and the newly issued short Lee Enfield Rifle Mark 3.

The men stood at ease awaiting the order to come to attention, the four pipers took up their positions ahead of 'A' Company and the officers and senior N.C.O. of each company stood facing their men ready to give the necessary orders before moving off. Roylance stood at ease with both hands behind his back; his face looked pale and more bloated than usual in the grey light. Colonel Richie, the battalion commander, and Major Wright, his number two, were on horseback a little way ahead of the columns. They were talking to two staff officers, one British, the other French.

"How far to our first camp, Captain?" asked Richie of the Frenchman.

"La Valentine? 12 kilometres, Colonel."

The Colonel nodded. "That's about eight miles?"

"Oui, Colonel."

Colonel Richie turned to Major Wright. "Go and find out what the hold up is Jimmy," he said, inclining his head towards the battalion.

"Yes, Sir," replied Major Wright, who heeled his horse into a trot.

He found Regimental Sergeant Major Macrae impatiently watching the last wagon being loaded. "The C.O.'s getting a wee bit impatient Sergeant Major," called Major Wright from the saddle.

Macrae saluted. "Ma apologies to the Colonel, Sir," he said, a little red-faced. "The battalion is nearly ready."

Twenty minutes later the orders to attention, shoulder arms and right turn were given to each company. Then a pause, a moment of complete silence, before Macrae's bellow sent the Seaforths moving forward. Almost at once the pipers at the head of the column broke forth with 'Scotland The Brave'.

The regiment made a fine sight as they swung along with their khaki tunics, dark Mackenzie tartan kilts and red and white diced hose and glengarries; the magic of the pipes made fuzzy heads clear, chests swell and backs straighten. These were proud men of a proud regiment, first raised in the Highlands in 1778 and whose record was second to none.

Military and French policemen held up traffic and cleared the way for the battalion as it marched through Marseilles. The townspeople cheered and waved hats and scarves, red-cheeked women threw flowers from windows. There came shouts of 'Vive L'Ecosse' as dark-eyed urchins tried to keep in step with the soldiers.

Half an hour later, the town and the cheers behind them and the pipes now silent, the battalion marched through mainly flat scrubland. At almost noon they halted at two farm buildings lining the road. On a wooden notice painted in white were the words 'La Valentine Transit Camp'. A little while later the soldiers were busy pitching their khaki 160lb bell tents within the camp confines. Eight men slept to each tent; the beds were palliasses on wooden boards. The men slept in regulation order of heads to the tent walls, feet to the centre. There was a practical reason for this, for on the frontiers in India the Pathans, or musclemen as they were known, often came down from the hillsides to rob. Their method was to cover their bodies in monkey grease and steal into the army camps at night. They sought mainly rifles and blankets from the sleeping men. The Pathans were a very patient race and could move past the guards like shadows, with the grease on their bodies to prevent capture. The robberies, although small, were an irritant to the British Army. The soldiers were instructed that should one of them wake to find that their comrade facing them was being robbed, he was simply to lie still and alert the man opposite by tapping his foot with his own, then both could combine to apprehend the thief.

At La Valentine, the battalion was confined to camp, their time being taken up mainly by parades and inspections. Off duty the men wrote letters, played cards or speculated about the war. Colonel Richie and Major Wright were billeted at a farmhouse and it was there that the Colonel received a dispatch informing him that two French interpreters were arriving the following day, Wednesday, and would be requesting him to provide accommodation for them at the camp.

The following day the two interpreters duly arrived, and so did the rain. It poured down ceaselessly for two days, turning the camp into a quagmire. To the men accustomed to the heat of India, it was a cold, miserable place. They were glad to hear that their stay there was a short one.

Saturday, 1.00pm, the battalion said goodbye to the La Valentine Camp and marched nine miles to D'Arenc railway station. They arrived in the cobbled station yard a little before 4.00pm and had an hour and a half to wait before transferring into straw-strewn cattle trucks. In the meantime the cooks had set up a field kitchen, hot tea, bread and tinned beef was dished out to the soldiers of each truck. It was dark before the train slowly steamed out of the station, to much cheering from the men relieved to be on the move. The station clock stood at 8.30pm.

Donna and Robb sat together in the tightly-packed truck, their backs up against a wooden wall rocking with the train. There was a smell of oil, leather and cattle. Few words were spoken, most men content with their own thoughts or listening to the crank and groan of the train's wheels

"What'll ye do when ye leave the army?" asked Robb.

His companion shrugged, then realised that in the darkness Robb couldn't see him and so said, "Och, I don't know, what about you?"

"Ma father has asked me to consider leavin' the regiment next year and help run the farm we have in Sutherland. Ma dad's no' as young as he was," said Robb.

"No, none of us are," replied Donna, dryly. "Have you no-one back home who could help?"

"No, they're all married now," replied Robb. "Ma sister used to help, but then she married a magistrate six months ago." He grew silent for a moment, then said again with a derisive laugh, "A magistrate!"

The conversation intrigued Donna. In all the time he had known the Highlander this was the most he had ever spoken of his family. And why the sarcasm in his voice when he mentioned the magistrate? These points puzzled the Englishman, but he said nothing. There was little talk between the two men after that. As for the rest of the soldiers, they were sleeping or tying to sleep, heads resting on small packs or curled in the foetal posture. In the darkness a couple of cigarettes glowed

The speed of the train seemed to have hardly increased since leaving D'Arenc. Donna felt inside his tunic for his pocket watch; the luminous fingers said 10.20. He felt the smooth oval shape in his hands for a few moments; not unnaturally his thoughts drifted back again to the Indian sub-continent where he had spent the last three years. He was happy there. No, not happy, a soldier is never really happy, except maybe under the anaesthesia of a dram or two. Content, yes, he was content in India; he enjoyed it for its exotic beauty and warm climate. He remembered buying his pocket watch in Poonah the previous year. Reminiscing, he wondered what were the hindi words for watchmaker? 'Mistery Wallah'. Yes, they were the words. Very appropriate.

He watched the two cigarette ends glowing in the darkness, like two eyes he thought. He was smiling to himself now. It reminded him of his encounter with the tiger.

It occurred during one of his five mile runs. He had stopped running this particular evening about half a mile from the camp and had decided to walk the rest of the way along one of the dirt roads that ran through the mainly flat farming area. The light was failing rapidly as he padded along the track listening to the insects and frogs beginning their night's clamour. He approached a three foot broken down dry stone wall, which bordered the track at a point by a bend to the left. As he drew level with the bend a huge head appeared like a ghost above the stones, its yellow eyes were opalescent fire fixed upon him. Donna froze in mid-stride. His heart jumped. From the corner of his eye he could see the distant lights of the barracks, so very near and yet so far. Not daring to blink and keeping his eyes transfixed on the tiger's yellow orbs, his mind raced, weighing up his predicament. The road was deserted; the animal was no more than six feet away from him. If he turned and ran it would have him before he could cover a few yards. A cold sweat broke out on his forehead and he stood there for what seemed an eternity. Then, very slowly, not daring to take his eyes off the beast, he inched backwards towards the pile of rocks that went to make up the wall opposite. After another age he sensed the wall behind him. He groped frantically and with his right hand behind his back he managed to loosen a sizeable rock as a weapon.

The tiger's position had not altered. In the gloom the yellow eyes were still hypnotically anchored to its prey, the great mouth half-open. Donna, keyed up, waited, first for a snarl, then for a rush as it sprang at him. The man and beast stared at each other for perhaps a minute, then miraculously the animal turned its head slightly, sniffed the air and with a soft snort vanished. The tiger had probably scented a more appetising victim back down the track, perhaps a cow or a goat. However, Donna did not wait to find out but fled away. It was pitch darkness when he arrived back at camp, but he told no one of his experience, and not being a fool he made sure that his future runs were done earlier in the day. He knew now why the natives called dusk 'the beasts' light'.

****

The troop train rumbled on into the French night and, still thinking of India, Donna fell asleep sitting up.

Early the following morning the train halted at a small village station to take on coal and water. Colonel Richie and one of the interpreters had stepped down and were conferring with a French railway official on the tiny platform. R.S.M. Macrae, whose truck was some way down past the platform, jumped down onto the track then marched back along the lines and came to a halt just behind the small group. After a minute Colonel Richie looked at him enquiringly.

"Yes Mr. Macrae?"

The R.S.M. saluted. "Permission fur the men to stretch tha legs, relieve themsels, sur?"

His C.O. pondered for a moment and then said, "Yes, sarn't major, and while we're at it we may as well eat. Be so good as to inform Sergeant Mullins and his bobhajis."

"Thank ye, vera good sur," said Macrae, saluting and marching away straight-backed.

There was a mutual respect between these two men despite the obvious difference in rank. They were alike in character and had much in common. Both their families had served in the Seaforths for generations, both, although being professional soldiers, were religious and regular kirk-goers. Reading was a way both men liked to relax, with Macrae it was the classic works of Scott and Dickens, whilst his C.O. enjoyed reading the life stories of great generals.

Two hours later the train moved off again, slowly shaking its way through the hills of central France. Campbell and Laidlaw, contrary to orders, were sitting at a doorway with their legs hanging over the side of the truck. Occasionally the train passed through villages whose names the two men found impossible to pronounce. They grew tired of this after a couple of hours and picked their way through the other occupants to where a game of cards was being played. There was little conversation save for the murmurs around the card school. Most of the men were bored, bored with the scenery, bored with the slowness of the train, bored with their surroundings, and some tried to doze the monotony away. All of that day and all of the next day the dreary journey continued, broken only by the odd stops to eat and answer nature's call. At 11.30pm on Monday evening the train shuddered to a halt under the lights of Orleans railway station.

In light rain the battalion de-trained and formed up on a road outside. It was 1.00am before they were ready to move off. They marched westwards, bones numb and sore, to where the camp, like La Valentine, consisted of a few wooden huts by open land. Here in the now heavier rain the men pitched tents by the light of oil lamps. It was 3.00am before the first of the soldiers slumped wearily into damp beds.

Reveille was at 8.00am, two hours later than usual, and for the rest of the day, save for a parade muster and weapon inspection at 11.00am, the men were allowed to relax and recover from the journey.

The following day leave was given barring defaulters. The majority of the battalion, after being cooped up in a train for three days, not unnaturally headed for the nearby town. The little place bustled with military activity. The railway station was one of the busiest venues; wagons loaded with shells rolled towards the front at regular intervals, troop trains came and went, and a Red Cross train passed slowly through the station, travelling at approximately four miles an hour loaded with wounded French soldiers. From the partly opened doorways wafted odours of carbolic and putrefaction. There were occasional moans also, sounds that the onlookers remembered long after the train had gone.

In Orleans itself the hostilities seemed to have had little effect on its inhabitants; foodstuffs, fruit and vegetables were plentiful, eggs and poultry were in abundance. In the estaminis (café bars) there was plenty of cheap wine to be had. A few of the soldiers already in Orleans carried souvenirs, German helmets and pistols. A soldier in the West Kents tried to sell Campbell a watch, which the man said he'd taken from a dead German officer at a place called Le Cateau, but he was given short shrift by the big Highlander and told to "fuck off".

The following day the battalion marched to the firing range a mile from the camp. There each squad of men was given instructions on the recently issued Mark 3 Lee Enfield rifle. The new rifle was lighter in weight and shorter in length than its predecessor, 8 lbs 10.5 ozs and 3 ft 8.5 inches respectively, but of far more import to the infantrymen was the fact that the new Lee Enfield had a magazine which held ten rounds of .303 ammunition in two five round clips with a muzzle velocity of 734 yards per second.

This being the first occasion the men had had to try out the weapon, their first five rounds were fired at their own speed so as to ascertain and correct any slight trajectory fault when taking aim on a target. 'Get to know yer best friend,' droned the instructors (meaning the rifle). After the initial five rounds were fired came 15 rounds rapid fire, or the 'mad minute' as some of the soldiers christened it later. It consisted of 15 rounds of aimed fire on target within 60 seconds. It said much for the standard of musketry of the battalion that nearly every man achieved the rapid-fire test within the minute.

In the afternoon the battalion's machine gun teams opened up at targets from 100 to 300 yards range. Firstly came Lewis and light machine gunners practising at various angles and distances with the drum-fed magazines, which held 147 of .303 ammunition. After this the two Vickers six-man machine gun squads took up positions. Each team consisted of a number one who fired the gun, number two who fed the 250 round belt of .303 bullets into the breach, number three who kept number two supplied, while numbers four, five and six kept the tins of belted ammunition supplied. The team practised reversing roles, then lastly, once the spout had cooled sufficiently, they dismantled the gun and changed the barrel, which had a life of 80,000 rounds, blindfolded.

To Donna, a member of Lieutenant Roylance's squad, the 'new' Vickers machine gun was, but for a few slight modifications such as lighter in weight and a lesser rate of fire, 550 rounds per minute to the Maxim's 600 rounds, just a copy of the one he had become so expert at in India.

The following morning the battalion paraded in a blustering wind where a visiting British General addressed them. The high-ranking officer sported a monocle in one eye and his talk centred on the war and how our soldiers were holding the huns, and how he was sure that with the Seaforths' help the hostilities would be brought to a favourable conclusion within a few short months. He droned on for the best part of an hour. Most of his words, however, were lost to the rear ranks because of the wind, which got perceptively stronger the longer he spoke. The officer's face and neck got redder and redder the more he battled to be heard. In one of the rear ranks, first Donna, then quickly followed by Campbell and Laidlaw, then half a dozen others, stuck their identity discs into one eye and assumed the very essence of attentiveness, although they hadn't heard a word the windbag had uttered. At the end of the pep talk the R.S.M. called for three cheers for the General, but only the front ranks responded, the rest mimed.

As Donna left the parade ground accompanied by Campbell and Laidlaw he spotted Lieutenant Roylance bearing down on him, a look of triumph on his fat face.

"Report to the company office tomorrow morning Private Donna – ye're on a charge."

The Lieutenant must have witnessed Laidlaw and Campbell's disrespect, but he said nothing to them.

In the afternoon the regiment route-marched in full marching order through an even countryside brown with autumn. They passed flat-featured farm workers, women and old men mostly. They stared without apparent interest as the Highlanders marched by to the creak and jingle of their equipment.

Half an hour later they met the Manchester Regiment marching in the opposite direction. As they drew level shouts of 'Ya goin' the wrong way Jock' and 'Only another ten miles lads' came from the Lancastrians. From the Seaforths' ranks someone shouted, 'Och away an' piss up a rope'.

A few hundred yards behind the Manchesters came columns of Indian sepoy soldiers, who, together with the First Seaforths, were part of the First Indian Army, having arrived in France in the same convoy. There was hardly a greeting as the two bodies passed each other, save for a solitary 'assalam alaikum' from a lone Scot's voice. This greeting was answered with a compulsory reply of 'alaikum salam' from the sombre-faced Indians.

The next morning Donna was marched before Major Wright and charged with parade ground insolence. He offered no defence and was duly given seven days extra duty.

At 6.45am two days later the regiment left the camp and marched to Orleans railway station. They entrained almost at once. Their destination was to be Merville, a town 170 miles to the east. It was a bitterly cold morning and for once the men didn't complain about how tightly-packed the trucks were, realising, no doubt, that it helped conserve heat. Presently the train creaked slowly away from Orleans and out into the open farm land, its speed gradually increasing to a maximum of about 15 miles per hour.

It was after 7.00pm when the train shuddered to a halt in Merville. It stopped in a siding where the line ran parallel to a paved road. The small wooden fence normally used to separate the two thoroughfares had been taken down to facilitate the detraining of troops. Shadowy khaki figures with lanterns waited at the gap in the fence to direct and assist in unloading.

The cramped stiff-limbed men stumbled down out of the trucks and lined up shivering on the roadway. There were mutterings of 'bastard cold' and 'fuckin' freezin' from a few voices in the darkness. Captain Shornberg (German John to the men of 'A' Company), feeling the bitterness of the night, approached Colonel Richie, who was grouped with other figures watching the proceedings

"What is it Captain?" enquired Richie.

"Just a suggestion, sir. If the billets are not too far away could not 'A' and 'B' Companies proceed, get 'em out of the cold and leave more space on the roadway?"

Colonel Richie nodded. "Good idea. The animals and transports will take a wee while yet."

He turned to a military policeman. The well-muffled, sour-faced individual shrugged. "No reason why not, sir," he said, and moved smartly away to lead the two companies.

Companies 'A' and 'B' were glad to be on the move. They were tired and hungry; they had not eaten since breakfast over 12 hours ago. With packs and rifles slung, they marched towards the lights of the town. After about 20 minutes they halted beside a huge building with many windows. On its big wooden door were the letters ARMY BILLET LINES in white paint.

The building turned out to have once been a textile mill, and no doubt when peace came would be so again, but now what floor space that could be easily cleared had been to accommodate the soldiers. To Donna the mill and the smells and creaks of the oaken floors were like letters from home. His first job when leaving school at 14 had been at Jones' Mill, not 200 yards from where he lived. He remembered going to the Mill Office with his school pal Bob Brady, where they had both been taken on and worked in the Winding Room on the second floor. He recalled he had enjoyed working there with Bob but got restless after about a year and left. As far as he knew Bob was still working there.

He bunked down on the bare floor and stared at the cotton fibre clinging to the stout wooden beams and roof pulleys. Despite the clamour and bustle of comrades settling down for the night he was soon asleep, reminiscing of happier times.

Merville was a neat little town with solid three-storied houses, a fine romanesque church and thriving little shops. Its main industries had been brewing, salt refining and textiles. The people of the town seemed cheerful enough, especially the shopkeepers, who did a roaring trade selling goods as varied as fruit to photographic equipment. Most spoke Flemish or pigeon English. In the market square residents sold produce direct from the peculiar three-wheeled Flemish carts, while the docile mules either dozed or munched on feed bags bored by the whole business. There was a preponderance of British uniforms, Gurkha soldiers with rifles slung across their shoulders bought bright fabrics and stuffed them into their tunics. A few Leicesters and West Kents were gathered around an organ grinder and from time to time dropped coins and the odd brass button into the operator's box. In the estaminets there was no shortage of weak beer or cheap sweet-tasting wine. The places were crowded, but there was no belligerence or unruliness, just talk of home and speculation of when the war would end. From time to time two military policemen appeared briefly and scanned the young faces, quite a few of them by now glassy-eyed. The M.P.s usually left the premises to hisses and rude noises.

Donna and Robb decided that the estaminets in the town were too crowded for comfort and sought to look elsewhere. In a quiet suburb on the Estaires Road they came upon a farm cottage with a notice saying 'Food and Drink' written in English. Robb led the way, opening the three-foot wooden gate in the fence corraling the building. A smiling, portly woman greeted them at the door, "Entrée, entrée," she said, and ushered them towards a stone-floored room on the right, a room from which a babble of voices could be heard. The two men removed their glengarries and unslung their weapons. Carrying both items they entered the dining room and sat down at an empty table by the fireplace. The talk in the place petered out and was replaced by an uneasy silence. Donna looked round at the other occupants of the room. The reason for the sudden hush was soon apparent, for sprawled at the other three tables were six or seven cavalry officers, and from the number of wine bottles on the table plus the silly expressions on most of their faces, they appeared to be the worse for drink. They stared at the newcomers with an undisguised expression of disdain

"The place is full of bastard officers," whispered Donna from behind his hand.

Robb nodded. "I know but ahm no movin' oot," he said from the corner of his mouth.

One of the silly faces stumbled to his feet, nearly upsetting his table. He lurched over to the newcomers and stood over them, swaying on his feet. The buttons of his tunic were undone. The officer tried to put on an authoritative expression, but his fat shiny face, heavy eyes and slack mouth were almost comic to Donna. He was a prime example of all he detested in the officer class, slovenly in dress, arrogant, bombastic and tyrannical to anyone considered not of their class. Donna couldn't help his own look of contempt at the bully

"Wash the hell," screeched the officer, "do you think you are doing in here?"

Robb tried to explain. "We didn't know, sir. There wasnee a notice."

A voice from the back barked, "Get to your feet man when you speak to an officer."

There were sniggers of laughter when the drunken officer suddenly grabbed Donna by the ear and began pulling him upwards. Donna felt himself going cold with anger. The blood drained from his face; he was being humiliated and he was now at his most dangerous. It wasn't his or Robb's fault that the place was for officers only. The woman had greeted them warmly enough and, like Robb had tried to say, there was no sign above the door saying 'Officers Only'.

Donna, now on his feet with bloated face still hanging on to his ear, looked with hatred into the officer's eyes. Then, hardly realising it himself, there was a thud and a yelp. The cavalryman fell back like a sack of potatoes, blood and mucous spraying from the officer's nose. The Englishman, with both his hands, full had butted his antagonist solidly in the face. In the next instant the two Seaforths clattered out of the farmhouse, down the garden path and taking the fence in their stride, raced back up the road as fast as their legs could carry them. After they had put some distance between themselves and the house, Robb, still running with a rifle in one hand and a hat in the other, gasped, "Ahm no surprised ye dinni take a dram much, ye never stay in one place fuckin' long enough." The two didn't stop running until they reached the marketplace and the anonymity of the other uniforms.

The next day the Textile Mill's fulling sheds were used as a bath house, the big vats normally used to dip and process the cloth were filled with hot steamy water and 20 or so men at a time revelled in the chance to wash and soak their bodies. Some of the men were loathe to leave the hot comforting water when their time was up and tried to hide below the surface, but the N.C.O.s' sticks soon fished the laggards out.

Part of Donna's extra duties included cookhouse fatigues, which meant being awakened at 4.30am by the night guard, after which he made and lit the fires to heat water for the battalion's breakfast tea. By 5.00am the cooks usually began appearing. Private Conroy was invariably the first to appear, shuffling into the stone building puffy-eyed and fumbling with tobacco makings. His greeting was always the same, "What's new?" To which Donna's reply was the same, and which never failed to bring a smile to the cook's face, "Fuck all".

Donna brewed two mugs of strong tea from a small dixy of boiling water balanced above the flames. The two then sat in silence, the early hour making them uncommunicative, Conroy rolling a cigarette, the other warming his hands around the tin mug. The two of them savoured these few quiet moments; they knew that soon Sergeant Mullins would show up with more duties.

At noon Colonel Richie received orders to mobilise the battalion. They were to join up with the 2nd Battalion Gurkha Regiment (billeted in a disused brewery on the Merville road). Under cover of darkness the two regiments were to march south. The order ended with map references and times.

At 6.30pm the Battalion fell in on the Mill Road. It was dark by now and a stiff wind had got up, pulling at packs and kilts. The soldiers moved forward leaning into the wind. The black sky made a screen for the red and white flashes of shellfire. There was no skirl of pipes; there was no talk amongst the ranks of grim-faced men, just the wind and the slog of feet on the cobbled stone. At the crossroads figures with lamps directed them along the road to the right. Black shapes of trees and hedges loomed up out of the night, giving a sense of unreality.

Pinpoints of light in the distance turned out to be military police posts along the roadside. A further cluster of lights ahead grew into a village. Without halting, the soldiers marched on through the market place and passed the medieval church, absorbing impressions in the darkness of cowed horses stood by guns and a house with a huge red cross painted on its wall. Through the village and out into the black countryside they went, the crunch of feet, the nuisance wind blowing across them. A mile on they passed a troop of cavalry stood off the road to allow the infantrymen to pass. Another mile and another collection of houses, in darkness this time. An hour later the battalion halted in a shell-blasted village called Vieille Chapelle. By now, the wind had abated somewhat, but then it began to rain, the light, clinging type.

The soldiers were allocated various roofed dwellings and marched off by their N.C.O.s. Every available premise, from converted barn to village school, was used to accommodate the men. The officers shared a billet in a château next to the church. It was 10.30pm before all the men were under cover and out of the rain.

Donna, Robb and eight others had been put into a small farmhouse where a huge hole in one wall had been repaired with sheet iron. Sacking covered the broken windows. The house contained just two artefacts, a wooden drawer from some long gone chest and an oil lamp. Donna leaned his rifle against a wall and balanced the straps of his packs from the muzzle in such a way that the packs didn't touch the floor. Then, after brushing the wetness from his tunic with hands and glengarry, he collected handfuls of straw scattered about the floor and placed them in the dead fireplace. He broke the drawer up with his feet to get a fire blaze going.

"Guid lad," said Corporal Williams to Donna. "Ye know how to make a sigri?" he asked, lapsing into the Indian word for fire.

"Aye," nodded Donna, "but this won't last long." He indicated the rest of the broken up sticks from the wooden drawer.

Corporal Williams turned to a soldier and said, "Mick, away and see if ye can root some wood."

The man pulled a face, nipped his cigarette out, stuck the stump behind his ear, then went out into the rain. The soldiers stood getting warm in a semi-circle around the fireplace. There was silence for a while, then someone complained about being cold, adding it seemed warmer in Merville, meaning the cotton mill.

"Well, ahm vera glad we're away from Merville ma'sel'," said Robb. "It got a wee bit too hot for ma liking," he added, looking at Donna with amusement.

Donna understood what the look meant and smiled. This triggered Robb to chuckle. The laughter became infectious as both re-lived the events of a few days ago, Robb vividly picturing again walking down the path of the officers' own farmhouse, politely knocking on the door, carefully wiping their feet and removing headwear before entering the dining room. Then two minutes later the two of them charging back out again like meteors, both hurdling the gate at full stride and galloping back up the road again as if the hounds of hell were after them. By now the two men were weeping with mirth as each re-lived the episode in their mind's eyes. The others in the farmhouse, not privy to the reason for the laughter, just looked at each other and shrugged.

It was during the merriment that the door opened and the R.S.M. and Sergeant Cooper walked in, rain glinting on their hats and greatcoats. The men automatically stiffened to attention, laughter vanishing.

"Stand easy," said the R.S.M. "Everything in orda Corporal?"

"Yes, sir," said Corporal Williams

"Sir?" said Williams again.

"Yes?"

"Will there be any supper tonight?"

"Ahm afraid no," said R.S.M. Macrae

"Will we be 'ere lang sir?" asked someone else.

Macrae looked in the man's direction. "No, we move agin some time tomorrer."

"Right sir," replied the soldier.

The R.S.M. took a last look around the room, nodded to himself, then leading Cooper, went out.

"Guid night."

"Guid night sir," called Corporal Williams.

Minutes later Mick returned with some wooden fencing to feed the fire. He grumbled whilst shaking the rain from his tunic. The wood was soon broken up and fed into the fireplace, where it hissed before catching alight. The place began to warm up and so did the men crouched around the fire. Outside the rain appeared to have increased, though the mumble of shellfire had died down. There was the usual murmurings of mundane talk from the group. Macfedris wanted to know what had caused the huge patched-up hole in one of the walls.

"Mice" came the wry answer from someone toasting his rear. One man, who sat poker-faced staring into the flames, shared neither the smiles nor the conversation. He was Private Harper, known as 'Slim' because of his build. He stood about five feet seven inches tall and weighed no more than eight and a half stone. Aged 25, he came from some obscure village in Lancashire, a gaunt, intense man. Donna, with his medical training, considered him something of a psycho who rarely forgot a slight.

The other men of 'A' Company were wary of the 'wee man'; there were too many instances in the past for them not to be. There was the time back in India when two of the company's card sharks had combined to skin Harper of his pay. Two weeks later the two cheats were badly burned; they had to be dragged from their beds in the early hours. Someone had put a match to their mosquito nets whilst they slept. Their injuries proved so bad they were invalided back to Britain for specialist treatment. The Pathans were blamed for this outrage. Although he did not say anything, Donna did not accept this.

There was another instance when Harper came off worst in a drunken brawl with a much bigger soldier from 'B' Company and a few weeks later Slim's antagonist was found nearly dead on some spare ground suffering from a fractured skull. There were other occasions of a lesser gravity which were never explained, and yet some thread of connection could be traced by the discerning back to the loner Harper. He was questioned more than once, but without the slightest shred of proof no action was taken against him. The other men of his company became wary of him and left him to himself, which was possibly what he desired most in the first place anyway.

Laidlaw was talking now. He was saying that the second battalion Gurkhas had left Merville five minutes after they had and were billeted in the village that the regiment had passed through a couple of miles back. Campbell's voice was heard next calling someone a "lowland bastart". Corporal Williams, sensing some past grudge about to erupt called, "We'd better away to our beds lads noo." To set an example he left the fire and, taking out a blanket and groundsheet from his big pack, made a bed on the floor, using his small pack as a pillow. The last man to leave the fire threw a couple of pieces of timber into the flames before turning down the lamp. For this he was admonished by a voice in the gloom for "saving non fe the morra", to which the offender countered with an expletive as he fumbled in the darkness.

It was quiet in the farmhouse, save for the crackle of the fire and the deep breathing of men sleeping. The flames from the hearth glowed bright and played on the rough grey walls. The soft glow hid the shabbiness and dereliction of the house, giving an illusion of cosiness and, to some of the men still awake, a reminder of happier times spent back home in cottages very much like this one in the Highlands of Scotland. Their reverie was soon disturbed, however, when the rumble of the distant guns opened up again.

At 1.00pm the following day the battalion left Vieille Chapelle and moved on towards the front, passing through the hamlet of La Couture and on to Richbourg St. Vaast, a distance of three miles. After once more being installed into various billets, Colonel Richie visited his men, informing them that the battalion was to support the British Third Division and that that night they were to relieve men in the trenches to the east. He ended his short speech with, "Get as much rest as ye can and good luck. Ghidich n Righ."

A little later in the afternoon, the armourer issued each soldier with 150 rounds of ammunition and two empty sandbags, which were to be pinned to the tunic front for easy access. Next, a brown paper-wrapped hardtack biscuit from the field kitchen was dished out to each man. It was during the handing in of excess equipment to the Quartermaster that the first couple of shells fell on the village, hitting the row of small shops in the market place. Next, the brewery and a house near to battalion headquarters were blasted. The shelling grew in intensity. Men indoors hid in corners or under bunks as the walls and roofs shook with each blast. The bombardment lasted for half an hour, but apart from one of 'B' Company's mules being killed, the guns missed their targets.

They left Richbourg St.Vaast at midnight taking their first line of transport. They marched south along a cold black road, moving in the direction from which the barrage had come a few hours earlier. There was no talk, just the metallic sound of mess tins and equipment and the clatter of wagons to the rear. They began to pass houses badly damaged by shells, some just heaps of rubble with just the odd wall standing. At crossroads they passed French cavalrymen bivouacking in some trees, their pipe-smoking sentries hardly giving them a glance.

Further on they came to farm buildings which were still burning. This, together with the odd whine of rifle shots, indicating they were not far from the front.

"Anee idea where'a we're goin'?" asked someone.

"Dinna ken," came the reply.

"They never'a tel ye' oot."

The regiment was halted just before the junction of another road where wagons and groups of soldiers were drawn up. The battalion's machine gun teams were fallen out and ordered to collect their ammunition and weapons from the transports. Soon after, the Seaforths were led by uniformed guides along the road to the right, which was covered with debris of all kinds and intermittently lined with the odd ruined farmhouse. Despite the chill in the air, Donna found it hard going and began to sweat. He also had a container of machine gun ammunition to lug. In the darkness he nearly stumbled over the legs of a dead horse which lay partly in the roadway.

For half a mile the soldiers fumbled forward until they were met by more spectral figures that directed them single file into trenches either side of the roadway. Donna, on the heels of another member of the gun team who was carrying the tripod, was about to follow him to the right but was stopped by Lieutenant Roylance and ordered to put down the ammunition tins and take the trench opposite to the left. This he did, but after scrambling down in the darkness and going forward, he found it was hardly a trench at all but a ditch stretching about 60 yards in length. As he passed along to take up a position next to men already there he found that the ditch and ground around was littered with dead soldiers, nearly all appeared to be turbaned Sikhs.

FOUR

Collyhurst

James Donna started school when he was four. His mother was sad that particular morning as she got him ready. The week before she had bought him a new jersey and a pair of trousers from the open-air market on Rochdale Road.

To dress him she stood him on a chair in the kitchen.

"You do look nice," she murmured quietly, trying to cheer herself up more than anything. He stood there, his little face looking serious, with his clogs highly polished, the long stockings pulled up to his knees and his baggy pants reaching almost to his shins. The jersey was too long in the arms and had to be folded back a couple of times at his wrists. The collar of his check shirt had become trapped under the jersey and she smoothed it out, saying at the same time, "Only yer hair to do now son." She wet a comb under the cold water tap and began teasing his hair into a fringe. There was a tuft at his crown, which refused to lie down even after more water and strokes with the comb, so she gave up and put the implement into the pocket of her pinafore.

She stepped back a little and looked at him again.

"Are you ready now James?"

The little lad looked back at her, his big blue eyes troubled.

"What's the matter luv?" she asked.

She wondered if the unfamiliarity of going to school for the first time was bothering him.

"You'll be all right at school," she said, reassuringly. "There's other nice lads there and games to play. Are you worried about school son?"

The little lad shook his head.

"Then what is it?" she asked, puzzled.

"Well," said the little lad after taking a deep breath, and with all the seriousness of a Prime Minister, "if I'm going to school and I've got a new pair of kecks an' a new gansey, can I have a new bandage on me leg?" His little dimpled hand pulled up one of his trouser legs to reveal a small dried-up wound on his knee.

"Oh!" cried his mother, clapping her hands to her face in mock horror, "I am a silly mam, aren't I?"

The little lad nodded smiling, delight in his eyes. She fixed a bandage from the medicine shelf a couple of times around the scab and then replaced his stocking.

"There, is that better?"

He nodded. She lifted him off the chair and held him to her for a few moments. He smelled of soap, clean and fresh. She kissed him on the cheek and stood him down on the stone floor. She searched in her pinny pocket for the farthing his father had left for him. The little lad stood looking up at his mother, his hands deep in his pockets.

"I like these kecks mam, the pockets are dead deep."

She smiled. "I know luv, but don't put yer hands in them while you're at school will you? The teacher might not like it."

She ushered him into the living room where his sister Elizabeth sat waiting for him. "Keep tight hold of his hand Tizzie," she said. "Don't let him run off into the road."

Elizabeth nodded. Her mother spoke again, more sharply to make sure the girl understood. "And don't forget to bring him home with you later on."

"I will, don't worry," replied Elizabeth irritably.

She stood watching from the front door as the two walked off up the street, the little lad one hand clasped tightly to his sister's, the other hidden in his baggy trouser pocket. He held his head a little to one side as he hurried to keep up with his sister's long strides. His mother sighed again. He looked so little to be taking his first step into growing up.

St. Oswald's Church of England School smelled of wood and polish. He would recall the smell long after he left. He stood outside the headmaster's office with two other lads who, like him, were starting school for the first time. The three stood in silence, a little bewildered wondering what was to happen next. One of the boys, with spikey hair and a front tooth missing, began to fidget with his clogs, placing one foot in front of the other then back again. The other, a sturdy red-haired lad, became bored and started picking his nose. Donna, meanwhile, had forgotten what his mother had said and had thrust his hands into his pockets. The pockets were so deep that his arms vanished up to his elbows. He stood there playing with the farthing inside.

The three lads were soon to get their first taste of school discipline, however. It came in the shape of the headmistress, a tall severe-looking woman with ill-fitting yellow false teeth. She came sailing up the corridor, papers under one arm, and bellowed at them:

"Get your hands out of your pockets, keep your feet still, stop picking your nose." She glared at them, wagging a finger. "I can't imagine what kind of homes you come from."

The three little boys stared up at her apprehensively. Spikey hair's bottom lip began to quiver.

"What's your names?" she snarled.

The red-haired lad answered first. "Robert Brady," he said.

She went as if to strike him.

"Robert Brady, Miss," she ranted.

"Robert Brady Miss."

Donna and spikey hair (whose name turned out to be Thomas Brophy) were quick to catch on and answered correctly. She ticked each name off a paper, then curtly said, "Come with me." She led the lads off to slim, pretty Miss Rothwell's class and more regimentation.

School held little pleasure for Donna. Not because he was a dullard, on the contrary he was a bright lad, but because it seemed to him that the regime was ruled by fear. He had forgotten the number of times grown ups had told him that teachers were very clever and knew everything and yet when he couldn't keep still once in class and dropped his slate, Miss Rothwell had slapped his cheek, her pretty face a mask of fury. Surely if teachers knew everything, she should know that it's impossible for some lads to keep still, even when asleep. He hadn't cried though. No, boys don't cry, not in front of the teacher anyway. Don't give the bullies the satisfaction of seeing tears.

Adults, it seemed, were always telling you off.

If you played football within 100 miles of a house they came out and chased you off. If you told ghost stories under the gas lamp at night they moved you on. If you didn't wash your hands and face 20 times a day they shouted at you. If you explained that you weren't dirty, or answered back, they called you cheeky. At home, if you were sitting down and someone wanted your chair, they would say, "Isn't it time you were in bed?"

Grown-ups sent you to bed at night when you were wide awake, then woke you up in the morning when you were dead tired. If you asked too many questions you were told to 'shut up'.

Girls were useless; they wore long frocks, they had long hair, they were very weak. Maybe it was because of their long hair that they had no strength. All your strength, they say, is in your hair. They can't climb or play football. They play house on the croft or play with dolls; they were useless.

Boys don't like big dogs that chase you and try to bite your legs. Cats are alright though; they don't bark at you and try to bite. You could pick cats up and stroke them and if they did bite or scratch you it didn't hurt much. Even horses were all right as long as you were careful and didn't stand near their back legs. It was a curious fact that horses were scared of little lads. Donna himself had patted two horses, the coalman's horse and the hot potato man's. Horses were dead big and strong, yet they were scared of small boys. The reasons, one of his peers explained, was that horses' eyes magnified everything they saw so that little lads appeared like giants.

For young Donna life was only worthwhile once the gong to end school had sounded, then free from his draconian betters he could give reign to his boundless energy. The halcyon days were when the school closed for the summer holidays. These days usually started with an early toast and porridge breakfast prepared by his mother, then off to Bob Brady's house. Bob, more often than not, was still in bed, so Donna usually sat in the living room trying not to fidget whilst Bob's mother inveigled her son to get out of bed. Minutes later Bob's feet would come shuffling down the stairs. He usually appeared in his nightshirt, carrying his trousers, socks and clogs, face puffy and hair like a haystack. He dressed in the kitchen, had a quick nominal swill under the cold water tap, then a couple of his mother's dip butties with a cup of strong tea, and the lad was ready for anything the day might throw at him.

Some days the two lads walked for miles; they loved to be in the sunshine, life was new and full of incidents. Time meant little or nothing and was gauged by only three factors: firstly, if the sun was up it was early; secondly, if it had set then it was late; and lastly, if they were hungry it was either dinner or teatime. The farmlands of Crumpsall and Moston drew them most days. Probably, although they were too young to understand, it was some minute stirring of a love of the land inherent from their ancestors.

On one of their sojourns they were caught chasing a farmer's chickens and as a punishment the despot made them remove their clogs, which he kept, and made the two youngsters walk all the way home bare-footed. Their tribulations didn't end there, for when they arrived home limping, they were promptly walloped and sent to bed without anything to eat. However, the worst punishment for these two free spirits was not the miles of unshod walking on small feet, nor the clips across the ears, nor was it the deprivation of food. No, the real torment was to be sent upstairs to bed whilst it was still early and being able to view other children through the bedroom window playing happily in the street outside. Life, Donna decided through his tears, was definitely unfair.

The clog-losing incident took place on a Monday, so it was Friday and pay day before Donna's mother had sufficient money to spare to buy her son another pair of clogs from either the open-air market or the second-hand shop on Rochdale Road. Bob's position was a little better; his mother (who was a widow) had been promised a pair of cast-off boots from one of her late husband's relatives. These, however, were not forthcoming until Thursday.

So, without footwear the lads' range was limited to the street, the croft and the River Irk. Bob called for Donna wearing the sleeves of an old coat tied to his feet. Donna couldn't find an old coat so he wore two pairs of tattered socks, and for comfort he twisted the holes around to the top of his instep. So shod, the two made their way up the rising Collyhurst Road and crossed the bridge in front of Pilkington's Works, then following a path along the riverbank they halted beneath the huge railway viaduct. It was this point beneath the arch that the river was at its broadest and flattest, the ideal place for playing ducks and drakes across its surface. To the boys the Irk was a fascinating river. It could change colour several times a day subject to whatever was worked by the dye process further up along its banks. Plus, one could never tell what object the river would bring down with it, wooden chairs, case balls, dead animals etc. Glass bottles were the best, though. When one was spotted bobbing along in the current there was always a scramble for stones to throw at it, the object being to smash it before the pace of the river took it beyond range. Yes, to hit, or better still to smash, a bottle as it swept past definitely made your day. Clogs or no clogs.

The following day, to the disgust of the boys it rained. Forbidden by his mother to go out Donna prowled about the house like a caged deer, gazing frequently through the windows to see if the rain had abated. He went upstairs into the front bedroom and started jumping from one bed to the other. The noise soon penetrated down to his mother who was baking in the kitchen and she shouted up to him to 'give over and come down'. He duly did and to occupy him she gave him some dough with which to make a pastry man. He washed his hands at the sink and began shaping the dough into a figure, with feet too big for the legs. He liked helping his mother to bake, his face was a picture of contentment as he finished his man with currants for the eyes and mouth, and carefully placing it on a saucer he left it to his mother to put in the oven. He wandered into the living room and began messing about with the wall cupboards by the window. His mother's voice came again from the kitchen.

"James, don't fiddle in your father's drawer," she said threateningly, adding, "You broke his pipe last time."

It was as he closed his father's drawer as carefully as he could so his mother wouldn't hear that his eyes came to rest on a red book lying in the recess between the drawers and cupboards. Its front cover had a Greek soldier on horseback in silver relief. On the first page in large letters were the words 'The Iliad'. He flicked through the pages, gazing at pictures of ships and battles and one of a huge wooden horse. Intrigued, he went back to the beginning and began to read.

Although the long words were beyond him he could read enough from the text to paint pictures of combat, honour and betrayal. He sat in his father's chair fascinated. His mother, concerned at his quietness, looked to see what he was up to. Glad that for a while he was occupied and out from under her feet, she started on her next labour, scrubbing the family's washing on the same table on which she had recently been baking.

By 12.00 noon the rain had stopped and the sky became decidedly brighter. Donna's mother, her apron front wet from the scrubbing, disturbed him in his reading.

"Go to Jackson's for me James an' get me 'alf a pound of bacon, a loaf, an' 'alf an ounce of pipe tobacco for yer dad, will you son?"

The lad pulled a face at being interrupted.

"Will you give me a note, and I've got no shoes mam, and it's wet anyway."

"Well then," she said deliberately, "have a look in the cubby-hole an' see if there's an old pair of Dan's boots in there. They'll do for going to the shop, it's only a cock-stride away."

She held out a shilling. "Hold it in your hand, don't lose it will ya? Oh, an' ask him to put a good jockey on each," she called as she returned to her scrubbing.

The word 'jockey' applied to an extra portion given by shops to attract custom and to ensure that customers were given correct weight, so that if someone bought a loaf of bread a small part of a loaf was added free of charge. If the purchase happened to be a pound of butter, a couple of ounces of butter were added on top, hence the word jockey. The shops that gave the biggest jockeys usually got the most custom.

The lad folded the corner of the page he was on and closed the book. He didn't bother looking in the cupboard below the stairs for a pair of Dan's old boots but opened the front door and surveyed the state of the pavement outside. It had stopped raining and by this time the sun was out, drying patches on its surface. He decided to go to the shop via the dry areas. He hopped and jumped from dry area to dry area, imagining them to be islands in a great ocean.

At Jackson's shop he was subject to the usual wait to be served. Not that the shop was crowded, on the contrary, there was only one other customer, a pale-faced girl of about 12. From beneath her long shabby dress he could see her toes poking out. She was barefoot also. She looked at him and grimaced.

"Have ya called 'shop'?" asked Donna.

"Course I 'ave," said the girl in disgust. "I hate coming 'ere, they allus make ya wait for ages, it's a wonder the place doesn't get robbed!"

There was some reason for the girl's lamentations for there were times when the Jackson family seemed most ill-suited to being in business. The trouble was that once Mr. Jackson (especially in the cold weather) got settled by the fireside he was most loath to leave its comforting warmth. When the shop's bell signalled a customer he usually inveigled his wife to attend them. If his wife was absent, or refused to be put on, then he usually cajoled his eldest son, Jack, to serve in the shop. At times when Jack was occupied or felt disinclined to do his father's bidding, Jack would pass on his father's command to Thomas, the youngest. Tom, aged ten, would then, under the influence of either a bribe or a thump from Jack, reluctantly stop whatever he was doing and proceed to administer to the shop's customers.

Once, when Donna and his sister Elizabeth were together in the shop, they could distinctly hear the Jacksons arguing amongst themselves who should serve the customers. Mr. Jackson's voice came through to them trying in turn to persuade, first his wife, then his two sons. After ten minutes of argument and counter-argument from within, Mr. Jackson's irate voice could be clearly heard bellowing into the shop: "Oh serve yer bleeding self."

One wondered how the business survived such slapdash management, but the fact was it had been run like this for a number of years. One day service good, the next day service atrocious.

Donna and the girl did not have long to wait today, however. Mrs. Jackson, a plump florid woman, appeared through the doorway curtain from within.

"Yes, luv," she said to the girl.

"A packet of Black and Green's tea an' two night lights please."

She served the girl, then turned to Donna.

"What can I do for you James Chadd?" she said amiably.

The lad looked up at her above the counter.

"Me name's not James Chadd," he said seriously. "It's James Donna."

She tried to hide a smile. "Oh I'm sorry, of course it's Donna, my mistake. What do ya want?"

Reading the note, he said, "I want a loaf, 'arf a pound of bacon, 'arf an ounce of pipe tobacco an' me mam said can you put a good jockey on each please?"

Elizabeth was in the house when the lad returned from the shop. She was slumped sulking in a chair because her mother had refused to give in to her constant badgering for a farthing for toffee. The girl suddenly turned her anger on him when he attempted to return to the book.

"Oh no you don't, that's mine," she said peevishly and snatched it from him.

The boy appealed to their mother. "Mam, Tizz won't let me read her book."

"You little melt, you're nowt else," said Mrs Donna to Elizabeth. "Let him read it, it's keeping him quiet." Then, more loudly, "And don't mither me any more for money for toffee. Yer dinner will be ready in ten minutes," and so saying she threw a handful of potato peelings on the fire.

The girl, not normally recalcitrant, gave in reluctantly.

After dinner the lad hopped his way round to his friend's house. Bob was in the kitchen sniffing from time to time as he sat cutting pictures from an old newspaper with a pair of scissors.

"Got any shoes yet?" asked the newcomer.

"Nope," said Bob gloomily.

Donna sighed. "Me neither. When I get bigger I'm gonna go back and batter that bastard farmer," he said intensely.

Bob sniffed again, then nodded agreement. Donna took a closer look at his friend. "'Av' yer been crying Bob?"

"'Ave I 'eck," said Bob defiantly. He jerked his head towards his mother, busily putting curtains up in the other room. "She can't hurt me."

"What happened?" asked Donna.

"Well, I was only tying the dog's legs up with the clothes line when she belted me for making it yelp, but I wasn't 'urting it," he said sincerely.

Donna nodded his sympathies, then a gleam came into Bob's eye. "Hey, why don't I give you an 'aircut? It won't 'urt, like it does when they use the clippers."

"Okay," said Donna. "Yer better not make a mess of it, our Janey gets married soon and I'm going to the do."

So, with a dish towel from the washing rack around his neck to prevent loose hairs going down his collar, Donna sat as still as he could while Bob set to work with scissors and comb. He started on the top of Donna's head, where a tuft was stuck upright, then proceeded to snip the surrounding hair to the same length, but not always in the same area. The result after ten minutes was that Donna's hair had varying lengths from two inches to half an inch, giving him the appearance of an alopecia sufferer.

The tonsorial session came to a somewhat premature end when Bob's mother entered the kitchen. She took one look at Donna's head, let out a screech, and then made a grab for Bob. She clutched him by the scruff of the neck, but he was a big lad for his age and struggled free, dropping the scissors and comb. She grabbed him again by the collar, but he twisted free and made a dart for the yard door. Alas, he ducked into the cord holding the washing rack to the ceiling, causing it to slide down around his mother's shoulders, restricting her movements.

"You wicked lad, you naughty sod, just wait till I get me hands on you. You sod, you're nowt else," she screeched.

Bob fled into the yard, closely followed by Donna, still with the towel round his neck. Later, when he arrived home he had to suffer a scolding from his mother.

"Wait till yer dad sees yer," she said, adding resignedly, "Yer don't half make a show of me, yer show me up no end."

As young as Donna was he noticed the difference in the ways the male and female members reacted to his appearance. Janey and Elizabeth just looked at him in disgust. Daniel didn't even notice his brother's savaged hair. He came into the house through the back door, and after washing his hands at the sink he had his meal in front of the fire, then fell asleep in the chair.

When Richard came home from work he took one look at Donna and roared with laughter.

"Hello porcupine," he said. He took his cap off and plonked it on Donna's head. "'Ere, you'd better wear this so the old man won't see your bonce."

Donna needed no reminding about what his father might say. With Joe in the army there was only his dad to see him now and he feared that the head of the family would be the most critical. He pictured punishments, like being sent to bed early for a week, which was a lifetime to a boy, or a few wallops if his father was in a bad humour. It was about seven o'clock when his father came home from the docks. He was a tall, lean man with grey hair and moustache to match. His mouth was set in a thin line, giving him a severe expression. He grunted a greeting and made his way to the kitchen. As he passed Dan, still dozing in the chair, he tapped him on the shoulder. "Hey, if yer wanta sleep, go to bed," he said tersely in Dan's ear. In the kitchen he unslung the bag he carried.

"I've brought you some vegetables," he said shortly to his wife. He removed his cap and coat and hung them on the back of the door.

Meanwhile, his wife bustled about, laying his meal on the white scrubbed kitchen table. Whilst he washed the dirt from his hands in the living room, Donna left his stool by the fire and began searching the cupboard for Elizabeth's book. Not finding it, he appealed to his sister, who was seated opposite knitting.

"Tizz, where's that book?"

She gave it to him from beneath her cushion, adding, "Don't bend the pages."

Meanwhile, Dan woke up and started blinking into the fire. Collecting his senses, he sniffed and focused his eyes on Donna.

"What's happened to yer hair?"

"Bob Brady was cutting it but his mam belted him before he could finish," said Donna.

"Good job she did," smiled his elder brother. "Has dad seen yer hair yet?" he whispered.

"No."

Dan raised his eyes to the ceiling in mock dread.

Not long afterwards Donna's mother came in from the kitchen and sent him to the shop for a new gas mantle. To do the errand he had to borrow a pair of Dan's old shoes from under the stairs. When he returned Dan and Richard were sitting in the kitchen arguing over a game of cards. Elizabeth had gone out, whilst Janey could be heard moving about upstairs, no doubt going over her trousseau. There was just his mother and father in the living room. She was doing some knitting for Elizabeth, he was reading the evening newspaper and smoking his clay pipe, each one too preoccupied to talk.

Donna placed the gas mantle and farthing change on the sideboard, then took up 'The Iliad' again, glancing from time to time to see if his father had noticed his haircut. He hid behind the book, but after a few minutes he became enthralled in the story and less aware of his surroundings. A cough brought him back to reality. He looked slowly across at his father, who stared back at him over his spectacles. His father then turned to his wife.

"Ya know Molly, I believe he's moulting."

The following week Janey married Jim Knowles at St. Oswald's Church. It was chaos in the house that morning. Everyone was up early, getting dressed up in their best clothes, new stiff collars and ties for the male members of the family whilst the women fiddled with each other's hair and monopolised the looking glasses.

Donna was the last one to get out of bed. He slept with his brothers. He'd been awake early enough; he was awake, in fact, when Richard and Daniel rolled reluctantly out of bed, but he had stayed put because he liked being in that big bed on his own. You could hide yourself in that huge expanse of blankets and sheets. The bulges your knees made you could imagine were great mountains leading down to a vast plain, or that the counterpane was a magic carpet whizzing you through the air to exotic lands across crocodile-infested rivers. After a while he grew tired of this and hung upside down from his repose to retrieve a matchbox lying beneath the bed. Inside was his pet ladybird, which he'd sneaked upstairs. He played with the scarlet beetle, watching it crawl up hills and fall off cliffs until he lost it amongst the pillows. Then he got up and put on his trousers and went downstairs.

He had to wash his face twice before his mother was satisfied it was clean enough. He then put on his best suit and a new pair of squeaky clogs. To hide his hair he had to wear a cap. His father had hired a posh coach to take the family to the church. It was decorated with silk ribbons with two splendidly turned out grey horses in front. James and Liz wanted to sit on top with the tall-hatted driver, but one stern look from their father silenced both of them.

"Take ya time driver," said Mr Donna gruffly to the coachman.

As the driver clucked his horses into motion the sun broke from behind the clouds, bathing the party with a comforting warmth. Some of their neighbours had come to their front doors to wave and cheer as the coach swayed gently over the cobbles of Fitzgeorge Street. Young James felt like royalty. Normally, of course, he walked to school, now he sat a little squashed between Daniel and Elizabeth. His father sat by the window. Jane, in her long white satin wedding dress, sat opposite him. Alongside her sat Richard, with Mrs Donna on his right.

"What's the matter with yer collar?" she asked Daniel softly.

"It's digging into me neck."

"Lean over." She fiddled nimbly and loosened it. "Is that better?"

He nodded, then said, "You smell nice mam."

She smiled gently, "Thanks darlin'."

Jane, who for most of the drive had looked rather pale and serious, suddenly leaned forward as the coach approached the arched railings of the church and grasped her father's hand with both of hers.

"Oh, I wish our Joe was here dad," she whispered.

"I know luv," said her father, "but our Joe couldn't get leave from his unit. Anyway, listen Janey, if you don't want to go through with the wedding you don't have to. Say the word and I'll turn this box on wheels around and we'll all go home."

Jane smiled and shook her head, squeezing his hand hard before letting go.

There was a small crowd of relatives and friends waiting by the doorway of the church. Mrs Chadd was there, wearing a splendid plumed hat. She sniffed and dabbed her eyes when she caught sight of Jane in her wedding dress.

"Oh you look beautiful Janey," she cried, and kissed her.

"It only seems like last week that I nursed you to sleep," she said. Jane hugged her. True to fact, after Mr. Donna's first wife had died, leaving him with two small children to bring up, Mrs Chadd, a widow herself with two waifs of her own, had done excellent work in looking after Jane and her brother Joe. Not unnaturally there was a strong bond between the two families, so much so that less discerning neighbours and acquaintances often referred to the children of the Donna household as Chadd.

The Reverend Lomax, clad in his long ecclesiastical robes, stood in the entrance of the church smiling and bowing his head in greeting, making a perfect picture of humble benevolence.

Young James shrugged his head away when the Reverend patted him on his hair. The youngster had little time for the clergyman. A few weeks before the Reverend had walloped him and his pal Bob Brady across the ear after he found them still in the playground after school was over for the day.

The wedding reception was held at the Donna house, a modest affair of a small plate-sized cake, chicken and salmon sandwiches and crates of bottled beer. Before paying the driver off, Mr Donna bade him and his mate enter the house and gave each a large glass of whisky. A little later more friends, Mrs. Chadd included, squeezed into the living room to toast the bride and groom. Then Mr. Donna gave a speech, looking very serious in his stiff collar and his flattened down hair, and everyone clapped him. Afterwards Mr. Kershaw, a relative of Mrs. Donna, took out his accordion and began to play. It was at this point that young James left the merry-making and went to look for Bob.

The newly-weds had managed to obtain a house to live in not far from the church in Forest Street. The rent was a shilling a week and for months before their big day the two of them had spent countless hours cleaning and painting the place in readiness. Young James and Tizzie had helped by carrying pots and pans, curtains and other household necessities from Fitzgeorge Street up to the house. More often than not Jim Knowles would already be there beavering away with a paintbrush, or whistling as he fixed new shelves in the kitchen. He was a tall, fair-haired young man, not given to loud talk but quiet and sensible. Young James liked him.

A few months after the marriage of his eldest daughter, James Donna senior, now in his sixties, left his job at the Pomona Docks and opened a small shoemaker's shop a few doors away from Jane's new home. The long hours and travel to Salford and home each day wearied him so much that he spent most Sundays in bed. He was grateful now that he had a skill to fall back on. He never tired of speaking fondly of how his stern father had made him learn a trade in his rebellious youth to try to keep him out of trouble.

A few months after opening the shop he discovered his biggest profit was in repairing footwear, 'sole and heeling'. He charged a penny to three halfpennies for putting new irons on clogs. About this time Daniel was almost at school leaving age and his father had offered to teach him the trade, but Dan had declined, explaining that he preferred a job outdoors. More to the truth was that at times his father could be impatient with him and placid Daniel envisaged being constantly harangued if he was to do things in the shop less than perfectly. Anyway, a strong lad could always get a job at Higgins' Brick Works, which preferred to employ boys rather than men, so saving on wages. If nothing better came along, he intended trying there.

On rainy days young James often pottered about the shop. Although too young to learn the shoe-making trade, he nevertheless enjoyed waxing the tatching ends used for sewing the upper to the sole, or softening the sheets of leather in the bath of water. For polishing a dozen pairs of boots and shoes, his father gave him a 'clodd' or penny. When not helping he'd watch his father at work, observing how he filled his mouth full of half inch rivet nails, then after scoring the new sole with his thumb nail, driving the rivets home with a single blow of a file and finishing them off with the hammer.

Sometimes, when in a good mood, his father hummed to himself. The tune was always the same, 'Queen Of The China Seas'. This was usually after his favourite hotpot dinner brought by Jane from her home a few doors up the street. Still in his apron, he'd relax with his feet on the counter, smoke his clay pipe and hum away.

One day, whilst helping in the shop, young James accidentally knocked over a full bottle of black shoe stain. His father's wrath was instantaneous. "You clumsy sod," he roared over his glasses. "Quick, use them rags to soak it up." He was icily silent as he watched his son quickly right the bottle, then frantically mop up the black dye from shelf and floor.

"Never mind," said his father when his anger had abated somewhat, "Little apples will grow again." It was a saying he uttered usually after every catastrophe, minor or otherwise, and one he'd first heard his own father use.

In spite of the odd upset, young James enjoyed going to his father's shop. He loved the delicious smells of leather, wax and blacking; these aromatic odours were pure nostalgia in later years whenever he entered a cobbler's or shoemaker's premises.

Young James broke his arm whilst bird-nesting in Queens Park and had to go to the Infirmary. He gingerly walked the two miles or so into the centre of Manchester, swearing from time to time, not without reason for with each step his arm throbbed. His pal, Bob, accompanied him, stopping from time to time to pick up stones and throw them at birds or cats. James could have found his way to the hospital blindfolded, for in the past few months he'd been treated there half a dozen times with injuries ranging from a gashed head to a fractured toe.

"Not you again?" said the thin crab-faced nurse in the office. "Well, what have you done this time?" she asked rather resignedly.

"'E's 'urt 'is arm," said Bob

She frowned. "I'm not asking you, I'm asking him. Anyway, are you here for treatment?" she asked Bob pointedly.

Bob shook his head. She looked back at James.

"How did you do it?"

"'E fell out of a tree," said Bob again.

The nurse's face went crimson. "Get outside and wait in the corridor," she barked.

The lad gave her an insolent look and sauntered out.

Still angry, she once more turned to James.

"What was you doing up a tree?"

"Bird-nesting."

She tutted with annoyance, then went to a cabinet and flicked through the cards. "Donna, wasn't it?"

He nodded. She fished out his medical card.

"Come on," she said shortly, and led the way out of the office and into the doctor's consulting room where sat three other patients, one a wretched-looking woman of about 20 with a black eye and badly cut face.

"How did you do that?" the doctor was asking her as Donna entered the room.

"I fell downstairs," she said in a flat voice.

He peered more closely at her battered face. "Did the stairs have a ring on them?" he muttered sarcastically. She drew away slightly as he dabbed at a deep gash by the side of one eye.

"Hmm, half an inch over and you'd have lost an eye. It needs stitching," he said, straightening up. She whimpered. "Now now," he said, his voice softening. "We'll only put a couple in. It needs more but we'll make do with two."

Although they took the unfortunate girl to another room to stitch her face, the remaining patients still in the consulting room could hear her cries quite plainly.

'They always lie to you,' thought Donna. He automatically felt his head where he'd had six stitches inserted a few months ago. He silently mimicked them, 'Oh yes, just a couple of tucks to make the wound heal quicker, won't hurt son.' Not 'arf. The sods always put more stitches in than they said and it hurt like hell.

"Well, what have you done this time?" said the doctor when it was Donna's turn to be looked at.

"I've 'urt me arm," said Donna.

"I can see that. How did you do it?"

The lad told him. The doctor, who was not without humour, kept a straight face and asked Donna if he fancied living at the infirmary and becoming his apprentice. The thought of having to administer stitches to patients made Donna shake his head gravely.

Fifteen minutes later, and with his arm splinted and in a sling, he headed out of the hospital. It was only when he was halfway down the stone steps that he remembered Bob. He looked about him, but there was no sign of his friend. He went back into the infirmary and searched the corridors without success. Deciding that he must have got bored with waiting and gone home, he resigned himself to doing the same. He hadn't gone far before laughter and a small crowd grouped around one of the bronze statues which stood in front of the hospital drew his attention. Closer scrutiny revealed the small shape of Bob, busily bandaging the head of one of the stern-looking figures.

Daniel left St. Oswald's and was taken on at Higgins Brick Croft. Later that evening he told his parents that the manager had thought he was older than 14 because he was so tall and well-built. His mother smiled at him and brushed his thick brown hair off his forehead with her hand, pleased because he was pleased with being thought of as older. His father, who'd been reading the newspaper, laid it aside.

"Aye, well don't work there for too long, Dan. The weather's mild now but in the winter with the rain and snow it's a different matter on that open site. Anyway, I don't want none of my lads suffering from rheumatism and bad chests in later life, undoing all the good food yer mother's put into you." With these profound words he lit his pipe and picked up the newspaper again.

With Janey now married and Joe in the army, there was more room for the family to get together before the fire in the evening. All that is save for Mrs. Donna, who rarely sat down before 10.00pm, busying herself amongst other things with washing up, preparing the lads' lunches for the next day, or just brewing tea for the family. Elizabeth usually knitted or played 'cat's cradle' with a loop of thin string, where when you held the string taut with palms facing, the lines described the shape of a pair of scissors, a bicycle or a cross. The only trouble was it needed two people to play the game, one to take the string from the other's hands to achieve a different form and vice versa. It was usually Dan or her mother who played with her before they in turn grew bored with the game and made excuses of having other things to do. Richard, who was nearly 16, had lately taken to smoking a clay pipe. There he was trying to read a book and suck on the pipe at the same time and the thing going out every two minutes, causing more than a few comical glances from his father.

"How's your toothache Dick?" he asked gruffly.

"Oh, don't remind me," moaned Richard, finally giving up on the pipe and laying it on the mantelpiece.

His father pulled the corners of his mouth down when he spoke.

"Well, I've told you time and time again, you have too much sugar in yer tea, it's not good for you. You'll have no teeth by the time yer 20."

Richard didn't answer, he just went on reading his book. Mr. Donna got up from his chair and raked the fire with the poker, causing the burning coals to settle lower in the grate.

"Go and get a shovel of coal from the yard Jim," he said to his youngest.

James, just about to have a drink from his fireside cup of tea, protested. "Can't Tizz go instead? I've no clogs on."

His father looked at him sternly. "No she can't, she's a girl and it's dark out there. Go or go to bed now."

Young James looked daggers at his smirking sister and did as he was told, stopping only to pull his clogs on in the kitchen.

"'Aven't yer finished that book yet?" asked Daniel of Richard.

"Shurrup," said Richard, not looking up

Daniel looked across at his father with a twinkle in his blue eyes. "You know he can read now Dad," he said, inclining his tousled head towards the reader.

"Aye?" replied his father in mock surprise. "Well he spent long enough in Standard Four." Reference to Standard Four always brought back Richard's boyhood infatuation with the class teacher Miss Shaw. Now talk of it embarrassed him and made him angry.

"Right, that's it," Richard exploded, "I'm going out." He snapped the book shut and stood up. This was met with roars of laughter from Daniel and his father.

"Don't be so bloody touchy," said his dad, trying to keep his face straight. "We never said anything about Miss Shaw," realising he'd said the forbidden name and trying to hide his laughter behind his newspaper.

Richard, his face like thunder, turned his fury towards the hilarious Daniel. "I'll thump you," he threatened.

At this point Mrs Donna came bustling in from the kitchen. "What's going on here? Shame on you," she shrieked, firstly to her husband and then to Daniel. "Can't you leave him alone instead of always taking the Mickey out of him?"

"I didn't mean anything," said the still smiling Daniel. "Honest, mam."

Though angry, she gazed into his upturned, innocent face. Of all her children, although she'd hardly admit it to herself, she probably loved Daniel the most. She cherished memories of him as a baby; how not long after being born he'd smiled up at her just as he was doing now. How as a child he had suffered the pain of teething and infant infections with hardly a whimper. She was fond of recalling waking up instinctively in the night and by the dim glow of the wax nightlight finding him awake in his cot, the cherub face flushed with fever but making no sound save for his soft, rapid breathing.

"My poor little lad," she'd whisper, feeling the hot little forehead. Despite this Daniel never gave her sleepless nights and in the years that followed his good looks and cheerful manner, especially if her husband had been stern with her, was a strength she drew on.

"Come in the kitchen Richard and I'll make you a nice cup of tea," she said coaxingly. "Take no notice of these two."

But Richard's face was set. "No, I'm going out," he said adamantly, snatching his coat from the back of the door as he left the house.

After he'd gone she stood for a moment shaking her head, then went back to her work in the kitchen.

Elizabeth got fed up with the string and went to help her mother in the scullery. Young Donna left his stool and sat in Richard's more comfortable chair and began to fidget. Presently, his father put away his newspaper, spat in the fire, then looked at him sternly over his glasses. The lad thought he was going to be told off for not keeping still and he drew breath and stiffened. His father was a stern man who could terrify you with his roar; a smack from him was something you remembered for months afterwards. His mother had felt the back of his hand on more than one occasion and had to bury her face in her apron to muffle the tears. As a father he was respected more than loved.

The stern moustachioed face spoke: "Yer mother tells me you were seen climbing on the railway arches the other day. Is it true?"

"Er..."

"Is it true?" roared his father.

The lad nodded, frightened.

"Get to bed and think yourself lucky I didn't wallop you."

Young James fled upstairs. He hated being sent to bed early. He wished he'd gone out and ducked the encounter with his dad. At that minute he hated his mother for telling on him. Yes, his parents had warned him about the danger of climbing on the high arches before, but he was a good climber, he wouldn't have slipped. Some nasty sod of a neighbour must have spotted him and Tommy Brophy looking for pigeon eggs.

His eyes were full of tears as he watched forlornly the kids playing 'Ralivo' in the street below from the bedroom window. He felt caged and frustrated. A thought came to him. If he went into the backyard on the pretext of using the lavatory, he could no doubt slip away and be free for a couple of hours. He dismissed this thought after a while, however, realising that his two or so hours of freedom wouldn't outweigh the hell he would have to pay when eventually he returned. Sighing resignedly, he undressed and got into bed. He had a bed to himself now, for when Jane married and moved into her own home, it left Tizzie with a bed to herself. Not to be outdone, he'd asked his mother to make up his brother Joe's bed for him. About 9.00pm he heard his mother's step on the stairs; he could always tell it was her by her habit of pausing half way up. She carried a night light in a saucer of water in one hand and a small plate with a sandwich on it in the other.

"'Ere," she said quietly, "don't let him see," indicating downstairs. "When you've finished hide the plate under the bed and I'll take it down tomorrow."

"Thanks mam."

She placed the night light on the chest of drawers which stood between his and the big bed where his brothers slept, then sat on the edge of his bed.

"Before you 'ave your butties, will you see if they've left any underclothes under their bed son?"

"Course I will."

He was under the big bed in a flash, reappearing a few seconds later with a singlet and two odd socks covered in fluff. His mother shook her head

"I don't know," she said resignedly.

She took the garments from him then moved to go back downstairs.

"Goodnight, God bless, Jim."

"'Night mam."

Now, with a chicken sandwich inside him, he lay in the soft glow for a while before the night light flame made his eyes grow heavy and he fell asleep.

Sunday in Collyhurst was quiet, with hardly a vehicle on the roads. The few shops that opened for newspapers and tobacco were closed by noon. It was a day of best clothes, church and Sunday School. In the morning the mission band tramped the streets clad in ill-fitting uniforms, stopping at corners to play tunes like 'Nearer My God To Thee' or 'Onward Christian Soldiers'. This invariably caused the dogs to bark and go on with themselves, bringing many a silent curse from those still abed recovering from a hangover or simply trying to catch up on lost sleep.

The public houses were the only establishments that opened normal hours on Sundays, and by midday these places began to fill up with late sleepers and men returning from church. The law forbade gambling in public places, so usually by 2.00pm the casual observer could discern a group of half a dozen men leaving the pub to make their way down Collyhurst Road and climb a local landmark, a high steep mound called the 'tip'. Once on top and hidden from view from below, they played 'pitch and toss', a game of chance played with coins, while one of the group acted as a lookout.

The patrolling policeman had a beat that included the railway's wooden fence which overlooked the tip. Here he could spy while being concealed from sight. The gamblers knew about this vantage point and when big money was involved the lookout sometimes brought a spyglass. There had been quite a few attempts by the coppers to apprehend the law-breakers. At Whit Week eight constables had converged on the tip from different directions, but the lookout had done his job well and all the gamblers had escaped. Willie Stringer had the closest call in having to dodge between two policemen on the tip's edge and roll to the bottom before picking himself up and haring down Collyhurst Road towards Angel Meadow.

If the weather was fine the young eligible lads and lasses spent the Sunday afternoon going walking, usually in twos. They strolled along in their best clothes hoping to strike up an acquaintance with someone they fancied. One of the most popular walks took them along Collyhurst Road parallel with the River Irk, then across the iron bridge, before climbing the steep fifty-three steps over the railway line, which brought them out of the vale to 'Barnie's Hills', a high, undulating plain of rolling grassland dotted with yew and birch trees. Despite the rail freight lines, Barnie's was a quiet, desolate place where ponies grazed in peace, and because of its air of tranquillity the gentle hills were a favourite, not only with Sunday promenaders but also with lovers and courting couples.

On Sunday evenings the Temperance Society came round and held open-air meetings. A small man with a red nose usually led the group beating a bass drum. The croft behind The Grapes pub was used as a preaching place, or if the weather was bad, then the deep office doorway of Jones' Mill was used instead. The proceedings were nearly always the same, a bearded elder would loudly extol the evils of drink and the suffering it caused family life. Other members of the group would then speak in turn of how drink had nearly ruined their lives before they had found God and salvation, and so on. Then, led by the man with the drum, the little band would move off down Collyhurst Road towards Angel Meadow and Goulden Street.

One Sunday, as the meeting neared its end, an unusual thing happened. The drummer motioned that he would like to say a word or two. He went on in a rather gruff voice, much in the same vein as his predecessors had, of how he'd redeemed himself and hadn't touched a drop of the devil's brew in years. He'd obviously got carried away with having an audience (which was mainly children and youths) and by his own oratory, for he closed his address thus: "An' so, ladies and gentlemen, yer see me now reborn." Then, forgetting himself, "I'm so 'appy now I could jump through this fucking drum."

One day young James was punished for making a noise in class. Mr. Carter had ordered the children to put away their slates and sit up straight. James had fumbled his and it had clattered to the floor. It wasn't waywardness, as Carter assumed, but feverishness which had made him lethargic in his movements, for when he'd got out of bed that morning his head had ached and he felt hot. He'd hardly touched his breakfast. His weak plea of not feeling well had gone unheeded by his mother in the morning rush and bustle to get the rest of the household off to work.

"Get out here and bend over my desk, and hurry up about it," snarled the puce-faced teacher.

The three strokes of the cane numbed James' buttocks, then seconds later they began to burn red hot. He clenched his teeth hard and screwed up his face; he wasn't going to cry, not in front of the class, not in front of that bully Carter. He limped back to his seat and sat down, but now there was new agony; it felt like sitting on hot coals. He managed to sit by leaning slightly forward, taking most of his weight off the inflamed area. He shivered from time to time, his face pale. He felt weak and humiliated. Weak because he was ill and humiliated because he'd been punished in front of the rest of the class, especially those silly girls.

The rest of the morning seemed like a year in passing, but after dinner he discovered that his feverishness was transitory and he began to feel better. Although his bum still hurt, he knew that eventually the stinging would also ease. The afternoon seemed like another year before the bell went and it was home time at last. He was free of the 'horror house'.

"We're going to the park," said Bob Brady, nodding towards Tommy Brophy who was standing nearby. "Are yer coming with us?"

"Naw, I'm going home, I don't feel so good," said James

"Okay, see you tomorrer, so long."

"So long."

Young James set off home, walking slower than usual because of the caning. As he reached Forest Street he thought of calling at his father's shoe shop but decided not to. He never knew what kind of a mood his dad might be in.

Instead, he made his way to the redhills fields, which were skirted at the lower end by Fitzgeorge Street where he lived. He was almost halfway across the fields when he came upon Eliza Jones seated on one of the sandstone humps from which the fields got their name. He shuffled past, but her voice made him stop.

"Does it still hurt Jim?" she asked, her dark eyes all serious. He looked at her and brushed the hair from his eyes.

"No," he replied, feeling a little awkward as he always did when talking to girls.

"He's rotten isn't he," she said, (meaning Carter the teacher). James just nodded.

"Never mind, Jim," she said sympathetically as he went to walk on again. "You'll be all right tomorrer, ta rah."

He didn't answer, he found it hard to swallow and he felt tears coming to his eyes. Only half turning his head, he waved to her as he moved off. 'Mustn't let anyone see me cry,' he thought, now walking with his back to her so she couldn't see the tears streaming down his cheeks. Oh God, it felt terrible to be young and small. This had been a bad day for him from first getting out of bed. He'd felt ill, been ignored, then shouted at, been beaten and humiliated and then when all the world seemed his enemy, a few kind words from a silly girl had touched him, so making him do the unforgivable thing, cry. He wiped the wetness from his cheeks as he neared Fitzgeorge Street. 'Mustn't let anyone see,' he thought.

The Rice family lived two doors away from the Donna household. John and Ethel, harmless and inoffensive though they were, were considered a little slow by their neighbours, or to the less polite, 'not a full shilling'. He worked in his father's clog shop on Rochdale Road whilst she looked after their home. There was talk that the reason for John's slowness was that his mother breast fed him until he was eight years old, even going up to school at lunch break to give him a feed through the school railings. How true the talk was had little relevance to most residents of Fitzgeorge Street, who liked the good-natured Rices and were amused by their antics. For instance, he arrived home late one night a little the worse for drink to find that Ethel had bolted the front door, locking him out. His hammering on the front door brought her to the bedroom window where she flatly refused to grant him access. All his entreaties to her were of no avail, so deciding on another tactic he shouted up to her:

"Let me in or I'll show you up in the street."

"Go on then," she answered defiantly, her elbows resting on the windowsill.

"Right, I will," he shouted back. "I fucked you before we were married."

"Well, that's nothing," she sniffed disdainfully, "so did your brother and your two cousins."

Another time it was her turn to be locked out. He appeared triumphantly at the bedroom window, indifferent to her pleas despite the heavy rain that began to fall.

"Please let me in," she wailed, "I'm getting soaked."

"No, go where you've had yer beer."

"I 'aven't been drinkin'."

"I don't care. You locked me out the other week," he said with satisfaction.

"Ah, go on, let me in, I'm freezin'."

"No."

"I'll get a policeman."

"Get as many as yer want," he replied and closed the window. Thirty minutes later, with the rain still falling, there was a banging on the front door. It was Ethel again, but this time with two six feet tall policemen.

"What do ya want?" said Rice from the bedroom window.

"Come on now, open up," ordered one of the policemen, "or we'll run ye in."

"Piss off."

With that the two caped officers ran at the door with their shoulders in an attempt to burst it open, but the door hardly budged. They swore and stood glaring up at him in the rain. They threatened him again, then lined up for another run at the door. It was then that the rain appeared to come down in torrents and halted them in their assault on the woodwork.

"Bleedin' 'ell, the dirty get's emptied the piss pot on us."

For a full five minutes the air was blue with effin and jeffin and threats of imprisonment for life and so on and so forth, but the man at bay in the window was unmoved.

The leader of the two policemen tried another approach; he started to speak reasonably to Rice.

"Listen John, why don't yer let yer missus in? She's getting very wet. It's not fair yer know, she'll get 'er death o' cold, an' you wouldn't like that would you now?"

Rice stuck his chin out.

"I don't care."

"Aw, don't be like that John. Yer name is John, isn't it? An ya do luv 'er, don't yer?"

"I might do."

"Of course ya do John. Now lad, why don't yer just open the door a little to allow her to slip inside an' we'll be on our way. An' we'll forget yer threw the contents of the chamber pot on us, won't we?" he said to the other policeman.

For nearly an hour the coaxing and inveigling went on, first with one policeman, then the other, until finally Rice left the bedroom and came downstairs. He called out from behind the front door.

"Are yer still there?"

"Aye, but we're just off now John, goodnight."

The two officers didn't move but stood poised as the bolts were drawn back. As the door moved inwards a fraction of an inch they crashed into the house, punching and kicking poor old Rice all around the living room.

****

Roundabouts, railways and rivers have always been the beguilers of boys, risk and danger of little consequence.

"Should we see if we can climb it then?" asked Bob.

It was evening and Brady, Donna and Tommy Brophy were sitting on the step of Bob Greaves' bakery shop, one of their favourite meeting places, if only for the delicious smells which lingered there, even when the shop was shut. The object of their conversation was the dark outline of the high tool warehouse, built sheer on the edge of the Irk's only tributary in the vale before its waters vanished beneath the Collyhurst roadway.

"How will we get up?" asked the bespectacled Tommy.

"Easy, cross over the bridge, then climb up to the top of the wall, walk along the top on the other side of the river, then climb the drainpipe to the roof. Easy," Bob said, matter of factly.

"I don't know about that," said Tommy dubiously. "It's dark ya know."

"Ya don't have to climb it if ya don't want to Tom," said Donna.

Tommy shrugged. "I know."

The three lads stood in a loose circle, hands behind them. In unison they did a flee-fly-flow-bang to determine who went first. Donna lost and so had to lead, with Bob next and Tommy last. Like three shadows the boys climbed the parapet of the bridge and slowly walked along its flat top. Below they could hear the river gurgling in the darkness. From the parapet they climbed onto the roof of a small adjoining building, from where the lads could reach out and grasp the drainpipe which led to the roof of the tool warehouse. Donna reached out and grasped the pipe. He tested it by shaking it. It felt firm. He started climbing upward, using feet and knees for maximum grip. It seemed a long climb and he was breathless when he reached the roof, partly with the effort and partly because he was a little scared the drainpipe might be old and come away from the wall. It was chilly up there on the warehouse but the view was worth it. He could see lights for miles around. Leaning forward he walked up the slope of the roof to the apex to get an even better view, but as he gained the new vantage point he stumbled and because of his posture went legs first over the apex and began sliding down the slates on the other side. He threshed about trying desperately to stop himself, but if anything he seemed to go faster.

His legs shot off the edge of the roof. In an instinctive act of self-preservation he covered his head with his hands. It was at this heart-stopping split second that his downward rush was suddenly jerked to a halt. He felt himself swinging slightly in mid air. Far below him he could hear the water mocking him when he dared to move. He found that a guttering bracket had caught under the front of his jacket and had saved him from going off the edge of the roof to certain death or serious injury. He hung there for a moment getting his breath back. High above him he could hear Bob calling him in the darkness.

"Jim, Jim, stop hiding. Where the fuck are you?"

Gripping the wooden guttering with both hands, Donna gingerly eased himself carefully back onto the lip of the roof, then back up the roof's rake to the comparative safety of the apex. Bob gave him a look of reproach.

"Where yer bin 'iding?" he demanded indignantly.

****

"Leave the vinegar alone," murmured Donna's father to him absently. "It isn't mineral water."

It was Sunday afternoon and Donna Senior was sitting peering covertly through the kitchen window into the back yard. Now and again he'd chuckle to himself. James, seeing his father's attention was elsewhere, took another quick swig from the bottle before replacing it on the kitchen shelf. The lad was very fond of the occasional mouthful of vinegar, apart from its sharp acidic tang it left a clean feeling to his mouth and teeth. He wiped his mouth with his hand, then moved curiously to where his father sat. Squinting through the lace curtain the object of his father's attention was revealed at a glance, for Richard and Dan were circling each other wearing boxing gloves. At that very moment Richard, the elder of the two, threw a straight left, then a right cross which caught Dan in the face and knocked him back on his heels.

It wasn't an unusual thing for the lads, young Donna included, to exercise on a Sunday afternoon with Indian clubs or spar with boxing gloves in the art of self-defence. In fact, it was a regime their father had insisted on from the boys' earliest years. Their half-brother Joe, now in the army and eldest of the lads, had instructed them when Donna senior was unable to officiate. However, the watchers through the window could see that today this was a no-punches-pulled bout. It had probably begun as a routine sparring session, but with Daniel rather unwisely taking the mickey out of Richard, Dan was now paying for his lack of tact. Richard stuck out another straight left, which again caught Dan in the face, making it redder, but before Richard could follow it up Dan poked out his own left, which spun his brother round. In the kitchen Donna senior chuckled.

"Cover up, cover up," he whispered behind the curtain as Dan came in for some rough treatment from Richard.

"Why don't yer go an' stop 'em," said Mrs. Donna reprovingly, "before one of 'em gets 'urt."

"Shush," said her husband, waving her away.

At the bottom of the back yard Daniel again got the worst of an exchange, but this time as Richard moved in on Daniel, who was now covering up, the latter swung a right which caught Richard flush on the point of the jaw, knocking him into oblivion. Richard crumpled to the ground, his head by the yard water grid. Daniel stared down at his brother for a few seconds, then stalked off towards the kitchen door, pulling off the boxing gloves as he went. Donna senior motioned James and his mother quickly into the living room and pretended to be preoccupied with his newspaper.

Daniel said nothing when he entered the house, but his bruised face was set in an expression of distaste. He stripped off his shirt and washed his face and head at the sink, pulling a clean towel off the clothes rack to dry himself while his father watched him covertly from behind his paper. A minute later Richard came into the kitchen. Like Daniel, his face was set, but he ignored his brother and for the next week an uneasy silence hovered between the two lads, even though they slept in the same bed.

Mr. Donna was usually the first to rise in the morning. His wife still in bed could hear him cough occasionally and, aided by the sounds he was making, visualised him raking out the ashes to build a new fire in the grate. She lingered a moment or two, then got out of bed, dressed and went downstairs. Mr Donna was brushing dead ashes from the hearth whilst the fire, with its shovel and newspaper draught blower, roared up the chimney. She rinsed her face at the sink and, with the fire now established, made porridge on the hob and boiled water for the family's breakfast. Meanwhile, her husband, his main household job done, washed and got ready to go to his shop. Mrs. Donna, having made the tea, ladled the porridge into five basins and put them into the oven to keep hot.

Next began the ritual of getting the rest of the family out of bed. From the bottom of the stairs she'd call and plead, informing Richard and Dan that the hour was later than it was, in an effort to generate some sort of urgency in the brothers. (It didn't matter so much with Elizabeth and James because they were still at school and could lie in a little longer). However, the ruses rarely worked. All she got in response to her strained vocal chords were a few murmured promises followed soon after by renewed snoring. She shook her head in a gesture of hopelessness and turned to her husband, who by now had finished his breakfast and was filling his clay pipe.

"Shout up to those two will you? I've got a sore throat trying to get them up."

His technique was somewhat different to hers, but considerably more effective. He stood on the second stair up and thundered in his foreman's voice:

"Dick, Dan, Up, Now. The pair of yer allus leave it to the last minute, then yer rushin' to get to work."

Immediately there was a response from above. Bangs and feet could be heard. Daniel was the first to show himself, carrying his boots, socks and shirt. His hair was sticking out at all angles and there was a crease in his face where he'd been lying on a fold in the pillow. He slumped down in a chair before the fire, still not properly awake. His mother let him be and didn't try to ply breakfast on him. She knew from experience how irritable he could be until properly awake. Richard, on the other hand, once out of bed was quite placid first thing in the morning, providing his teeth were not hurting him. He had a peculiar habit of hopping two-footed all around the living room, clutching his boots and socks, cheerfully whistling a tune. This kangaroo-like dance plus his cheerfulness sometimes incited Daniel or his father to remonstrate with him, but he refused to be provoked and continued to hop about until he finally sat down and put on his boots.

After breakfast it was Daniel who generally left the house first because he had the furthest to travel, the brickworks being half a mile distant. The Collyhurst Finishing Company, where Richard worked, was just a few hundred yards from Fitzgeorge Street.

Most of young James's time in the morning was taken up at the sink washing, paying particular attention to his hands and fingernails. He scrubbed them in water warmed from the kettle until they became red and sore. His fastidious attention to cleanliness was endured not from any sense of vanity. On the contrary, in the school holidays he tried to avoid soap and water as much as possible. However, now the halcyon days were over he was particular about his appearance, especially if he was to satisfy the teacher's scrutiny. The children were inspected every morning before lessons. They were made to stand to attention at their desks, displaying in front of them their hands and fingernails, clean and neatly trimmed, necks and knees scrubbed and shoes and clogs polished to a deep shine. The daily classroom inspection the children were subjected to would have satisfied the most discerning matron in any infirmary.

Young James woke in the early hours of the morning to the sound of the wind playing about the outside of the house. He lay there in the darkness, the night light having burnt itself out, eyes open listening to the strange noises a house makes at night. He lay alone in Joe's bed and in the darkness he could just make out the big double bed where Richard and Daniel slept. He listened to their soft breathing and the occasional movement one or the other made in sleep. The wind outside grew stronger, then died away to nothing. The bedroom was quiet. Then something tapped twice on the window. The lad's imagination began to stir. He heard the stairs creak, then creak again. He visualised some horror creeping slowly up to his bedroom with large staring eyes, intent on doing away with him. His heart began to beat faster. His scalp grew tight. He regretted now the occasions when a few of the local lads gathered on the bakery steps after dark, frightening themselves by telling stories of ghosts or giant men with huge bulging eyes who lurched about the roads at night.

The wind gusted suddenly outside the house, rattling the window frame. Then from the stairs came another creak, but louder and nearer the bedroom door. That was enough, or rather too much for the lad. He slipped out of his bed and, fumbling his way over to where his brothers slept, dived between their two slumbering forms. He used his elbows to gain more space for himself and lay in the darkness feeling safe. But being between Richard and Daniel in bed made him hot and he soon began to sweat. He could feel beads of it on his forehead and rivulets running down his body beneath the bedclothes, but he refused to move, preferring a feeling of safety to all else.

FIVE

Stand-to

In darkness they heaved the corpses over the back of the ditch and dug in hurriedly. They filled the sandbags and laid them two high in front to make a parapet. Word had been passed up the line that an attack was expected at any time. They waited anxiously trying to penetrate the darkness in front of them, every little bump and shape seemed to take on a sinister movement if stared at long enough.

"What time is it?" whispered Jimmy Robb.

Donna felt in his tunic. "Half-three."

Way over to the left a machine gun fired off a short burst; this was answered by a spate of rifle shots, then quietness once more.

The battalion's headquarters were about 300 hundred yards behind the trenches in a damaged farm building on the La Bassee Road, the same road that the troops had used as a jumping off point for the trenches and soon re-christened 'dead horse road' by the soldiers.

They stood-to, cold and hungry through the hours of darkness, their brogue shoes and tropical tunics inadequate for the last day of October. From 7.20am it began to grow light, although a mist kept visibility down to a few yards. It was sufficient to reveal that the dead around them were more widespread than realised. Also, there were white officers lying stiffly amongst the bearded bodies.

As the mist began to lift more details came into view. To the right of the Seaforths, about 60 yards forward, was a trench containing the remnants of the Royal West Kents plus a few 47th Sikhs who had managed to scramble in after their previous day's ill-fated attack. Facing them about 120 yards away were the German front line trenches, distinguished in the flat farmland as a line of low brest works.

Donna viewed the terrain with interest. To the right of the trench in no-man's-land were two derelict farm buildings, which during the hours of darkness he'd mistaken for trees against the night skyline. To his left a road led through shell-holed farmland to a village about a mile or so distant. He could see smoke rising from the ruins, although the steeple of the little church near the roadway was intact. To the rear there was more open farmland, and about 800 or 900 yards distant what appeared to be a line of enemy reserve trenches. 'Dead horse road' was lined with shattered trees.

They were still stood-to when the first shells came over. During the night someone in the trench said he'd heard that the Germans weren't expected to use their artillery because their own trenches were too close by. However, here they came now, woofing in the distance, the noise and turbulence growing in intensity until the soldiers covered their heads and bent double, convinced that the monsters were coming right on top of them. The shells landed about 30 yards in front with tremendous crashes; earth and parts of dead Sikh showered down on the cowering men, black smoke from the explosives was everywhere.

This was Donnna's first time under fire and his heart was in his mouth. He thought his last moment had arrived. He rose cautiously on shaky legs and looked through a gap in the sandbags, then quickly crouched down again at the sound of more shells on the way. Two exploded behind him, one hitting a cottage, the other demolishing a garden wall, throwing the bricks sky high. The enfilade continued throughout the morning causing dreadful shrapnel casualties. 'B' Company had an officer and three men wounded by murderous flying metal. One man had his lower jaw torn away; he sat in the bottom of the trench dazedly watching the blood seeping into his tunic. The stretcher-bearers, struggling to take casualties to the field aid post, were shot at as they hurried along 'dead horse road'. Donna watched as the rear man was hit in the back, the force of the bullet turning him completely around to face the enemy trenches before he fell. The Seaforths answered with a fusillade of rapid fire at the German parapets. The spent bullet cases came flying from the rifles like confetti in the withering hail. It felt good to be having a go back.

Gradually the firing tapered off to a temporary lull but for the odd rifle crack from the Germans, answered for good measure by two from the Scotsmen. They were grateful though for the respite while sentries watched the German positions in case of a sudden attack. Most men were slumped down in the fortified ditch having a smoke or trying to catch a few minutes shut-eye. They were hungry and tired not having slept or eaten for nearly 24 hours. Their faces were dirty, quite a few minus hats. One or two of the more adventurous tried softening the issued hard tack biscuits each man carried by pouring water over it, but after many minutes of mastication the thing still had the taste and consistency of compressed cardboard.

Donna and Jimmy Robb were filling their pouches with ammunition when the sentry above suddenly fell back across the two of them. There was a fist-size hole in the side of his head. He lay with his shoulders across the Englishman's legs, his mouth open, his breathing shallow and rapid.

Robb was the first to react. He gripped Macfedris, who was sitting next to him, and bellowed, "Away and get a fucking stretcha." After a few moments the badly wounded man started snoring. Donna looked at Robb and shook his head. By the time the stretcher got to him he had stopped breathing. Donna brushed blood and bits of brain from his kilt apron, then took his place at the parapet. Through a gap in the sandbags he cautiously scrutinised the churned-up terrain. Everything appeared quiet and deserted except for the khaki-clad dead, some lying mutilated like sides of beef a few yards in front of the trench. One dead Sikh had lost his turban; the long black hair trailing back about two feet reminded Donna of a biblical painting.

The Germans started to bombard again, this time with a smaller high-velocity shell. Giving little warning of its approach it exploded in the air, scattering shrapnel in every direction. The whoosh and explosions went on incessantly throughout the day, lessening in intensity with the onset of nightfall.

The order to 'stand-to' was met by quite a number of moans. Laidlaw was particularly vocal. "Wat the fuck have we bin doon all day?" Though there was a perceivable drop in temperature, the darkness was welcomed by the infantrymen. Under its cloak the wounded could be removed, badly needed rations and ammunition could be brought up and maybe, despite the cold and the enemy, an hour or so of blessed oblivion in sleep could be had.

That evening two staff officers visited Colonel Richie, who had made his headquarters in the cellar of a house. Both were about 25 years old, well turned out with highly polished riding boots and fleece-lined coats to keep out the cold. The spokesman had a thin moustache and carried a cane.

He saluted. "Good evening, Colonel," he said. Then his eyes turned to the map on the table. "I've been asked to come along and brief you as much as I can," he said briskly. As he finished speaking a shell burst close by, causing the house to shake and dirt to fall on him from the ceiling. The other staff officer quickly stepped forward and brushed him down. Richie glanced at his Number 2, Major Wright, with a look of amusement. The staff officer caught the smile and blustered on even more briskly. He prodded the map with his stick. "As I was saying, Colonel, yesterday's attack was a poor show."

"Why was that?" asked Richie.

The officer blew the dirt from the map before replying. "Well now, after a bombardment from our artillery and some French 75s," he prodded the map with his cane, "here and on the left, Indian infantry and sappers attacked the village whilst on the right the 47th Sikhs attacked the German line at this point."

"What time did the attack go in?" asked Colonel Richie.

The officer looked at his companion for confirmation, then said, "10.00am."

"What was the weather?"

"Bright sunshine."

Richie pulled a face.

"Anyway," said the officer, eager to get on, "at the village, after some fierce fighting the Indians drove the Germans out but the Sikh attack was halted on the right flank here," indicating the position which the Seaforths had now taken.

"Do we still hold the village?" asked Major Wright.

The staff officer shook his head. "No such luck. Soon after the failure of the Sikhs to get to the German trenches, the Germans counter-attacked the village and unfortunately re-took it."

From outside a distant maxim gun began stuttering. Richie scrutinised the area where the Sikh's attack had foundered. It was flat, open farmland. "How long did the artillery blast the enemy at this point?" he asked.

"Well, I understand a few shells were fired but I'm afraid the division is rather short on ammunition."

Colonel Richie shook his head in disbelief and began searching his pockets for a match for his pipe. The red-banded staff officer went on unperturbed.

"No, Colonel, I believe had the Indians skirmished when they came under fire from the German line I'm sure the enemy trenches could have been breached!"

He sniffed derisively. "Instead, they only got to here," he said, rapping the map with his stick.

"Aye," barked Richie, unable to control his wrath at the rear line expert, "and most of them are still there but they'll no' be getting up."

Out in the darkness two more shells exploded, causing more dirt to fall within the cellar.

The officer dismissed his aide's valeting attentions and changed his line.

"I notice Colonel that you have left a gap in your positions in front of the deserted house. Is it not a possibility that the Germans could practically walk through whilst your chaps were being heavily shelled on the flanks, or during the early hours of darkness?" He paused, looked at his companion, then went on. "I understand that on an early morning reckie in this area one of our chaps visited the Gordons' front line position and discovered nearly all the officers and men asleep on the bottom of the trench.

Major Wright felt his C.O. stiffen. "Ah ye sure," he roared, "that your chap didne make a mistake with these men and in fact they had frozen to death through lack of proper clothing?" He thrust his pipe towards the staff man. "Listen, don't you bother aboot my men, they're Seaforths and I wouldne swap one for any ten others."

"Er, I did not infer," stuttered the officer.

Major Wright, anxious to relieve the tension, interrupted. "What type of troops are we facing?"

"Prussian jägers Major."

"What are they?"

"Elite rifle Battalions."

Unable to find a match Colonel Richie lit his pipe from the lamp, but he was still angry.

"What about propa winta clothing for ma men? Did ye know they're still wearing shoes?" he rapped.

The second officer fumbled for his notebook. "Leave it to me Sir," he said, trying to be reassuring. "I'll report it to Divisional HQ."

Richie, now calmer, drew on his pipe. "Ah already have done... twice."

The staff officers left soon afterwards promising to arrange to have the dead Sikhs removed and buried.

In the trenches men from each platoon were detailed to fetch the rations up. Although cold and dog-tired, Donna volunteered to go with Lance Corporal Littler and three others back about a mile to the field kitchens in the reserve lines.

The four man ration party climbed up out of the trench and started picking their way diagonally across the previous day's battlefield. It was pitch black and they were careful in their tread to avoid the corpses and equipment that littered the ground. Halfway across the zap of a stray bullet made Harper turn sharply and stumble onto a body. It made a long groan as the air was driven from it; the sound made Donna's hair stand on end but it appeared to have little effect on Slim Harper.

"Sorry cock," he said as he fished about retrieving his dropped rifle.

As they climbed onto 'dead horse road' two shells exploded bright red 50 yards away. They flung themselves down flat and stayed there until the whine and rush of flying metal had ceased. Later they were challenged by a patrol.

"Halt, who goes there?" came a voice from the darkness.

"Seaforth ration party," answered Littler.

"Advance one man and be recognised," said the disembodied voice again. This he did and had a light shone on him.

"Who the fuck were they?" asked Donna when they were allowed on.

"Lincolns ah think," said the Lance Corporal.

At the canvas-covered field kitchen they loaded up with bread and dixy tins of hot stew

"Where's the tea?" asked one of the party.

"Coming up, but ahm afraid it's only gunfire," answered one of the cooks. This was received with groans and swear words. (Gunfire tea was hot tea minus milk and sugar).

"Call yersels baawarchis (cooks)," grumbled Private Caine.

"Nae use blamin' us," wailed one of them, "the Army Service Corps wagons ah late."

Donna searched the steamy oasis for a familiar face.

"Where's Conroy?" he asked

"Roon tha back" was the reply.

He found the kitchen wallah gloomily peeling a huge pile of potatoes by the light of a lamp.

Although Conroy was older, Donna greeted him brightly, "How ya doing son?"

The Londoner, Conroy, had to look twice before he recognised whom it was.

"Oh hello Donna, didn't know ya at first, black face and what not." He nodded towards the mountain of spuds, "Look at this bleedin' lot."

"You're better off here than up front though," said Donna gravely. "Collins got one through the head today. He was standing next to me and he just keeled over."

"Aye, so I heard."

The need to get back to the ration party prompted the Englishman to raise the real reason for the visit.

"Listen Andy, have you got any buckshees?"

The cook vanished into the darkness, returning a few minutes later with a tin of corned beef. He held a finger to his lips. "Say nothing," he said conspiratorially.

Donna nodded. "Thanks Andy."

On the journey back with the rations Donna caused some amusement when he stopped in the darkness to stick a branch of a tree down the back of his webbing.

"What's that for?" whispered Macfedris.

"Well," he said laconically, "I'm thinking of having my own Christmas tree."

As they neared the trenches the Germans sent up a flare. The group froze stock still in mid-stride as the ghostly light bathed the land in an eerie glow. They felt terribly exposed there on the road, expecting a burst of machine gun bullets to slam into them at any moment, but nothing happened. The flare arched and slowly dropped to earth and darkness once more. There was a unanimous breath of relief and audible mutters of 'thank fuck for the dark'.

In the trenches many of the platoon had fallen asleep; they lay curled up in the darkness to conserve body heat. Sergeant Cooper shuffled amongst them, a dixy of rum in his hand. "Come on, my brave lads, one tot each, this'll put some life in yer."

The meagre rations didn't last long but the stew, though hardly warm by now, tasted wonderful. Donna broke part of the branch across his knee and made a small fire in the side of the trench. The heat helped to take away the hunger from the small group crouched around the beacon. Most were dozing, rifles propped between their legs.

"Praise ta Prometheus," muttered Robb.

"Who's that?" queried Campbell.

"Who's what?" asked Robb.

"Promiscuous."

Robb smiled. "Prometheus? According to Greek legend he was punished for giving man fire."

"How was he punished?" asked Macfedris.

"His liver was torn oot every morning by a huge eagle, then in the night it grew back again ta be torn oot at the morn once more."

"Huh," said Campbell, "ye' are no making it up?"

Robb laughed and shook his head. "Well noo, there's no doubt them old Greeks were barbari bastards."

A little later the fat face of Lieutenant Roylance appeared in the firelight. He seemed quite matey as he told them to be extra vigilant as the enemy might try to raid the trench or infiltrate the farmhouses during the night.

After he'd gone Donna relieved the coughing Haskins as sentry and leaned on the trench wall peering into the blackness of no-man's-land. God, he felt cold. What he'd give for a pair of the old man's boots right now. In front the German lines appeared quiet and still; he was glad of that. Away to his left he caught the occasional flash of a rifle from the enemy's right flank. To keep his mind from the cold he watched for the rifle again, noting first the pinprick of white light, then a second or so later the distant cough of sound. Peering again, his eyes tried to penetrate the dark mass of the ruined farm buildings in no-man's-land, but it made his eyes hurt. Above, the sky had a ceiling of dirty grey cloud and from somewhere beyond the German trenches the nostalgic, rather touching, call of an owl. He sighed despite himself and strained intently to hear it again.

"Everything all right?" asked a voice close behind him, breaking his reverie. It was Sergeant Cooper with an armful of empty sandbags.

"Yes, Harold," said Donna.

"See anything?"

"No."

"Hear anything?"

"No."

"Good," said Cooper, who started to move away.

"Harold," said the Englishman, "give us a couple," indicating the bundle.

"Aye, I see what yer mean," said the sergeant, a hint of approval in his voice. "It'd keep yer warm fillin' them up."

Donna said nothing. Cooper was only half right, for when he'd vanished Donna merely stuck the canvas bags into his thin tunic for extra warmth. A few more fires dotted 'A' Company's line. Donna could see the reflected glow on the back of the trenches and shadows moving about repairing the line, glad no doubt to be able to keep warm by being active.

At 11.00pm, to add to the cold and discomfort, it started to rain heavily, turning the clay of the trench bottom into a morass of clinging mud, or it collected in pools which grew deeper by the minute, slopping over the sides of the infantrymen's shoes to saturate with numbing wetness. Some of the soldiers stood on sandbags in an effort to keep above the water, but after half an hour these too became waterlogged. The men had wrapped their groundsheets about them to keep dry. They stood hunched as the rain lashed down and the water rose slowly up their puttees.

Since arriving in France the travelling and sameness of each day's duties had caused many men to lose track of time and reflect on happier past evenings. "Fucking Saturdee neet, in ah shit pot like this," said a voice bitterly.

It rained all through the night, easing off at the first greyness of dawn. Of the Germans there appeared little during the night, even when some of the sentries had opened fire to relieve the miserable boredom. Now, as though to let the Seaforths know they were still there, they opened up with rifle fire, knocking up dirt and debris all along the parapet.

The strafing lasted a few moments, then trailed to a stop, leaving the sound of the wind and rain to take its place. The Highlanders watched across a hundred or so yards of mud and water-filled shell holes. From the German trenches smoke could be seen rising in various parts of their line.

"Tha bastards, wil'ne come noo," growled Campbell softly. "They're away ta breakfuss."

Leaving sentries up they tried to bale out the foot deep water in the bottom of the trench, but their efforts had little effect on the level. The atrocious conditions could not extinguish the wry humour of soldiers in adversity, however. Red-eyed Jimmy Robb watching Macfedris wading with great difficulty to cover a couple of yards informed him straight-faced that new orders had come up saying they should be on the lookout for submarines. However, for the most part they were too wet and weary for much talk, most had developed coughs or runny noses, a consequence of having feet constantly submerged in freezing water. They were given a tot of rum and some breakfast that morning.

The food had been brought up the previous night and kept in sandbags until the morning. There was bread, a twelve-ounce tin of corned beef divided between four men, some dry tea and a tin of Tommy Ticklers plum and apple jam, the last item especially welcome as most young men are partial to sweetness. Also, the jam had a dual use. Apart from being spread on bread it could be used to sweeten the tea.

Wood, mostly branches from the shattered trees which littered the roads, had also been brought up, though wet. In no time tea was being brewed in mess tins over small smoky fires.

After the German's initial burst of rapid rifle fire, they sniped continually and with deadly accuracy at the Seaforths. It was tantamount to suicide to show, even for the briefest moment, any part of the head above the parapet; ricochets were almost as lethal. Lance Corporal Littler had his right forearm broken while rolling a cigarette. He was crouched well clear of the top when the bullet zapped up the trench, missing other members of his platoon but knocking him over. When he tore away the red-stained sleeve, blood gushed upwards in a scarlet arc. The bullet had severed the radial artery.

George Campbell surveyed the pale N.C.O. "Ye lucky cunt, ye'll get to Blighty wi' tha'," he growled, partly with envy but mostly to reassure Littler. The big Highlander quickly tied a bandage from his small pack tightly over the spurting wound, but his handiwork failed to stop the bleeding, the blood dripping rapidly into the muddy trench water. Campbell looked towards Robb for help. "Tha' fuckin' thing wil'ne stop," he said.

Roylance came lumbering up looking like the rest of his platoon, bedraggled and covered in mud. "What's tha problem?"

Campbell nodded towards the wounded man. "Canna stop tha' bleedin' sur."

The officer, aware that his men were watching, fastened another bandage above the wound and used a stick to tension the binding into a tourniquet, but this hardly had any effect and the Lance Corporal appeared to get paler.

"Ah see it's slowed doon," bluffed the officer. "Take yersel away ta tha regimental aid post, but keep ye heed doon."

Before the N.C.O. could obey, Donna, who'd been watching and thinking that the wounded man would never make it to the aid post, propped his rifle against the side of the trench and crouched by the wounded man's side. He took hold of the injured arm with one hand, while with the other he felt for the brachial artery in the man's biceps. Having located it he pressed the artery with his thumb against the bone of the upper arm. The bleeding stopped.

"Now ya can do that yersel," said the Englishman, showing Littler where to apply pressure with his good hand.

"Thank ye Donna."

"It's nothing. Watch how ya go."

"Ye know," said Jimmy Robb thoughtfully when Donna had returned to his position, "ye're a wee fool, ye could be outa this, ye could be on easy street working with the M.O. The orderly he has noo does ne know his elbow from his arse'ole, ye should be in there."

Donna shrugged, easing his chafing webbing from across his shoulders. He said with a wry grin, "I'd miss being soaked to the skin, and being shelled and shot at."

Robb looked into his face, then continued the charade. "Oh precisely my boy," he said, putting on a posh accent. "I myself could be the Duke of Fullers Earth but ah hate wearing a fucking tall bonnet and tails."

However, in the following months Donna was to reflect bitterly more than once on the wisdom of his friend's words.

During the night the Germans had got into the two ruined farmhouses near their lines, giving a greater field of vision on the British positions. From this vantage point they turned their artillery on what was left of the Royal West Kents, dug in, forward and to the right of the Seaforths. For half an hour they blasted and tore at the Kents' position. Jimmy Robb, watching, shook his head in disgust. "Poor bastards," he said, gripping his rifle then squirming off down the line in search of the officer. He found Roylance, head down watching the barrage through a gap in the parapet.

"Can ah have a word sir?" he shouted, his teeth showing white in his black face.

Lieutenant Roylance nodded.

"Could'ne our guns flatten them houses? Tha Kents ah getting murdered an' it'll be us next."

Roylance nodded to indicate he understood, then motioned Robb to go back to his position.

It was later in the morning, during a lull, that the first shells began hitting the Seaforths' central positions, sending great spouts of brown earth and sandbags flying high into the air or exploding in mid-air in a mass of black and bright red, shredding shrapnel in all directions. Around midday the shelling tapered to a stop, but was then replaced by intense rifle fire from the German trenches. Opposite, the Highlanders opened up in reply, but it was almost impossible and foolhardy to see what effect the infantrymen's fire was having on the enemy. Roylance almost paid the ultimate price for his curiosity, a bullet exploding into a sandbag less than an inch from his head.

Number 2 platoon were less fortunate; they lost two men, both shot in the head, their blood colouring the mud and water in the trench. The dead men's waterproof groundsheets were used to cover them over. Later in the afternoon it was the Seaforths' turn to be shelled again. This went on, varying in intensity until darkness brought a blessed relief.

Under a pitch black sky at 2.00am the following morning Lieutenant Cameron and six men, having removed cap badges and other insignia, slipped over the parapet into the blackness of no-man's-land and groped their way forward. Ten minutes before, Sergeant Cooper and five volunteers from Number 1 platoon had crept out and now lay in extended order in line with the ruined farm buildings. Facing them was the German front line trench 200 yards away. Donna was one of the five to volunteer to act as cover for Cameron and his men, not because he felt more daring than other members of his squad, but because apart from Harper he was the only other Sassenach in No. 1 platoon and felt compelled as an Englishman amongst these Scots to volunteer for this dangerous mission.

Lying doggo in the darkness, his hands numbed with cold, he could see the glow of a fire in the enemy trench. In front Campbell lay like a corpse ten feet to his left and there was another figure a similar distance beyond him. To his right loomed the black mass of the farmhouse, ominously silent. He wondered about a sentry, or indeed if there was anyone in the place. Then, as if in answer to his thoughts, he heard a slight scraping sound from within the matrix, then close by the sound of soft running water. Very slowly Donna inclined his head towards the sound. No more than a dozen yards from where he lay and merged within the darkness of a wall was a German soldier urinating. The Englishman watched riveted, for as the Jerry finished and turned to grope his way back into the house, a shadow moved quickly along the wall and clubbed him senseless. As silent as pathans (Indian hill tribes), the raiding party swarmed into the building. To the men lying outside there came firstly the thin shaft of light from within followed by a shot and a scream. Seconds later Cameron and his men stumbled out and were racing back towards their own trenches.

Donna eased the bolt of the Lee Enfield.

"Now for the fucking fireworks," he muttered. From the German lines he could hear frantic shouts of 'auf, auf', and then shouts of 'tommies". His mouth was dry. 'Here the bastards come,' he thought, but they didn't. Instead, the whole of their parapet lit up with rifle flashes, bullets whined around above him and zapped and slammed into the cottage like hailstones. Two hundred yards to the left a German machine gun opened up with long bursts of diagonal fire. This was returned with white flashes from the West Kents and Seaforth positions.

Donna felt a bullet tug at his shoulder strap. He tried to press himself deeper into the earth to escape from the fire. As the inferno raged inches above their heads the support squad began crawling back towards their own trenches. It was almost dawn before Donna dropped wearily back into his own company trench; he was filthy and numb with cold. Despite this he curled up against the wet clay and fell asleep.

By daylight two of the night raiders hadn't returned. It was hoped that perhaps they'd lost their way in the darkness and scrambled into a trench further up the line, possibly the West Kents, which was forward of the Seaforths. However, as the day and the sniping and shelling wore on, no word came and concern for them was replaced by the will to survive.

After eight days of being slouched in mud and freezing water, of inadequate food and winter clothing, of being shelled and sniped at, a new torment manifested itself. Lice. Unable to wash, the soldiers discovered their bodies and clothing were infested. The lice lived on the blood of the infantrymen, debilitating further their meagre reserves of energy.

After fourteeen days the Royal Scots relieved the Seaforths. Although the relief began at 9.00pm, it was 2.00am before the troops were billeted at Lacouture a few miles distant. To the soldiers the roughly converted barns and outhouses were heaven. There were hot baths and each man was given stew, a measure of rum and a blanket where he could roll up and go to sleep by a constantly attended fire.

The first three days were spent in sleep and de-lousing; clothing was steeped and washed in huge vats of boiling water. Any equipment lost or torn was made up or replaced. Donna discovered he had eleven holes through his tunic. He didn't care to speculate too long on how he'd attained them or their significance.

On the fourth day the battalion marched through heavy rain to a village called Le Hamel, three miles to the west. They were to stay at Le Hamel during the day, then return to the trenches near Givency under cover of darkness. However, the village had been badly knocked about by shell fire and the billets where the infantrymen were installed were little more than shattered walls, most without roofs, scant shelter against the rain and cold. Each soldier knew that these billets, though cold and basic, were immeasurably better than what they were going back to.

SIX

Partings

"That's not a throstle," said Donna's father when the lad revealed the fledgling he had carried home so carefully inside his jacket. They were in the kitchen, the man seated at the table, the boy stood before him carefully holding the bunch of downy feathers.

James was disappointed; it showed in his face.

"No," said his dad shaking his head, "that's a bramhall. Same spotty chest, same colour, but it can't sing like a thrush, better take it back Jim to its nest."

The lad shrugged and gently returned it back inside his jacket. He wanted to please his father and also make amends. A couple of weeks before, the skylark the family kept and whose song in the mornings used to ring out throughout the house, died. Young James blamed himself for the death of the bird. Usually his dad had fed it on a mash of butter, breadcrumbs and chopped-up egg, but a couple of days before the songster's demise, the lad had fed it a big black worm he had dug up on waste ground. The bird had gobbled up the offering readily enough, but the bacteria within the worm's body must have been too much for its small constitution to take and the next morning the household awoke to an unusually quiet dawn, finding a pathetic little bundle in the bottom of the cage.

"Can I take it back tomorrow?" he asked his father. But he knew his answer before he asked. His father just looked stonily at him. Without another word he left the house and traipsed back the two miles to parkland where he had found the nest. Since Mr. Donna had left his job on the docks and opened up his shoemaker's shop, footwear was hardly a problem now for the family. Boots and shoes apart, he had also made a jerkin for Richard and a pair of breeches of soft leather for Daniel.

His latest skill as a shoemaker soon became known. One lady whose daughter had deformed feet regularly made the journey from the outskirts of Harpurhey to his little establishment for specialised footwear for her child. His skill with leather enabled the girl to walk almost normally.

Although he ran his own household strictly, as his father had done before him, he had a heart and for the very poor, whose request was simply to repair or re-iron clogs, he either accepted in payment whatever they could afford, or waved away their proffered pittance with the words, "Pay me when yer become rich". Because of this, and his sobriety, he was respected in the neighbourhood.

In August, Joe got ten days leave from his unit, embarkation leave they called it. He was sailing to Egypt shortly afterwards. He looked grand in his walking out uniform with its red coat, gold buttons and blue trousers. Everyone said how tanned he looked and hadn't he got taller? Mr. Donna, who rarely showed any emotion, was very proud of him. It told in his face.

Joe had brought presents with him, a posh briar pipe for his father and a bottle of scent for his stepmother. What struck young James most about his stepbrother was the smell. Quiet Joe smelt of metal polish and blanco. Whilst at the army camp Joe had won the guards' novices light heavyweight boxing tournament, the medallion and chain which was his prize he gave to his father to keep.

The boy loved to sit listening to Joe and his father talk. He'd perch on the stool by the fire, enthralled with stories of army life and foreign lands. He liked Joe and didn't mind giving his bed up. Besides, Joe gave him sixpence to clean his kit whilst he was on leave, a task he'd have been glad to do for nothing.

The days of Joe's leave seemed to fly past. Then, when he'd only a couple of days left, Mr. Donna brought out the parcel of layers of cotton wool he'd purchased a few days previously.

"Here Jim," he said, "fetch me Joe's tunic and thread me a needle and some red cotton – yer eyes are better than mine."

The lad did as he was bid, then watched intrigued in the milky light of the gas mantle as his father carefully sewed the layers of wool into the chest lining of Joe's scarlet coat. The lad was curious. He fidgeted on his stool, longing to ask questions but reluctant to interrupt. Instead, he watched as his father's large black stained fingers deftly dog-stitched the wool into position.

"What have you done that for, dad?" he asked as his father smoothed and fussed the padding into an even contour. His dad stuck the needle into the bib of his leather apron, then looked at him over his glasses as always.

"It's to prevent Joe being shot if there's any trouble when he goes abroad."

The lad stared at him puzzled

"How will that stop a bullet?"

His father yawned, took off his spectacles and rubbed his eyes before answering.

"Well," he began, "you'll notice now that the chest area is no longer flat, the cotton wool padding I've sewn in has contoured that vital part of the chest area and made it round."

"Would that make a bullet or a spear glance off it then?" asked the young James intelligently.

"Exactly. An old sweat who once served with General Gordon in the Sudan swore the padding his mother had stitched into his tunic had deflected the fine points of two bullets and so saved his life." Mr. Donna emphasized the point with his finger. "It's the shape that's important, not the padding."

The male members of the family took Joe for a farewell drink in The Star on his last night of leave. Friends of the family, despite his polite refusals, kept buying him drinks. These he slipped to Richard and Dan until by 11 o'clock both lads were quite tipsy and had to be helped home to Fitzgeorge Street by Joe and their father.

The following day, as he was about to leave he called to see Mrs Chadd, the widow who together with her own two youngsters had cared for Joe and his sister Jane when their own mother had died. She greeted him with sad eyes and after a few moments, when it was time to go, she suddenly hugged him and kissed him on the cheek. Joe felt a little embarrassed and gently scolded her for being silly, but as he left her house he found it hard to swallow.

Janey came down to see her brother off. She watched tearfully with Mrs. Donna and Tizzie as Joe, with his father carrying his kit bag, left for the railway station.

Earlier that morning, Mr. Donna, in an attempt to lift the gloom of Joe's departure, had joked about he himself impersonating Joe by blackening his hair and going abroad in his son's place, but once they had left Fitzgeorge Street and begun to climb the steep cobbled Bridenvilla Street, they spoke little until they reached London Road railway station.

"Don't forget," said Mr. Donna, "let us know what ship you are leaving on and I can check its progress at the shipping office in Cross Street."

His son, so like him, nodded. Joe spoke through the carriage window.

"I'll bring you something back dad."

"Just bring yerself back, Joe," said his father, raising his voice above the hiss and noise of the train station.

Minutes later, as the train, accompanied by whistles and shouts of 'stand clear' and clouds of steam, slowly began to move, they shook hands very firmly. In the noise and emotion of the moment it was seconds before Joe realized that his father had pressed into his hand two gold sovereigns. The two watched each other, waving from time to time until the train was out of sight. Mr. Donna sighed, then sighed once more before wearily turning for home.

****

Tizzie left school at Easter and got a job at Frankenbergs millinery shop on Rochdale Road. She worked from eight in the morning until eight at night Monday to Friday and received ninepence a week wages.

Mr. Frankenberg had originally come from Germany and spoke with a thick accent. His wife, Sadie, was a tall, dark woman with lovely expressive hands. They had a son, Coppul, about the same age as Tizzie, who suffered from a bad stammer.

Tizzie, a bright girl, was quick to learn and very polite with the customers; the couple soon became very fond of the pretty husky-voiced redhead. She endeared herself to them further with her patience, especially when in conversation with their handicapped son. She would listen with her head slightly to one side as Coppul formed his words. Her presence had a calming effect on the lad and made him more coherent.

Tizzie, for her part, liked her Jewish employers and often shopped for bacon for them at lunchtime, a meat that their faith really forbade them to eat, but which they found delicious. On special Holy Days, when the Frankenbergs were not allowed to undertake the most menial of tasks, she'd make her way through the dark cold streets to the shuttered shop where she'd find them seated cold and in the dark, whereupon Tizzie would make a fire for them and light the gas mantles. For this they paid her two pence or gave her something from the shop, which she accepted reluctantly. However, the good-hearted girl never once asked for payment for her efforts, often blushing with embarrassment when Mr. Frankenberg pressed the coins or article into her hand with the words: "Here my liebshen - take it."

Bob Brady called for young James one evening, looking rather secretive. "What's up?" asked the latter once the two were out of the house and away from the adults.

"Do you remember that unknown woman that was found strangled in Angel Meadow?" whispered Bob from the side of his mouth.

James shrugged and shook his head. Bob became impatient and gesticulated with his hands.

"You must remember, it was in all the papers."

Young Jim thought for a bit, then said he remembered, but he didn't really because he never read the newspapers and he suspected that Bob didn't either. His friend had probably heard his mother talking about the foul deed to some neighbour.

"What about it?" asked Jim

"Well, they've laid her out in Bootle Street police station and they're asking members of the public to see if they recognize her," said Bob. "Shall we go and see if we know her?"

Jim nodded, a little awed at the prospect of seeing a dead body.

The two civic-minded youngsters set off on a fine summer evening down the cobbled Collyhurst Road, past beery smells from the open doors of The Grapes. They dodged young girls playing top and whip in the office doorway of Jones's cotton mill. On their left was the huge corporation tip and they could see lads they knew playing on its steep sides. To their right were the openings of Bebbington, Appleton and Bratt Streets. A little further and they were in the shade of the Collyhurst Finishing Company buildings. Strolling on they lingered by the short iron bridge that spanned the evil-looking River Irk at the foot of the 53 steps. The steps led up to Barnies hills. They threw stones into the river, then, fed up with this, they ambled on, stopping only when they were opposite a row of two-storied dwellings on the far bank of the River Irk.

Because of the fine weather quite a few of the residents had left their front doors open. Bob antagonized a severe-looking man who was sitting staring into the dirty brown depths by calling him fish head and pulling faces at him across the water. The poor chap tried to ignore the taunts at first, but then his patience snapped and he suddenly leapt up, waving his fist and threatening all kinds of injury to Bob, to which the lad, reassured by the natural barrier, threatened all kinds back.

The small school of St. Catherine's was next to receive the lads' attention. They rattled the railings with sticks until the school caretaker chased them off. A passing railway cart took them the rest of the way to Angel Meadow. They clung like monkeys to the back of the heavy horse-drawn vehicle, unbeknownst to the driver, only dropping off at the junction of Goulden Street so they could watch the blacksmith shoeing a big docile horse in Redbank.

"Well, what do you two want?" demanded the desk sergeant at Bootle Street.

"Can we have a look at the murdered woman in case we know 'er?" asked Bob.

The policeman looked down at the two lads suspiciously for a moment, then nodded. "Have you ever seen a dead body before?" he sniffed. "Not a pretty sight!"

"Course we 'ave," said Bob, "plenty of times."

The officer's eyes narrowed. "What's yer names?"

"Robert Brady."

"James Donna."

"Right," he said after writing them down, "follow me." He motioned the lads around his desk, then led them down a corridor.

"Now then, take a good look and tell me if you know 'er," he growled.

He opened a door to a room and ushered the lads inside, at which point the officer was suddenly called away by a superior.

"Back in a minute," he grunted, leaving Bob and Jim alone in the mortuary.

The body lay on a trestle table covered by a shroud. As far as they could see it was the only occupant. What struck James most was the heavy smell of perfume in the air. Bob didn't seem to notice.

"Let's have a look at her," he whispered unperturbed, and marched up to the corpse and began ascertaining which end was the head and which the feet. He removed the cloth from the poor wretch's head and gazed for a moment at the waxen face. The woman had been found strangled, so the newspapers had reported. Also, during the foul deed, a scarf had been stuffed into her mouth, which was now evident because part of the fabric was protruding through the dead woman's teeth.

Unlike young James, Bob appeared completely unaffected by his surroundings and became fascinated with the task of removing the scarf from the dead woman's mouth. He reached out and tugged one way, then the other, at the inch or so of silk material, but to no avail. Then, while young James watched, Bob's frustration got the better of him and he suddenly climbed up onto the corpse and sat astride the dead woman's chest, as one would a horse. Now, with both hands free he could pull with greater effect, which he proceeded to do, jerking the deceased's head up and down like a yo- yo.

James watched mesmerised until a sound like thunder from behind made him nearly jump out of his skin.

"What in the effing name o' Gawd's goin' on?"

It was the police sergeant. They'd both forgotten about him. He stood there, his face purple, his eyes nearly popping out of his head in disbelief.

"What in the effin 'ell are you doing?" he roared, grabbing Bob by the head and lifting him off the table.

"I... I was only trying to get the scarf," he spluttered.

"Trying to get the scarf?" thundered the policeman. "Trying to get the effin scarf? I've a good mind to throw yer in a cell and swallow the key. Yer a criminal. What are yer?"

He carried Bob by the head down the corridor towards the door of the police station.

"Now then, if I see either of you two around here again I'll swear it was you that did the murder an' you'll both 'ang. Now fuck off."

****

Summer school holidays seemed to hurtle by for young James. These were halcyon days for the youngster, where the sun always seemed to shine. There was lots to do and time didn't exist; if it was light you played outdoors, when it got dark you went home. If you were hungry and the sun was out, it was lunchtime; if you were hungry and the sun had set, it was teatime. Eventually, when it became too dark to play and the gas-lit streets echoed to the shrill calls of parents for their children, there was always home and supper and an hour to listen heavy-eyed to the rest of the family as they grouped chatting in the living room Then it was into the small kitchen for a wash at the slop stone, then up the stairs to bed, where his tousled head was soon a prisoner of Somnus, the Goddess of sleep. In these glorious days of no school, young James couldn't know that this summer would be the last one the Donna household would enjoy as a complete family.

In August, Richard had a birthday. As usual his mother made a cake and lit 17 candles. Then, after the family sang 'Happy Birthday' and tugged Dick's hair two extra times for good luck until his eyes watered, she removed the candles and broke them up with her fingers.

"Why do you always do that?" asked Tizzie. "They've hardly been used."

"It's bad luck to relight birthday candles," replied Mrs Donna.

"Why is it?"

Her mother just shook her head. "Because it is," she said without explanation.

One evening, Daniel got a telling off from his father for entering the kitchen with his dirty boots.

"Look at the sodding place, clay all over the floor," moaned Mr Donna. "I've told you before, don't come into the house with your boots on, leave 'em in the yard."

Daniel, as usual, didn't answer his father back. Instead, he got the handbrush and began to clean up the loose clay which had fallen on the stone floor. His father (who must have been out of sorts) still picked at him. "Yer not doing it right, look you've left some there, see," he nagged.

Mrs Donna, busy making the meal, looked at her husband appealingly. "Leave the lad, he's doing his best," she said quietly. "I'll clear it up later, besides its raining outside."

Mr. Donna looked hard at her.

"Don't tell me its raining outside, woman. It's still no excuse for turning the kitchen into a midden." He looked about the living room. "Where's the paper?" Richard was reading it, but without a word he closed the Evening News and handed it to his father.

The evening meal was eaten in silence by the family, only the ticking of the wall clock and the rain on steamed-up windows intruded on the group in the kitchen.

Richard was the first to finish this evening. He placed his knife and fork together to the left of his plate amongst the bones of chicken and half a roast potato.

"That was nice mam," he said, getting to his feet.

"Yer welcome," she smiled, still busy with her own food.

In January the household found it had another resident. Tizzie was the first to be aware of the uninvited guest. She'd gone upstairs to fetch something from the bedroom and caught a glimpse of something small and furry vanishing up the chimney. She yelled and dashed back downstairs, refusing to go back up again. Richard picked up the poker and went to investigate. He found that, whatever it was, it was causing soot to fall into the unlit fire grate and somewhere high up in the chimney he could hear the thing coughing. It turned out to be a cat and all kinds of entreaty couldn't tempt the terrified animal down again. So it was unanimously decided to leave the cat to Daniel to deal with when he got home from work.

After tea, it took Daniel two hours to coax the pathetic creature down with milk and some cooked meat. At first the half-starved wretch snatched at some meat, then tried to dart back up the chimney. But Daniel had anticipated that and grabbed it by the scruff of the neck, all the time talking to it in a soothing tone until he had quietened the terrified thing. He spent another hour gingerly stroking and cleaning the filthy black and white fur until he had won its confidence. He watched as the cat, in between coughs, ate ravenously, then darted off under his bed. The cat was allowed to stay only because no member of the family could catch it. With Daniel it was a different matter. The animal would come down the stairs at the sound of his voice and follow him around the house, quickly acquiring the name of 'Magnet'.

As weeks went by it became so attached to Daniel it would leave the house at the appropriate time and wait at the corner of Fitzgeorge Street for its master to come home, meowing loudly when it caught sight of him approaching. Once home, Daniel would clean his boots in the yard, wash his hands at the sink and feed the cat before he sat down to his own meal.

One evening, his mother stood looking at Daniel's broad back as he bent washing his hands in the kitchen. She was strangely troubled. He caught her watching him as he turned and began to dry his hands.

"What's wrong mam?" he smiled.

She shook her head slightly. "Nothing luv." Continuing with a rush, she said, "Oh, Dan, why don't you leave the brick works and get a job indoors somewhere? You could always get taken on at Jones's mill or the Collyhurst Finishing Company. It must be really rough working outside in this weather."

He brushed his hair from his eyes and said, "Alright mam, I will."

Mr Donna came in a little later, his coat glistening with rain. Young James and Daniel were still eating at the table.

"Here you are," he said to Daniel. "I hope it lasts longer than the first one." It was a new leather apron.

Mr. Donna said little and ate his meal in silence. Richard said he didn't want anything to eat, he'd got toothache. As he reached for the tincture from the shelf, he knocked over some other bottles. As he hurriedly set them upright again, his father, who was in a sober mood, intoned a phrase he'd heard from his own father, and one he often used in the aftermath of catastrophes, large or small.

"Never mind, little apples will grow again."

As the evening wore on Roy Blunstone, a friend of Daniel's, called at the house to see if he wanted to go out, but Daniel said he felt tired and was going to have an early night. After his pal had left Daniel made his way into the kitchen, where, hidden from view, he swigged from a bottle of cod liver oil. Calling 'goodnight', he climbed the wooden stairs to bed, followed as though on some invisible lead by Magnet. The two went to sleep, one in the bed, one under it, to the comforting sound of a steam train crossing the high viaduct above the street.

The following morning young James awoke with a thumping headache and sore throat. He was lying between his two brothers in the big bed. He heard his mother calling the boys, each one by name. Dick was the first to stir. He moved the covers aside and rolled out. Young James, with eyes closed, could hear him hopping about in his characteristic way as he dressed himself.

"Dick, will you tell mam I feel ill?" croaked the lad

"Alright," said his brother, scampering off bare-footed. A moment later his mother was in the bedroom urging Daniel to get up.

"Come on Dan, you're going to be late."

James felt his mother's cool hand on his forehead.

"You're boiling up lad, better stay off school today and stay in bed and keep warm. I'll bring you some medicine later."

She turned her attention once more to Daniel. "I shan't tell you again Daniel," she said, injecting some sternness in the tone of her voice.

Daniel leaned up off the pillow, his thick brown hair stuck out at all angles where he'd lay on it.

"I don't want to go to work today mam," he said seriously.

"Are you ill?"

"No, I just don't feel like work today. I rarely have time off work, you know that."

His mother sighed, then went back downstairs again.

A little while later, Mr. Donna's voice boomed from below.

"Daniel, if you're not out of that bed in one minute flat, I'll be up and drag you out."

Daniel knew better than to ignore the threat. He rose slowly, reluctantly dressed himself and left the room followed by the cat.

Young James, now alone in bed, painfully opened his eyes to gaze through the window at the grey overcast morning. He looked at the sideboard by the wall, at the fine cracks in the ceiling and the black scorch mark on the pale blue distempered wall where the gaslight had been lit too near the plaster. He closed his eyes and tried to sleep, the sound of the front door being opened and shut in quick succession telling him that some or all of his family had left for work.

Despite his fever, he smiled to himself. His keen ears had detected the soft tread of the cat in the bedroom as it made its way to its haven under the bed. A little later, when he heard the door to the house open and close for the last time, he heard his mother's footsteps climbing the stairs.

"Here you are Jamey," she said a little breathless. She carried a bowl of cold water and flannel in one hand and a bottle of medicine and spoon in the other. She laid the bowl on the chest of drawers while she carefully spooned two big doses of Febrifuge into him. From the flannel she made a cold water compress and laid it on his burning forehead. It felt good. She stayed for about twenty minutes, speaking gently to him and changing the compresses when they lost their coolness. His mother could always make young James laugh. As he lay there with his eyes closed, she said softly, "My word, you're hot.

I'll bet I could boil a kettle on your head. Shall I go and bring one up?"

James smiled and shook his head. His eyes felt heavy. After a while she left James to sleep while she went to get on with the housework.

It was just after noon that a loud banging on the front door woke James up. A man's voice cried excitedly, "Mrs Donna, Mrs. Donna, it's your Dan, he's been in an accident at the works."

"Oh God!" he heard his mother exclaim.

Next came a babble of voices. He recognized his father's amongst them, speaking quickly, question coming on question. "How's my lad? Is it bad? Where is he now? For Christ's sake answer me will you!"

"I think they've taken him to the infirmary Mr. Donna."

"I'm going there."

The voices grew fainter as his father and the other man moved off down the street. As he heard the front door close and his mother moving about in the kitchen below, Young James slipped out of bed and, clad only in his night shirt, went down the stairs on unsteady legs. He stopped two steps from the bottom and peered around the side of the staircase at his mother walking aimlessly about the kitchen wringing her hands.

"What's happened to Dan mam?" he asked weakly.

She'd been too preoccupied to hear his feet on the stairs. She looked up suddenly.

"Oh, he's had an accident at work. Mr. Roberts and your father have gone to Sam Lawlor's for a cab to take them to the hospital," she said absently. Then she pulled herself together somewhat.

"Go back to bed, son, and keep warm."

He did as his mother bid and eventually fell asleep. It was a deep sleep. He dreamt he was in a wood being pursued by a giant and no matter how fast he tried to run the thing seemed to be gaining on him, and then, mercifully, the dream changed and he was in a rowing boat on a gravel lake on Barnies hills. It was nice there and he was rocking gently with the boat's motion.

He woke up to find Janey gently shaking him by the shoulder

"Wake up Jim, wake up."

She looked serious. "How do you feel?"

The sleep had done him good and he told her so. She gave him some more medicine.

"Would you like something to eat?"

"Yes."

She straightened his pillows.

"How's Dan?" he asked a little hoarsely, watching her back while she struck a match and lit the wall gas light in the darkening room.

"He's very ill," replied Janey quietly with her back still to her stepbrother. She sighed and then busied herself again with the bed. "Keep warm and I'll bring you something to eat later," she said.

The following morning he felt much better. He was allowed to get up, provided he kept warm and wore his clogs. Normally when indoors he liked to discard his footwear. His father always chastised him for this practice, never tiring to point out the harm that cold could do through the bare foot, causing any number of fatal complaints in later life, such as stomach ailments and TB. However, today no one took much notice of him, being too preoccupied with poor Dan's fight for life.

In the living room he found his mother being comforted by Janey. Richard was sitting quietly, gazing into the fire. His father, unshaven, grey-faced and looking old, was asleep in the chair. Tizzie, now fourteen and quite the woman of the house, was making a stew in the kitchen. James went and seated himself next to Dick.

"How's Dan Richard?" he asked softly.

Richard just shook his head and carried on gazing into the fire.

Janey answered the question for Richard.

"He's still very ill. Dad and Mr. Roberts have been at the infirmary all night."

"Will Dan be alright?"

Janey sighed and shook her head. "We just don't know."

At this, his mother wept softly in her apron. Her voice broke as she sobbed.

"My beautiful little lad. He gave me the least trouble of all of you. Oh God." Pictures of him as a baby came to her, especially the time he was burning up with fever and had tried to smile up at her. "Oh God, why him, oh God."

"Shush mam," said Janey gently, "he's very strong, he'll pull through alright."

With her face still buried in her apron Mrs. Donna wept. "I had a feeling something was going to happen to him. I told him the other night to leave those bastard brickworks. The same warning must have come to him because he didn't want to go yesterday, he was made to go," she said, weeping bitterly. James had never seen his mother so distraught before and it upset him. He hitched nearer to Richard, who, without a word, put his arm around his younger brother.

Partings

Daniel died in the infirmary two days later; he'd hung on to life for nearly three days with a hole in his back the size of a football. The hospital doctors were amazed that he'd lasted so long in such a mangled condition. His arm and the back of his head had also been damaged. The surgeons expressed their sorrow and deep regret to Mr. Donna, saying they'd never known a young man with such a strong constitution to fight for life like his son had.

With tears in his eyes, Mr. Donna replied brokenly: "He was only sixteen, not even a man."

More details of the accident came out from Dan's workmates later. It appeared that he had been working near an unguarded clay-cutting machine and somehow his new apron had caught in the gearing. He had instinctively put out a hand to stop himself being drawn in. With great strength, and despite his hand being mashed, he managed to free himself and turn away but then fell back on the wet muddy ground into the huge cogs, which gripped his shirt and bit into his back and head. Dan's friend Geoff Taylor, working on the other side of the track, on hearing his cries above the din, had ran and shut off the monster machine.

Mr. Donna received £16 compensation from the Higgins Brick Company for the loss of his son, a pound for every year of his life.

The family's grief was deep and constant, even the house itself seemed to mourn Dan as though its very fabric had somehow absorbed the sorrow from its inhabitants.

Long years after, when young James was a man, he still felt the hurt and remembered vividly on many occasions going into the bedroom and finding his mother lying prone in Dan's half of the bed crying bitterly. When she noticed him she would pull herself together somewhat and say she was just having a lie down. It affected his father in other ways. The tough old ex-guardsman withdrew into himself and rarely spoke, staring for hours into the fire, not going to bed. His inner torment must have been unbearable.

After Daniel was buried, Reverend Lomax visited the house. Mrs Donna let him in whilst her husband appeared apparently oblivious to the visitor. Mrs. Donna, more welcoming, bade him to sit and gave him a cup of tea. Still Mr. Donna didn't acknowledge his presence. The cleric offered his sympathies, saying he would pray for Daniel and the family for strength to meet this tragedy. He went on in a more philosophical voice: "The Almighty moves in mysterious ways, his actions at times like these are hard to comprehend, but if we have faith his wisdom will reveal itself."

At this Mr. Donna, still staring into the fireplace, said in a quiet threatening voice, "Get out of my house."

There were other visitors of course, friends and neighbours who called, caps in hands, speaking quietly and asking if there was anything they could do. They didn't stay long. There were the Stringers, Mr and Mrs...; they were both Irish, she from the south, he from the north. The Roberts, Beckets, Murphys, Mcloughlins and others. Most of these had at some stage lost children through illness or disease and knew the pain the family was enduring. Mrs Chadd, who lost her husband when her children were a few years old, stayed the longest, comforting Mrs. Donna in the kitchen.

The half full bottle of cod liver oil from which Daniel had taken his last swig the night before the accident, plus the torn and bloody shirt he'd last worn, were carefully placed by his father, unwashed, in a cupboard in the living room where Mr Donna kept his shoemaking account books and personal things.

Dan's cat, Magnet, left the house the day Dan was buried. It was as though it knew he wasn't coming back. It had been seen waiting at the corner of the street for him the day of his funeral. But, strangely, it was never seen again.

One month later the Donna family, unable to live in the house any longer, did the same and moved into a vacant house in Brydenvilla Street.

The adage 'Time heals all things' is not always the case. Though Daniel's death touched every member of the family in different ways, as time passed the pain lessened, as it must if life is to continue. But this wasn't the case with Mr. Donna. He was never the same man. He became more remote and, apart from working in his shop, he rarely left the house. It was as though a fire had gone out in him. In the evening he would arrive home, wash, have his evening meal, read the newspaper, then doze in the chair until it was time to retire for the night. He seemed to have a desire to hide from the world in sleep. In February a letter arrived from Joe in Egypt. Mr. Donna was the main writer of the family and normally would have answered Joe's letter in half an hour. Now it took him a week to reply.

One day after school, young James called at his father's shop to ask what he would like for tea that evening. As usual he stayed a while watching his father at work putting rivets into his mouth, then hammering them into the sole of a new pair of boots he was making. As he was shaping the uppers on the second boot, the drag knife slipped and sliced through his apron and trousers and put a deep gash in his thigh about three inches long. After the first initial curse, and with little fuss, James watched cringing as his father, with hardly any sound, sewed up the gaping wound in his leg with the needle and waxed thread he used to sew the boots and shoes.

"Jim," said his father a little hoarsely, "will you get me a bandage from our Janey?"

The lad ran off to his sister's house nearby and sped back with a dressing and bandage.

Later, as he walked home through the grass of the Redhills, a new and strange emotion stirred within the boy. All his young life he had respected and feared that big grey-haired stern man. Now he reasoned, with a maturity beyond his years, that his dad must have been preoccupied in his mind when he allowed the knife to slip. And as he watched him stitch the wound, then quietly ask for a bandage, his father had for a moment allowed the steel shield he carried around him to slip, enabling the lad a glimpse of the vulnerable man within. For the first time in his life he felt sorry for his dad.

SEVEN

Givency

It was gone midnight, but mercifully the rain had stopped when the battalion returned to the trenches. The four days rest seemed to have sped past. The soldiers on sentry duty stood hunched against the cold, the others improved the parapet or replenished the trench stock. Sleep was out of the question. In any case, 'stand-to' was only a few hours away.

Donna had helped the machine gun team dig out a ledge in the clay and position the weapon with sandbags to give it maximum sweep. Now he and Hoskins were seated on ammunition boxes trying to keep their feet dry when Sergeant Cooper found them.

"Just the very lads I've been looking for," he said genially.

"We're just having a smoke Sergeant," said Hoskins by way of explanation.

"That's alright son, but when yer done I want the two of you to go back to 'B' communication trench, then make yer way to shell box road where you should find Corporal Littler with some boxes of bombs. Help him bring them up."

Cooper then picked his way further up the trench, calling back, "An' don't get lost in the dark."

There were only four boxes but it took the three men nearly two hours to complete the task. Donna didn't mind, at least to some degree it kept one warm, though the feet still felt like ice.

"What's in them?" asked Robb of the rather unusually stout boxes.

"It's a new secret weapon," said Donna.

"Go on," invited Robb.

Donna couldn't resist it. "They're exploding senna pods."

Robb was equal to the leg pull, however. "Hmm, I suppose we throw 'em at the Jerries, he eats one, then fucking well blows his arse off does he? Very clever."

Just before dawn the soldiers stood-to, ready with rifle and bayonet, but the enemy didn't come. Then, as it grew lighter and the German brest works could clearly be seen, thin spirals of smoke were observed rising up into the cold grey morning.

"The bastards are having breakfast," said someone on the line.

Soon after, leaving sentries up they stood down and got breakfast. It consisted of bread, strips of bacon and gunfire tea, the former being brought up the lines in empty sandbags. Though not the most hygienic way to transport foodstuffs, nevertheless, after cooking the fatty bacon over fires from the end of their bayonets, the smell was delicious and it tasted beautiful.

About nine o'clock, sniping from the German trenches started and continued on all through the day, interspersed with heavy shells. Donna was fearful of a shell landing near to the bomb boxes and kept as far away as possible, but as darkness fell, around four o'clock in the afternoon, the shelling stopped, and this was greeted with relief by everyone. The soldiers hated the shells; rifle or machine gun fire is a different matter. One usually knows in advance the direction of gun fire and can fire back. With shells, however, you have a split second to decide where it's going to land, then even if it misses you by yards the bursting shrapnel can still take a head or a limb off and there's nothing you can do about it except pray the next round doesn't have your name on it.

"You know," said Hoskins between coughs, "once this lot is over I'm going to get out of the army."

He and Donna were sitting in a small dugout covered with wood and sacking.

"Are you married?" asked Donna.

"Not yet, but I've got a woman back home. We went to school together. Here, have a look," he said, fishing out a photo from inside his tunic.

Donna's eyes were tired and heavy and in the dim light of the small candle he could hardly see much of the girl's features, but he said, "Very pretty".

Hoskins had another coughing bout, then rolled a cigarette.

"Yes, she's a grand lass. She wanted to get married before I went to India but I said no, let's wait until I get back." He raised his eyes and looked about him. "Now this fucking lot."

"Never mind," said Donna reassuringly, "they say it'll be over by Christmas."

"Yes, but I'm not so sure," said Hoskins miserably.

The rations came a little later, bread, bully beef, tea and a square of cheese, which the Englishman didn't eat but slipped into a pocket instead.

It was quiet the next day, no shells and hardly any sniping, a time to repair the trench and dugouts. Donna and Hoskins were sandbagging further up 'A' Company's line. They worked mostly in silence, being too weary through lack of sleep to talk much, taking turns filling the bags and pushing them carefully between gaps in the parapet. About 70 yards to their right in no-man's-land stood the remains of a cottage, now reduced to a heap of bricks save for one wall about four feet high with a couple of fair-sized holes blasted out of it.

"Let's have a rest," sighed Donna after about an hour. In their debilitated state the simplest of movements took maximum effort. They slumped down on the fire step and leaned back against the trench wall.

"Do you want one of these?" enquired Hoskins, pulling from his tunic his tobacco tin. Donna shook his head, resting his eyes. Hoskins brushed his hands on his kilt apron and proceeded to roll a cigarette.

High above a bird called, then another. Donna kept his eyes shut, trying to imagine he was somewhere else for a few precious moments. Then a cloud of aromatic tobacco smoke drifted across his face. He was about to take up Hoskins' offer of a cigarette when the sentry ten feet away hissed a warning, "Cooper."

Hoskins reacted first, throwing the stump of his fag away and standing up. Almost immediately came the crack of a rifle, then a whack as his head jerked to one side, followed by a sound reminiscent of an eggshell being crushed.

Hoskins pitched sideways into the bottom of the trench, his glengarry gone, the side of his head a bloody mess. The hole was huge. He moved once and then started to snore as though going into a deep sleep, which he was but from which he would never awaken. The water in the trench began to turn red around him.

"Man hit," came the call.

Donna, now fully alert, was trembling. "Where did that fucking shot came from?" he yelled at the sentry.

The man shook his head numbly

Carefully Donna rose from his haunches and peered through a gap in the sandbags. The trenches opposite looked quiet and deserted, as they had earlier, yet he knew that there was a sniper out there just waiting for a moment's carelessness. His eyes switched to the wall and the heap of bricks. Considering the angle Hoskins fell, the shot could have come from that direction. Then, as if in confirmation, he thought he saw a slight movement at one of the holes, or was it a bird or was it his imagination?

Sergeant Cooper lifted Hoskins' identity disc, and as he withdrew his paybook from the breast pocket he also took a photograph, which dropped into the water beside the corpse. It was a picture of a girl. He looked at Donna. "What happened?"

Donna motioned him onto the firestep. "The bastards are using dumdum bullets. I think he got it from there Sergeant," he said, pointing towards a heap of bricks that was once a farmhouse about a hundred yards distant.

"Right," he said after squinting for a moment through a gap, "keep yer head down and warn anyone else around. I'll send Macfedris up to help you with the bagging." Someone threw a groundsheet over the dead man and stuck a board up saying, 'Danger, Sniper'.

The Germans shelled at 12 o'clock, but this time they were answered by British guns half a mile behind the Seaforths' lines. They fired not on the German trenches but beyond, in an effort to knock out the enemy's batteries. The shelling lasted perhaps half an hour with the Germans stopping first.

An hour before 'stand-to' another man was hit in the head and covered with a groundsheet. The bodies were removed after dark by the soldiers who brought the rations up. It rained incessantly that night, some said it was because of the shelling, most said nothing, intent on trying to keep their bodies out of the rain, although with regard to their feet they had given up long ago. With the inadequate shoes they wore their feet had been wet from day one.

Donna reflected more than once: 'What I'd give for a pair of the old man's boots right now.' Ever since Hoskins had got it through the head the Englishman had spent some part of the day observing the flattened ruins of the farm building. He'd watched at night through the rain and cold whilst on guard, but saw nothing. However, on the morning of the sixth day, his patient vigil was rewarded. As the mist cleared and the order to 'stand down' came, he had stayed, just concentrating his gaze on the heap of rubble, then after an hour and when he was about to give up, he noticed a difference in the inside of the holes. The interior of one hole was grey black whilst the other was jet black, as though something was filling it. 'Could it be bricks?' he pondered. Then, as he watched he spotted a slight movement. His heart began to quicken. 'That's got to be the muzzle of a rifle,' he told himself.

He nestled the butt of the Lee Enfield into his shoulder and aimed into the middle of the black hole. Taking first pressure on the trigger, he held his breath, hoping for another movement.

From his left he heard Macfedris whisper, "What is it Donna, have you seen something?"

He didn't reply or move a muscle, but mentally answered with a couple of choice swear words. He wanted no distractions in this private dual of life. and death. His eyes ached watching for the slightest movement, real or imagined. Then, when it came he fired dead centre of the hole. He felt the recoil jar his shoulder as he put another two rounds of rapid fire into the same place. He then watched anxiously for the smoke to clear. He didn't wait long as a few seconds later the black covered head and one arm of his adversary fell into view.

"Got the bastard," hissed Donna. The soldiers either side of him cheered, which brought others out from the dugouts to see what the noise was about. Lieutenant Roylance appeared, his fat pasty face grunting as he pulled himself onto the parapet and peered carefully through. Then, with hardly a glance at Donna, he jumped down into the trench, calling over his shoulder, "Good shot Macfedris."

Jimmy Robb and Harper looked at each other in amazement, then at Donna and at the retreating Roylance.

"That cunt needs glasses. I'll away after him and tell him it was you afore he makes his report," volunteered Macfedris.

Donna shook his head. "No, leave it be."

The little group stood around for a while shivering to keep warm and then drifted off, which was just as well because the Germans began shelling the trench again. One monster landed in the sap head and blew the soldier crouched there to pieces. Donna flattened himself into the trench wall and covered his head with his arms. The air was filled with noise, smoke and the stink of explosive. He felt something thud into the clay beside him. When the shelling ceased, still deafened he looked to see what had almost claimed him and discovered a human hand embedded in the trench wall less than a foot from where he cowered. He was relieved at noon and wearily pushed aside the sacking door of the dugout, which some wag had christened the 'Taj Mahal'.

"Here ye are hot shot, take a dram of this," growled Laidlaw, proffering his water bottle. Donna, his mind fuddled by a lack of sleep, took a deep swallow, then nearly choked, his throat on fire – it was whisky. Too tired to talk he nodded his thanks and slumped down on a makeshift bunk. Despite wet feet and the lice he was asleep almost as soon as his head touched the bare wooden slats.

He had a strange dream. Not a particularly religious man, he dreamt that Jesus appeared before him, bearded and dressed in long white robes. His gaze was compassionate, but what puzzled the dreamer was that Christ held a short broad dagger in his right hand, with the blade flat against his chest, the point upwards.

The dream faded, then far away he heard voices and was shook into consciousness by his friend Jimmy Robb. "Stand-to Donna." He wearily forced his body off the bunk and, grabbing his rifle, stumbled out into the cold air.

The light outside was fading and he took his place amongst the other soldiers lining the firestep ready to repulse any sudden attack the enemy might launch. The black undulating morass of no-mans-land was quiet and only the occasional back glow of light from fires gave any indication that the German trenches were occupied. He fumbled in his tunic pocket for his watch. He'd slept four hours; he felt much better for it. He thought of Robb, who had let him sleep to the very last minute knowing how vital it was to the body. He doubted he'd ever met a finer man than James Robb.

His thoughts turned to the strange dream he'd experienced. Could it have anything to do with the sniper he'd killed that morning? Instinctively, he looked across to the heap of bricks and the low wall. Yes, he could just about make out the crumpled form, but minute by minute the corpse was beginning to disappear into the blackness of the oncoming night.

At 6.00pm 'A' Company stood down, men not detailed for duties scurried for the best dugouts or tried to avoid being detailed. Donna was fortunate, for although the 'Taj Mahal' was crowded with bodies, a place was made for him by Campbell. The air inside was thick with tobacco smoke and the fumes from the small oil lamp, but at least it was warmer than outside.

"You fellows know where the monkey sleeps?" asked Donna as he squeezed down next to the big redhead. His remarks drew only the barest of grunts in response, chiefly because most of the soldiers were asleep or dozing.

The monkey saying was an old Indian adage which meant one who was artful and wise. Laidlaw, who was slumped with his head against an earth wall, suddenly snored loudly, then went quiet again. Campbell glared red-eyed at the sleeper.

"Drunken bastard," he muttered, then turned on Harper who was mechanically blowing smoke towards the roof. "Turn it in slim, yer like a fucking train."

Harper carried on as though the big Highlander didn't exist. The Englishman could sense the irritability in Campbell.

"George, why don't yer try for some sleep, yer look as though you've not slept for an age. If Cooper comes in for a volunteer, I'll go."

Campbell opened his mouth to say something but just nodded. He pulled his glengarry forward over his eyes and let his head sink onto his chest. Two minutes later he was snoring like most of the others.

Donna, forever hungry, felt for the hard tack biscuit in his tunic. He began to suck it in an effort to soften it up so as to be able to bite a bit off, but the biscuit was as hard as iron and the tiny particles he managed to loosen tasted like wet sawdust. He gave up and let it drop into the mud. He fumbled about in his pockets and brought out the bit of cheese he'd stowed away so carefully days before and swallowed that.

"Why do ye do that?" enquired a voice. It was Robb, who Donna had thought was asleep yet who had been watching him through half-closed eyes.

"Why do I do what?" asked the Englishman. "Save cheese up?" Donna was quiet for a few moments, then said, "What would ye consider was the worst wound ye could receive here?"

"Och, one that would cause lingering pain I suppose."

"Like a stomach wound?" asked Donna.

"Aye, like one in the belly," replied Robb intrigued.

"Well it's my medical experience that cheese lines the stomach and could slow down the intestinal fluids escaping too fast in the event of being shot through the gut, a man might even survive. It's only a theory."

"Hmm, very interesting," said Robb. Then, with some humour he said, "Now ah suppose it's nay only 'dead-eyed' Donna but Doctor Donna."

They got jam with their rations that night. 'Tommy Ticklers Jam' said the label. One tin was shared between four men; the sweetness was like Ambrosia. The rations were soon devoured and the dugout was packed so full condensation ran freely down the walls. Most of the men were smoking, which helped to dull any lingering hunger pains.

Later that night there were the usual trench repairs to attend to and supplies to be brought up from the rear and patrols. Harper and Donna had managed to evade Cooper by moving up and down the trench whenever the sergeant's voice could he heard, thus avoiding being detailed. Their luck ran out at 10.00 pm when Corporal Littler found the two and told them they had to go with him back to the supply lines and bring wooden stakes for the wiring parties.

The supply wagons were drawn up alongside the Givency La Bassee Road, a mile to the rear of the trenches. Because of the cloak of darkness the trio didn't bother sloshing blindly down the communicating lines, instead they climbed up on the level ground and, careful to avoid water-filled shell holes and the odd corpse, picked their way towards pinpricks of light in the distance. To the right on the outskirts of La Bassee, the orange flashes of British field guns were visible. At the supply wagons they loaded up with wooden stakes and picked their way back along Crater Road. It was here, while being stopped by a patrol, that one of the patrolmen was killed by shrapnel from one of the huge German shells nicknamed 'Jack Johnsons' which landed 50 yards away.

They did three journeys that night for wood. On the last trip Donna managed to scrounge a few potatoes from his friend Conroy, which were roasted and eaten later in the quiet time from 1.00am until 4.00am.

'A' Company tried the bombs out later that morning. They were round and had a fuse, which was ignited and then thrown towards the German barbed wire. They proved ineffectual; the vast majority didn't explode. It did, however, have an adverse effect. It brought withering rifle fire from the Germans which lasted nearly two hours, causing quite a few casualties, not least through ricochets.

That night Donna and Corporal Littler heaved themselves over the top of the trench into the black stillness of no-man's-land. They were thankful there was no moon, just a high ceiling of dirty grey cloud. They crouched, listening, then moved outwards.

"This'll do," whispered Littler. Harper appeared next over the trench with an armful of wooden stakes. He stood upright, unconcerned.

"Where do you want these?" he asked, his breath coming out as vapour in the cold air. "I've told Laidlaw to stay put and feed the wire out."

"Shush," rasped the N.C.O., "you'll waken the fucking dead."

With hammers wrapped with sacking to deaden the sound, they tapped the stakes into the ground about a yard apart and trellised them with barbed wire, hanging empty jam tins on the foremost wire to give an advance warning of any likely surprise attack at night or in the early morning mist. It was hazardous work, with frequent stops to listen, but Harper seemed oblivious to danger, muttering all the time about the cold and his feet. They wired further up 'A' Company's line until the early hours of the morning, when fatigue made them careless and their activities brought flashes and rifle shots from the darkness of the German positions.

The adverse conditions in the trenches brought a further malaise to the debilitated, vermin-ridden infantrymen. 'Neuritis of the feet' the medical officer called it, due to them being immersed for prolonged periods in water. Men suffering from this found that their feet became black and swollen and they lost all feeling in their lower extremities. The M.O.'s treatment was something of a joke amongst the men. His panacea for influenza, bronchitis and swollen feet was a big white number 9 pill. One man who hobbled painfully with a wrenched knee was almost put on a charge for dumb insolence. When given his treatment, instead of swallowing the number 9 he instead rubbed it vigorously over the painful joint.

The Germans attacked in the early hours of the morning. It didn't come as a surprise. For three nights before they'd amassed troops and supplies in support trenches. Their wagons and transports could be heard rumbling for most of the hours of darkness in the British lines. In the very ghostly light they appeared from the earth with spiked heads, like demons from hell.

"Hold your fire, hold your fire," called the officers to the Highlanders. When the Germans were almost at the barbed wire came the scream, "Fire at will". At this the parapets exploded into one continuous roar as men almost shoulder to shoulder opened up with rapid fire at seemingly unmissable targets. The first two waves of Germans went down in a line, a few impelled by their impetus fell into the Seaforth trench, dead. More lines of Germans came and the rapid musketry of the British downed them, as they'd done to their predecessors.

There was a lull.

"Ceasefire" came the order, and no sooner had this been given than the Germans came again. "Fire at will". They were mown down as before until the ground immediately in front of the British barbed wire was almost three feet high with the dead and badly wounded.

Harper watched a German soldier lose his rifle in his frantic rush forward. The point of his bayonet touched the uneven ground and was snatched from his grasp. Unable to stop, and realising his peril, the soldier, with mouth wide open and hands that shook, fell amongst the barbed wire. Harper shot him in the head from three yards. Donna had to use his glengary to hold his rifle, the prolonged rapid fire caused the barrel to get so hot it burned his hand.

They came again, but not en masse, until the attack petered out mid morning, leaving no-mans-land piled and littered with grey-clad bodies. Half a dozen Germans had managed to get into 'C' Company's trench, but they had been quickly killed.

The Seaforths stood-to all day, ready for any further offensive, but none came. That night spectres could be seen in no-man's-land. The order was passed up the trench not to fire at these figures – they were collecting wounded. No shot was fired. During the unofficial truce, Campbell brought in a wounded German officer and propped him up in the Taj Mahal. He was conscious but very weak and Campbell had to hold his head to give him a drink of water. Attempts to question the officer were received with a slight shake of the head from the wounded man. So Captain Shornberg, who could speak German, was sent for.

"Guten abend Oberleutnant," said Captain Shornberg. The German slowly opened his eyes and stared at the speaker for a moment as though he had trouble focussing.

"Ah, good evening Capitan," he said softly in near perfect English.

"So, you speak English. What is your Unit?"

The German replied with a question. "Where are all your machine guns?"

Captain Shornberg looked puzzled. "We have only one machine gun."

The wounded man's lips curled. "Lies, we were told that each of your men had some sort of machine gun."

"Oberlautenant, I do not tell lies, but tell me why do you in the Imperial German Army allow your men to use dumdum bullets?"asked the Captain quietly.

The German was incensed. "None of the 16 Bavarian Infantry Regiment under my command are allowed to," he snarled. Then he realised he'd given away his unit.

The ashen-faced officer looked at Shornberg through narrowed eyes and said, "You are very clever Capitan, but you will not win this war!" Soon after he was taken away to the Field Aid Station.

Two nights later, the Seaforths were relieved by the First Battalion Royal Scots Regiment.

During the rest period, after George Campbell and Slim Harper had recovered somewhat, Campbell persuaded Harper go with him on a visit to Bethune. Campbell said he wanted some French postcards; saucy ones to take home when he next got leave.

The two spent most of the day drinking in an estaminet with some Connaught Rangers. In the afternoon they decided to go to the marketplace to watch the street jugglers and acrobats. The streets as usual (apart from the locals) were filled mostly with soldiers and a few military policemen. There were also nuns from the church with collection boxes begging money for the poor, "Pour les pauvre, s'il vous plait."

But not all was as it seemed. Hidden under a tall nun's skirts was a khaki figure, who, once the M.P.s had passed, came out of hiding and before making off said to the nun, "Thank you sister for hiding me, but before I make myself scarce, I must say you have a lovely pair o' legs."

To which the nun answered in a deep voice, "Thanks mate but had you looked a little higher you would have seen a lovely pair of balls also. I'm on the run meself."

EIGHT

Army Life

After his son's death, Mr. Donna withdrew even more into himself. He sold his shoemaker's shop because of the memories it evoked. It was there he had made the leather apron which had dragged Dan into the machinery. He blamed himself for that. Now he spent his days at home doing hardly anything. Of course he bought newspapers and read them for hours on end. However, Mrs. Donna knew he wasn't really reading. The loss of his son was almost too much for him to bear.

If the weather was fine, and with much prompting from his wife, he'd take a tram to Chain Bar, reputedly the highest point in Manchester, and wander through the countryside, returning home late at night and hardly touching his evening meal. He usually sat staring into the fire or fall asleep in the chair. His cupboard by the window, where he kept his papers, account books, tobacco and clay pipe, now contained Dan's shirt, the one he'd been wearing when he was fatally injured. It was folded but unwashed. It was ripped and dried blood clung to the fabric. But, late at night when the rest of the family had gone to bed, he'd take it from the shelf and hold it to his chest with tears in his eyes. He felt torn and raw with guilt, a father's guilt for not having done or said the things he now would give his life to be able to say to Daniel. He himself had been brought up within a large family where it wasn't considered manly to show your feelings. It was alright for women to give vent to emotions, but not menfolk. Mr. Donna's terrible inner ache lasted for months, never really giving him peace until the day he died.

One day, in some kind of search for solace and to escape for a few hours, he rose earlier than usual and took a train back to the place where he had been born. He went to Lymm in Cheshire. Things had changed somewhat since his last visit years before. There were more houses and people but the Boat Inn by the canal and the dam and church overlooking the village were just as he remembered them. He walked up the hill away from the village past the church to the high ground and stopped at the gate of the farm his father had once owned and where he'd grown up.

114

He didn't go in; instead he stood there looking in at the farmhouses and outbuildings. After a while he sighed and turned his back on the farm and made his way towards the church. He wanted to visit his parents' grave. In a last letter written just before she herself had passed away, his sister, Elizabeth, had informed him where they were buried.

With the help of a church warden he located his parents' plot, but enquiries of the man about other members of his family were met with a negative response. But then the warden was young and had only been there for a couple of years.

Later, he called at the Boat Inn for a plate of hash and a pint, but again his quest for information concerning his relatives was met with a shake of the head. Wearily, he left the pub and headed back towards Manchester. He'd come here, he thought to himself, for what? For his roots? For his family? For strength? He hadn't found any of these things. Sleep claimed him on the journey back to Manchester and he was sorry when the train awoke him by bumping to a halt in Victoria Station. 'I wish I could sleep forever,' he thought, fumbling for the carriage door.

Young James and his friend Bob Brady left St. Oswald's that summer and were taken on at Jones's cotton mill on Collyhurst Road. They worked in the carding room where the huge bales of raw fibre were broken open and the cotton stuffed into machines which loosened and separated it. Afterwards, it became thread and was wound onto bobbins before going to the looms to be woven into cloth. The conditions in the carding room were anything but healthy; it was noisy and hot and the air was perpetually filled with the raw cotton fly. It piled up in great rafts on beams in the ceiling, on machinery and on ledges because there were no extractor fans. It irritated the eyes and throat, it got on the lungs and stomach of the workers.

"You'll get used to it," said old toothless Joe Klinka one break time as he watched James rubbing his eyes to get rid of the stuff. They were sitting in a small dirty room on the top floor used as a canteen. "It affects folk in different ways," went on Joe. "With me, it affects my stomach, gives me wind." He was quiet while he ate, his gums and lips revolving around his face. He slurped some tea, then spoke again, "I'll show you what I do to get rid of my wind."

He left the table and from a row of fluff-covered coats on one wall he took out a small box and came back to where the lads were still sitting.

James and Bob were intrigued and looked at each other, "What've you got there?" asked Bob.

"I'll show you," replied Joe mysteriously. Inside the box was a small green frog. Joe took out his grubby handkerchief and wiped the frog. He then opened his mouth wide, placed the frog on his tongue, touched its rear and the frog vanished down his throat.

"Bloody hell," yelled Bob, "you dirty twat."

"Now now," said Joe sternly, "don't be cheeky, it isn't dirty. What the frog does inside you is to clear your stomach of all the cotton fluff you swallow. A lot of us do it."

"What does it feel like gulping a frog?" Bob wanted to know.

"Nowt to it," said gummy Klinka.

"Well I'm not going to do it," butted in James, still with a look of disdain on his face. "I'd rather get another job first."

This he did, but not until he'd worked there for another nine months. He left the mill in March the following year and got a job a quarter of a mile away at the Irkdale Dyeing and Bleaching Company on Smedley Lane.

Bob Brady didn't go with him. He stayed on at the mill mainly because he'd become infatuated with a girl called Helen Kerr, who worked in the winding room.

The working conditions at the Irkdale were hardly better and in some respect worse for a growing young lad. The company washed, dyed and finished rolls of cloth sent from mills in the area. Operatives worked in conditions of wetness, steam, heat and chemical fumes, depending on whichever process room they were assigned to. James was lucky, unlike the other lads he was put to work in the folding room, which was fumeless, warm and dry. Another pleasant surprise was to discover that one of his uncles, John Foggaty, was employed there as a driver.

The Irkdale derived its name from the river on whose banks it stood, which was a ready vehicle for the mill's effluent and any other rubbish. Weather permitting, the favourite pastime at meal breaks was sitting on the banks in the shadow of the huge railway viaduct which crossed the river and watching whatever sailed by on the dark odious water. The game of ducks and drakes with a flat stone or slate was very popular with the young lads. The likeable Willie Stringer, a good-looking dark-haired boy, always excelled at this.

Tizzie was now nineteen and quite beautiful. She had a rounded shapely figure, pale pretty features and with her long red hair and husky voice was much sought after by the young men, although to her brothers, Richard and James, it was a mystery why these youths found her so attractive.

"They must all have bad eyesight," concluded Richard.

"Shut up," reproved his mother; "Tizzie is a lovely girl."

At the Frankenberg shop where she'd worked from being a young girl, males not normally given to buying wool or fabrics shopped there in the hope of being served and spoken to by Tizzie.

"I'm leaving the Frankenberg shop," announced Tizzie one evening when the family were seated around the fire.

"Oh, why is that?" asked her surprised mother.

"Well, there's this market trader who sells fruit and vegetables. He wants me to work for him."

"What's his name, this feller?" asked Richard

"George Ward," answered Tizzie. "He's not from around here. I think he comes from London originally."

"Where did you meet him?" asked her mother.

"On the market. I did some shopping for Mrs. Frankenberg last Friday but I've seen him before on the market. He has two barrows."

"Is he married?"

"I don't know," replied Tizzie shortly. "I'm only going to work for him."

"Have you told the Frankenbergs?"

"Not yet," said Tizzie softly.

"I think you're making a mistake," said Richard. "In the winter you'll be out in all weathers getting wet and cold."

"I don't care," shot back the spirited girl. "He's promised me a barrow of my own if I do well, then most of the profits will be mine."

"Hmm," sniffed Richard in derision.

Mr. Donna seemed oblivious to the discussion and just gazed into the fire, saying nothing.

The Jewish couple were sorry to lose Tizzie. Mr. Frankenberg refused to listen at first when Tizzie gave her notice, then offered her a rise in wages, but when he saw how determined she was he had to accept it.

Years later, Tizzie recalled that on the last day of her employment at the shop, and after she bade goodbye to Mr. and Mrs. Frankenberg and their son Coppull, tears came to the old man's eyes.

A week later two letters came from Joe, one in itself was always an event. However, two (though posted at different times) was of course doubly welcome.

Mr. Donna read both twice, then passed them to his wife saying, "He could be home next year Molly." She smiled and wiped her hands on her apron before taking them to a seat by the window to read. Mr. Donna often wrote to Joe, and before sealing his last letter he'd asked the family if anyone felt like adding a page or so of their own. Tizzie usually wrote a note. Young James sometimes did if he wasn't busy, as did Richard, but in Mr. Donna's last letter only Mrs. Donna had included anything. She wrote telling her stepson how Dan's death had affected his father but the one thing that cheered him up above anything else was a letter from him, so for that day at least Mr. Donna was almost like his old self. He would have been angry had he known the content of his wife's letter to Joe, preferring instead to give off a favourable impression of home and the family and not wanting to worry his eldest son.

At Christmas there was no Daniel so there were no coloured decorations and streamers in the living room. December had been very mild so the front doorstep and the stone flags were brown-stoned. Mr. Donna bought a large goose from the butchers on Rochdale Road and stuffed it with parsley and onions. There were pies and cakes, with Richard contributing two crates of beer from the pub. On Boxing Day Janey and Jim Knowles called with presents and were given a tot of whisky. The women kissed each other on the cheeks and the men shook hands, wishing each other 'all the best' and hoping for a better year than the last one.

The following day Johnny Kershaw called with Johnny Foggaty and was treated to the same hospitality. By about 6.00pm Kershaw left, returning fifteen minutes later with his accordion and a bottle of rum in his pocket. After filling everyone's glasses he started his repertoire with the song 'Silver Moon'. Then came 'That Ghost Of The Violin'. There were more songs, with Richard and Johnny Foggaty leading the voices. Mrs. Donna stayed mostly in the kitchen making sandwiches and passing them round. At 12 midnight, and because it was work as usual the following day, the party broke up, but not before Johnny played Mr. Donna's favourite song, 'The Queen Of The China Seas', twice. Mr. Donna saw his visitors to the door. Foggaty and Kershaw were relations and for an hour or so Mr. Donna appeared like his old self.

It was fitting that fate should decree a gathering of relations in such informal pleasure because Mr. Donna went slowly downhill afterwards. In September he developed breathing difficulties and could hardly climb the stairs. Dr. Mangan diagnosed pneumonia. The lads fixed up a bed for their father in the living room, and as he lost strength a fire was kept going day and night to keep out the cold. However, at the beginning of October his breathing was very loud and laboured and he slept most of the day. In his last few days of life he fought for breath, so Janey left her own home and slept on the couch to be near him. The night he died Richard attempted to give him a small amount of cod liver oil, hoping it would somehow work a kind of miracle, but their father slowly opened his eyes and shook his head slightly. A few moments later he gave a long rasping sigh and passed away, still holding Janey's hand.

She looked up tearfully at Richard. "Is he ....?"

"I think so luv," he replied gently.

Fittingly, the old ex-guardsman was given a soldier's funeral. After the church service a horse-drawn gun carriage carried the flag-draped coffin slowly through the streets. Behind the gun carriage walked his family and friends. As the cortege passed along the winding Fitzgeorge Street, where the family once lived, more people joined the mourners. The procession turned right onto Collyhurst Road and up the hill to Queens Park Cemetery. By the time his coffin reached the gates there was quite a crowd to accompany him on his last journey, so on an overcast afternoon he was buried in a common grave, as was his wish.

"Bury me with the least expense Molly, save yer money for the living," he often said. Even in death his wife had never disobeyed him. She would have much preferred that his last resting-place was with Daniel. The date was 13th October 1909.

In the following year the Donna household lost another member of the family, but in different circumstances. In August young James, without a word to any of his family, joined the army.

His reasons were threefold. A couple of years before Richard Haldane, Secretary of State in the then Liberal Government, had asked questions in the House of Commons concerning the dismal lessons Britain had learned in the South African war. A pacifist by nature, he wanted to know how the comparatively small force of Boer farmers, vastly outnumbered in many battles, had given the soldiers of Britain such a fight. It was his contention that if the army were to be the police force of the great British Empire then it would have to be overhauled and reconstituted. Having got the support needed, he set about his reforms, which amounted to better selection, better conditions and training and improved pay.

Unlike Bob Brady, who had married Helen Kerr, James wanted to see the world. He also admired the scarlet and blue dress uniforms of the regular soldiers he saw in the streets and pubs.

"What's yer name son?" asked one of the army panel at Ardwick Green Recruiting Centre.

"James Donna."

"Married?"

"No."

"Right, fill in this form, then come back here after you've seen the doctor," said the grey-whiskered civilian.

Forty minutes later James was standing smartly before the selection desk again.

"Right," said the recruiting officer, scrutinizing James's form, "what regiment would you like to join?"

"The Grenadier Guards," replied James.

The man leaned back in his chair and studied the would-be recruit. "No," he said at last, "I think you're a little too short for the Guards just yet son. I believe you'd be better off in the Medical Corps. Would you like to join the Corps?"

To James it seemed he had no choice, so a little disappointedly he replied, "Yes."

"Listen," said the officer, "I spent six years in the Royal Army Medical Corps as a doctor and they are in need of clean intelligent men like yourself."

"Right sir," said James with more enthusiasm.

"Good," smiled the man, "go home and wait until you're sent for."

Two weeks later he received a letter telling him to report to McGrigor Barracks, R.A.M.C., Aldershot, Hampshire.

If James imagined that the Medical Corps training was going to be any less hectic than the Guards, he was mistaken. A recruit's day at McGrigor Barracks began at 5.30am and consisted of inspections, parade ground drilling, lectures, more inspections, and more lectures, and more drilling. This regime lasted until 8.00pm and later at night, light permitting, the men's uniforms and kit had to be immaculately cleaned. If not, they were put on a charge. Three weeks of this was enough for the homesick James. One night he waited until it was dark, then slipped out of the barracks and made his way through the town to the railway station.

He found the platform deserted, but looking about he located a timetable showing trains for London. It was while he was squinting at the small print that he heard footsteps. He glanced up from the notice and his heart leapt. There coming towards him was a big military policeman.

James's mind raced. He didn't know what to do. If the M.P. approached him and took him back to the barracks then he was certain to be put in the guard room for being out without permission. That was the very least charge he would face. Should he bolt for it? Or try to bluff and act casual? He decided on the latter. He continued peering at the timetable.

The footsteps stopped a short distance behind him.

"Having trouble lad?" boomed a voice.

James turned. "Er, yes, I mean no, Sergeant." He was angry with himself for not being more decisive.

"Yes, no!" said the burly red cap, his hands behind his back. "Where are you heading?"

"London, Sergeant."

"I suppose you've got a pass lad?"

"Yes, Sergeant," answered James.

"Well, let me see it then."

James began going through his tunic pockets in an attempt to bluff, hoping the M.P. would tire or somehow be distracted by a train or something.

The sergeant waited, his moustachioed face partly in shadow.

"You've got no pass, have you lad?"

James ceased rummaging through his pockets. "No, Sergeant," he said resignedly.

There was a moment's silence. The M.P. looked him up and down, then in a softer voice said, "Go back to your billet and do your training lad. Army life aint so bad once you've done your training."

The would-be runaway nodded and began retracing his route back to barracks.

However, nothing can stop the passage of time and, at last, his initial training was complete. After a brief leave home to show off his uniform, Donna was posted to York Military Hospital.

On arrival he was befriended by a man from Leeds, a small shifty-faced old sweat named Quither, who liked a drink but was always short of money. He tried to tap a few of the new recruits the very first day, but to no avail. He amused Donna at first, especially after he'd been on the bottle, relating the dodges he'd used to avoid certain duties, but the reprobate Quither was to cause him much hardship.

One day Donna naively bought two pairs of army socks from him, unaware that the items had been stolen from the quartermaster's store. When a search revealed them in his locker, the luckless James was arrested pending a court martial and charged with stealing army property. Unbeknown to James, the obsequious Quither had panicked on hearing a search of lockers was to be made and had unloaded the socks on the fresh-faced newcomer – and even hinted where they might be found.

The man from Manchester wasn't aware of this intrigue until months later, at his short trial. He refused to name the person from whom he'd purchased the socks, but his defending officer was dubious, presuming that anyone in such a serious position would be only too happy to shift the blame from himself, but the obstinate Donna refused to betray Quither. After a short court recess, James didn't need to be told the verdict; he could see all too clearly the sword on the presiding officer's desk pointing in his direction.

"Private Donna, this court finds you guilty of stealing army property," said the seated officer. "You are a member of a trusted corps, you have betrayed that trust and you have besmirched the Royal Army Medical Corps. However, we feel because you have not been long in the army, you may have succumbed to temptation and we have decided to be lenient. 28 days detention in York Castle."

The military prison at York stood within the walls of the old Norman castle. It had been built originally as a civilian keep, but the army had taken charge in 1900. Donna was marched through the narrow streets under guard, across the Ouse Bridge and up the rising cobbled ground to Tower Street. The escort party halted before the huge wooden gates of the prison. After a few moments they were allowed inside, where the prisoner was handed over to the military policemen. From the gatehouse Donna was marched in double time out into the grounds of the prison complex, around the moat and high medieval Clifford Tower to the entrance of the prison building. Once inside he was dragged up a flight of stone stairs into a whitewashed room and brought to a halt before a white line drawn on the floor about ten feet from a desk, where sat a heavily-jowled officer with small piggy eyes.

Donna was sweating from the weight of his packs but couldn't help noticing that around the walls hung long wooden truncheons. After studying his sentencing papers, the man at the desk said, "I see you're living up to the Medical Corps tradition Private Donna."

James wasn't sure what he meant and said nothing.

"R.A.M.C. – Rob All My Comrades," the officer explained. "Now," he continued more matter-of-factly, "I see you're my guest for 28 days, but I'll promise you you'll wish you'd never taken anything belonging to another before you leave this place." With these words he motioned the prisoner and his guard out of the room.

From the Governor's office Donna was marched along a corridor, turning left and right in response to his guard's barked instructions until he was halted before a door marked 'Prison Doctor'. The doctor appeared to be about 60 years old. He had sparse grey hair, combed to cover a mainly bald head, a large red nose and smelled of whisky.

"Drop your trousers," he wheezed asthmatically. "Any skin diseases? Any chest trouble?"

"No Sir," answered Donna.

"Right, out you go then," the doctor rasped.

After the examination the prisoner was taken up several spiral stone steps to the top landing of one of the prison wings. The quietness of the wing made the boots of the two echo loudly. To Donna, the place had a peculiar smell to it, reminiscent he thought of the animal house in a zoo he'd been taken to as a lad at Blackpool.

His guard ordered him into an empty cell and then slammed and locked the heavy door, causing the sound to reverberate throughout the prison wing. Donna just stood there alone in the cell with a feeling of abject misery, regretting ever joining the army. His cell had a square barred window too high to look out of. Along one wall leant a bed, a board with three blankets and two sheets draped over it in alternate order. In one corner stood a small triangular wooden table with a chamber pot beneath. There was a small rope mat on the floor and a chair on which lay a card indicating King's Regulations and a diagram showing how an inmate's kit was to be laid out for inspection.

"That's not straight," snapped the big blue-chinned sergeant. It was the following morning. Donna was standing to attention in his cell, his kit laid out on the bed board. Donna said nothing.

"I tell you that pack isn't in line," insisted the warder. "Look," he said, pointing to the bed board.

The Manchester man turned his head to look where the N.C.O. indicated. As he did so the sergeant smashed Donna on the chin with his fist, knocking him into the far corner of the cell. By the time his senses had cleared and he'd picked himself up, blue chin had gone.

Life for a prisoner in York Military Prison was far from easy. From the moment they were allowed out of their cells after morning kit inspection every duty was performed at the double. They even washed and shaved at the double. In the washhouse two rows of men with towels tucked into their braces marked time with their feet before wash bowls. At an order from one of the M.P.s, the first row stepped forward and, still doubling, washed and shaved. After two minutes, to a barked command, the washers stepped one pace to the side and began to dry themselves, still doubling while the rear rank replaced them at the wash bowls.

The prisoners doubled for everything; they doubled for meals, they doubled on the parade ground, in the gymnasium while they lined up to vault over a huge wooden horse, they doubled!

"I don't think I can get over that sergeant," muttered Donna to the white-vested warder manning the vaulting horse.

"What, you can't vault this little thing," he replied mockingly. Then, in a more reasonable tone he said, "Well, have a try anyway."

Donna noticed for the first time that the man had a boxing glove on one hand.

The man from Manchester took a run at the wooden horse, and as he got near to it he jumped. It was while he was in mid air that he felt a blow under his chin. He hit the top of the horse but went over and landed in a heap on the mat.

"There you are," said the warder looking down at him, "I knew you'd get over."

When the prisoners were not being abused physically or verbally, they were given work that was performed in total silence. Such tasks included two-man log-sawing teams or picking and shredding oakum, which was a rope-type fibre used to stuff pillows and mattresses. The latter made the ends of fingers sore to men unused to such a menial task.

One morning, after Donna had served a week of his sentence, the blue-chinned sergeant tried out his 'kit' trick again, but James, whose jaw still hurt from that initial blow, was ready for him.

"That brass needs cleaning," the warder said. "Look."

Donna appeared to turn his head to look but his eyes never left the warder. As blue chin swung his fist, Donna ducked his head. The bully's fist slammed into the stone wall, causing him to let out a yell of pain and curses.

"You bastard," he wailed, cradling his damaged hand. "I've broke me 'and. I'll not forget this," he screamed as he left the cell.

The days in prison seemed endless, the only escape was in sleep, but even that was all too brief. Prisoners were not allowed to make up their beds before 10.00pm. However, it is written that all things come to an end, even the bad things.

By the time blue chin's hand had healed, Donna had five days to serve.

Then a new prisoner moved into the cell next to Donna. His name was Marrs, a big dark-haired man serving a six months sentence. James was always wary of blue chin at morning inspection. The Manchester man had learned from experience that the warder was most dangerous when he spoke casually, a ploy no doubt to put his unsuspecting victims off guard. However, the morning after Marrs had moved in, blue chin entered Donna's cell smiling and rubbing his fist, appearing very pleased with himself.

Later, when James and Marrs were engaged in the tedious task of oakum picking, the reason for the warder's mirth was explained. He'd hit Marrs, who was an army light heavyweight boxer, and stunned him.

"But I'll have the bastard," muttered the taciturn big man, "the first chance I get".

Marrs' chance came that evening at 9.30pm. Blue chin made his rounds of the cells to ensure none of the prisoners had made their beds up before the stipulated time. As blue chin stepped into Marrs' cell the latter, quick as a flash, slammed the heavy self-locking cell door shut.

"Now yer fuckin' bastard," snarled Marrs, "let's see how tough yer are when you've got a man face to face." There was fear in blue chin's face. Instinctively he tried to blow his whistle. As Marrs moved in on him, he swung his stick. However, the boxer easily parried the blow and then systematically began raining punches into the face and body of the warder.

In the cell next door James could clearly hear the bangs and thuds and blue chin's cries for mercy. It must have been five or ten minutes before the rest of the prison staff realised that something was wrong. Six of the warders came charging along the landing armed with truncheons. However, it was an hour before they managed to get Marrs' cell door open. He'd barricaded the back of it with the wooden furniture. Eventually they pushed their way two at a time through the narrow cell doorway. Still Marrs didn't give up, attacking them with a leg of the chair, but by now the prisoner was exhausted by his efforts and the warders fell on him from all sides until he collapsed bloody and unconscious. They didn't stop, however, but still carried on until their arms ached, often hitting each other in the confined space in their eagerness to injure.

There was nothing the other inmates could do. At the first hint of the disturbance they had been locked up in their cells. None of the prisoners ever saw Marrs again, with one exception. The rumour later was that the guards had beaten Marrs to death.

The military policemen taunted Donna on the morning he was released. He was standing to attention with full pack in the gatehouse, awaiting his freedom. Three of them took turns inspecting him, looking him up and down saying, "Yer brasses are filthy" or "Have yer slept in that tunic, lad?"

When eventually the door was opened and he was free to go, he marched out to more verbal bullying:

"Call yersel' a fucking soldier."

"Don't yer like it here?"

"Why don't yer stay a bit longer?"

"You'll be back!"

Donna's hatred for these men, who abused their authority to brutalize, cow and humiliate fellow servicemen in the name of army regulations was intense. As the prison door closed behind him he turned and spat onto it with pent-up venom. He watched the spit run down the wood of the door for a few seconds and turned and headed towards the town. He needed a drink before reporting back to his unit.

Later that day, after he'd returned to York Military Hospital, he was ordered before his Commanding Officer, Major Holt.

"Well," said the officer, "have you learned your lesson?"

"I didn't steal those socks, Sir," said Donna quietly.

Major Holt coughed and looked away, unable to meet the Manchester man's eyes. "But they were found in your locker, damn it," he said.

"I got them." James was about to say 'I bought them....', but he was interrupted.

"Yes, yes, I remember you saying that at the court martial."

"But it's the truth, Sir. I said it before, during and now after the trial."

"Anyway," said Holt, trying to lighten the dialogue, "it's all over now."

"But it isn't, Sir," persisted James.

"What do you mean?"

"Well, now that offence is on my army record!"

The Officer nodded. "Yes, I see what you mean. However, there is a way you could have that stain removed from your character as it were."

"How Sir?"

"Well, if I'm not very much mistaken, there is an army edict that states a soldier can have his record wiped clean if he volunteers to serve abroad." Major Holt paused for a few moments for his last statement to sink in, then continued: "However, the reason I sent for you Private Donna is to inform you that in two days time you'll be sent to Colchester. No, it's not a punishment. I feel you'd have a better chance there to settle down and do your work, a fresh start so to speak."

"Thank you, Sir," said James. For the first time since arriving in York he felt optimistic.

Later, he went in search of Quither but learned he'd conveniently been given leave. Donna's duties in his remaining couple of days at York were general. After his weeks in York Castle it was sublime to be able to work without being overseen and harried. He helped with the patients' meals and worked in the laundry. However, it was when he was detailed to clean the hospital mortuary that he was starkly reminded of the brutality of the army prison.

"Have you got any customers Corporal?" asked Donna lightly as he entered the mortuary carrying a long-handled mop and bucket of water. The N.C.O. was writing at a desk and answered without looking up.

Only one, snuffed it about three days ago."

James started his cleaning at the far end of the room, conscientiously mopping and drying until he'd worked his way down towards the trestle table where the covered corpse lay. The corporal left his writing and helped James move the table onto a clean part of the floor.

"He must be a big feller," commented Donna casually, adding, "Who is he?"

"A feller called Marrs," answered the corporal.

It took a second or two for his words to sink in, then James felt as though he'd been struck in the stomach.

He stared at the Corporal. "Say that again."

"His name was Private Marrs. Here, have a look at him." The N.C.O. was intrigued. "Did you know him Donna?"

James looked down at the battered head and dead face and sighed, "Yes, I knew him for a short time. What was the cause of death Corporal?"

"It says on his certificate death was due to multiple skull fractures occasioned by an accidental fall down stone steps. He was alive when they brought him in but he never regained consciousness," replied the N.C.O.

"The bastards," whispered James, "the dirty fucking bastards."

NINE

Festubert - over the top

The First Seaforth and Indian troops of the Meerut and Lahore divisions attacked the German positions opposite them on a bleak morning in December. Most men were dry-mouthed, oblivious to the cold, glad in some ways to be out of their own shallow, mud-filled holes. Beforehand they were told not to stop to help the wounded.

They advanced in extended order, skirmishing forward, then dropping to the ground before moving forward again. They were met by rifle and machine gun fire, sending some of them spinning. The shells began to burst in mid-air, firing chunks of red hot death in every direction. The noise was deafening.

Donna watched a man blown through the air amid clouds of earth. He covered his head against the blast, then dashed forward and fell into a shell crater. Squinting through the smoke and flying dirt he saw the German line, now about seventy yards away. To his right some of his men had got onto a farm track that ran towards the enemy trenches. He decided to head for that. Biding his time for the slightest lull, he was up and running and then to ground once more.

Ahead lay a Seaforth who was obviously badly wounded, the front of his tunic covered with blood, yet he appeared unconcerned and gave Donna a cheery 'thumbs up' sign. With rifle and bayonet at the port position, Donna went into action again, running forward and diagonally. It was during his next dash that the blast from an exploding shell bowled him over and over. The Englishman finished up lying flat on his back gasping for breath. He was too scared to look down at his legs, fearing that they may no longer be there, or perhaps badly mangled. Little by little his breathing became easier and slowly he inspected his lower half, thankful that he was still in one piece, minus his glengarry. He crawled to where his weapon lay and took stock of his surroundings. Apart from two dead or wounded men he couldn't see any of his company.

A dirt road lay a couple of yards away. "A' Company must be up ahead,' he thought. He dragged himself past the pile of bricks that had once been a wall and surveyed the debris-strewn narrow road that stretched before him. It was deserted.

He thought of his comrades. 'Where the fucking hell are they?' he asked himself. Deciding at least that some of 'A' Company must be ahead of him, he pushed himself up to a crouch and, using what was left of the wall for cover, stumbled into motion, ignoring the occasional ping ping of ricocheting bullets and shells bursting nearby. He'd covered perhaps thirty yards when something made him freeze in mid stride. Like a shadow he stealthily peered above the rubble of masonry and held his breath.

A German officer, immaculate in his highly polished boots and breastplate, was standing alone barely ten feet away. With his heart beginning to beat faster Donna took another look. The German had not moved; he stood motionless, hand on hip, gazing away from the concealed Englishman, watching the course of battle. The sun had shown itself, causing the silver eagle on the officer's hat to flash. This no doubt had alerted Donna to his presence.

James measured the distance between himself and his adversary. 'I'll give him the bayonet,' he said to himself, his heart beginning to pound. 'There're probably other spikeheads about.' Gripping his rifle and bayonet tightly he leapt at the German aiming for his throat, but the point of blade caught his unsuspecting victim under the chin, causing the latter to cry out. Donna, still shaky from being blasted by the shell, took no chances and, shutting his eyes, pulled the trigger of his Lee Enfield. He felt the officer go limp under him, the bullet had blown away the top half of his head.

Fearing that there might be more of the enemy around, he looked for cover and lay doggo amongst some bricks, his hands shaking. There was no sense of elation in killing the German. 'War is war, kill or be killed,' he thought gloomily. He'd seen many dead of both British and German since coming to France and the chances were, on another day in another battle, he himself would be lying in a crumpled heap as was his foe now. He shook these thoughts from his head and concentrated on his surroundings. The gunfire appeared to have almost stopped, so had the shelling. A movement to his right made him stiffen. He shifted the position of his rifle and took first aim, ready for anything that showed itself. A minute later he relaxed his grip on the weapon. Into his view came the head and back of an Indian infantryman.

The attack had started before dawn. In the darkness there had been some confusion, with Indian troops storming the Seaforth objectives, but as the light improved and co-ordination was achieved, the Germans began to lose heart and began falling back to a new position 150 yards away, abandoning wounded and trench mortars. Although the 80 yards of ground won was littered with British and Indian killed and wounded, the staff officers of the area were jubilant.

The captured German trenches were incorporated in the British line. The soldiers who occupied the new position were amazed to discover how better equipped the enemy was. Coal, coke and braziers were dug into the trench walls. Cheese and bottles of schnapps were found in the dugouts. Pumps had then been installed to keep the line free from the water that perpetually found its way in.

Despite these luxuries, the weather became even colder; the intensity of it seemed to freeze the very bones. It was bad enough for the British, acclimatised to the vagaries of the European winters, although quite a number of Seaforths suffered with frostbitten feet. However, to the soldiers from the Indian sub continent, the exposure to the bitterly cold conditions was something they had never before experienced. Some just gave up, succumbed to the elements and just died, and the dead man's groundsheet was pulled from his shoulders to cover his head. These bodies, as were the seriously wounded, were removed at night, the former for burial behind the lines and the wounded to the clearing hospital at Bethune. The medical officer dealt with the less serious cases in the trenches. The staple tincture of iodine dressing was used for what were considered minor wounds, the army's cure-all, the No. 9 pill, was for practically everything else.

Like the rest of the provisions, drinking water came up with rations during the hours of darkness, but its taste was always of taint due to the purification powder administered to it. Tea made with it was likened to hot soda, or worse. One way to a quick brew up was to fire a few rounds on the machine gun. When the water-cooling jacket on the barrel began to steam, all that was needed was a dixy and a handful of tea. Donna was convinced this method, though oily, improved the taste.

A couple of days before Christmas much activity could be heard as well as seen behind the German lines. This was stopped when the British artillery opened up with salvos of shells from the Le Touret Road. However, during the hours of darkness the rumble of German transport could be heard bringing up fresh supplies and men for a new offensive.

Each day a counter attack was expected and, although there was much sniping and almost continuous shrapnel bombs directed at the British front line trenches, no attack came.

Relief came to the Seaforths and the Indian troops in the midst of a swirling snowstorm, but these dirty, louse-ridden, half-frozen infantrymen hardly noticed. It was a four mile march from the front line trenches to the rest billets, where they were received with hot baths, a change of clothing, rum and food. These were indescribable luxuries, which could only be fully appreciated by men who had endured the extremes of conditions in front line trenches in winter. Many of the soldiers, although extremely under-nourished, once bathed, fell into unconsciousness, too tired to eat.

The following day Colonel Richie, together with the R.S.M., paid a surprise visit to the soldiers in the billets, most of whom were lying on bunks partly dressed, whilst others were still asleep rolled up in blankets. At the sight of the duo the men stiffened, put out their cigarettes and jumped to their feet. Others tried to awaken the sleepers.

"At ease, stand easy," intoned the Sergeant Major.

"No, let them sleep," said the Commanding Officer to those still trying to arouse the unconscious.

"I apologise for interrupting your rest and recuperation, but this is the first opportunity for me to congratulate you on your splendid effort at Festubert. Yes, I'm aware we lost 60 or so men, including that fine officer Lieutenant Camer, but Captain Shornberg, who was also wounded, should be back with us soon, which I've no doubt you'll be glad to hear. The divisional command is delighted with your efforts. Well done."

Later the same day, many men reported sick with various ailments picked up in the line. The majority had numb swollen feet. The medical officer diagnosed the condition as neuritis, caused by long periods of immersion in cold water. For treatment they were told to massage and bathe the feet in hot water and given temporary light duties.

After a more accurate tally of killed and wounded was taken, the battalion had a quartermaster's parade where missing kit was replaced. The most common item lost was the glengarry, but because the supply was exhausted the battalion was issued with the dark blue Balmoral headwear, minus the Seaforth's red and white dicing. But the most welcome item was a pair of boots to each man.

Although Christmas had passed, they got parcels from home. Donna received one from his mother; he could tell it was from her before he opened it by the handwriting. Inside was a cake, packets of tea, sugar and letters from Tizzie and Janey. He shared the parcel with Campbell and Slim Harper, who hadn't been sent anything.

Jimmy Robb invited Donna and Campbell to go with him to Bethune to visit some of the wounded and to have a drink. They had no problems getting transport, the cobbled roads were always a continuous stream of wagons going to and from Bethune and Richbourg. Though the town of Bethune was some miles behind the lines, it had not escaped the attentions of the Germans. Many houses and shops were smashed and holed. Heaps of bricks were stacked up by the sides of the road and broken glass littered the cobbles. Nevertheless, it was a busy town, commercially as well as militarily.

Their driver, a cockney from the West Kents, waved goodbye and dropped them off in the city square in front of the town hall, now sandbagged and used as headquarters by the army. They dodged and weaved through many differing uniforms occupying the pavements and found their way to the clearing hospital. By the look of it it had once been a school. Lined up in front of the building were ambulances, some motorised but mostly horse-drawn. The traffic seemed never ending as one ambulance left and another took its place. There was a steady procession of men being carried in up the stone steps. The entrance was chaotic, a confusion of voices and hob-nailed boots on the stone floor slabs. There were short-sleeved orderlies with bloodstained gowns tending the bandaged wounded on stretchers. Donna and his companions stood to one side and waited to be spoken to. Presently, a tired looking matron approached wearing a long rubber apron.

"You're in the way here," she said to Robb shortly. "What do you want?"

Robb produced a slip of paper from his tunic. "I beg your pardon ma'am but we've come to see these men."

She rubbed a hand tiredly over her eyes before focussing on the list.

"When were they brought in?" she asked, still checking the names.

"About ten days ago."

"Are you men related?" she asked. They all shook their heads.

"Captain Shornberg and these five men," she indicated to Robb, "have been sent to the military hospital at Calais. These two succumbed to their wounds soon after being brought in." She sighed, rubbed her eyes once more, then continued: "That leaves Private Laidlaw, chest wounds, we didn't think he would last the night when he was admitted, hence the reason for not sending him to the coast." The matron gave a weary smile, "but he's still hanging on."

"Can we see him ma'am, just for a minute?" asked Donna quietly.

"I can't see what harm it will do." She pointed upwards. "Up the stairs, along the corridor, first room on the left, and don't stay long."

The upstairs stank of urine and disinfectant. There were stretchers all the way down the corridors, handle to handle, with men swathed in bloodstained bandages moaning in pain or delirious.

A young black-haired orderly was tending Laidlaw when they found him. He was ashen-faced and the large dressing on his chest was making sucking noises as he breathed. He was conscious but very weak. The orderly washed Laidlaw's face with lint and warm water and did the same with his shoulders and armpits.

"Feel better now?" asked the youth softly.

Laidlaw barely nodded.

The medical orderly gathered up his bowl and pieces of lint.

"Don't tire him," he said as he left.

They stood looking down at him for a moment. George Campbell was the first to speak.

"How are ye, ye wee bastard?" he asked affectionately.

The wounded man then tried to say something but couldn't. He tried again, this time Campbell bent over him, his ear close to his lips. After a while, he straightened up smiling, his eyes wide.

"Well, I'll be fucked," he exclaimed, "he's jest asked me fer a dram."

Laidlaw started to cough, causing the dressing on his chest to depress and wheeze more. When at last the coughing subsided he closed his eyes. The three left, each squeezing his hand by way of farewell.

One hour later they were sitting in an estaminet. They'd tried the beer, which was warm and weak, at two sous a glass, now they were sampling the white wine or vin blanc at one and a half francs a bottle. The place was filled mostly by artillerymen all intent on getting drunk.

When they were two thirds through the second bottle of plonk, Jimmy Robb peered through the tobacco smoke at his companions. They had to put their heads together to hear him through the din. "If ever ah get hurt like some of them poor wretches, nay arms or legs, ahd be obliged to ye if ye'd put one through ma heed."

The table was serious for a moment. Then Donna, in an effort to chase away disquieting thoughts, said, strait-faced, "Ah, but what happens if you twist your ankle hoping for a trip to Blighty?"

He was, of course, referring to the time recently when George Campbell narrowly missed a charge of 'swinging the lead'. There was laughter at this, even from the big Highlander. They were at that soporific stage in drink, so when the gunners started to sing a rude song the Seaforths joined in, although they didn't quite know the words.

During the merriment two service corps men eased their way into the bar – the more youthful of the two wore the Mons ribbon – manoeuvring through the crowded tables and tobacco haze. He stared at Donna in disbelief. Unable to restrain himself, he blurted out above the noise: "You're Jim Chadd."

Donna stared up at the newcomer, recognition not dawning for a moment. "Fucking hell, it's Joe."

It was his friend from Collyhurst, Joe 'Gedder' Jones. To meet Joe like this, in another land far from home, was like finding some long lost brother in the middle of a desert. In his eagerness to shake hands, Donna nearly upset the table.

"Come, get something to sit on, you and your pal join us," he said half drunk.

Jimmy Robb waited until the two had got a drink and were seated and then turned to Donna with mock suspicion.

"Ah always had ma doubts aboot you Donna. A sassanach in a Scots regiment calling yourself James Donna. Now yer friend calls you James Chadd. Somethin' fishy there. Ah believe ye're a deserter from another regiment trying to escape a crime," he said dramatically.

This was received with howls of drunken laughter, and when Campbell, trying to be serious, said, "Ah agree an ahm gonna report ye," there was more laughter.

The only way the two could talk and be heard was to lean forward across the table like conspirators.

Newcomer Joe spoke: "I never dreamed the two of us would be having a drink Jim."

Donna shrugged. "What have you been doing with yerself?"

"Driving supplies up, ammunition, shells, rations, and bringing wounded back to the hospital here. I brought some of your wounded back over a week ago. I asked a feller called Macfedris, who'd been hit in the legs, if he knew you Jim, but he said he didn't."

Robb, who'd been listening intently, said, "Well he wouldna; if ye asked mysel' who James Chadd was ah wouldna ken who ye meant because our criminal friend next to me calls himsel Donna now."

More and more laughter and a few swear words from Donna. There was more talk and more wine, but all too soon it was night outside the drinking palace and time to go. They all shook hands before parting, Donna and Joe being the last to do so.

"Take care Joe, keep your head down," said Donna

"And you Jim. Oh, I nearly forgot, I got a letter from home – did you know that your Richard and our Elysa are walking out, they're courting."

"No, I didn't, but it's the best news I've heard in a long time," said Donna, by now drunk but mellow.

New faces appeared in the companies to replace those killed and wounded, the new men coming from a reserve battalion. One of the newcomers attached himself to Campbell; his name was Ralph

Findlay, a lad of about twenty from Inverness. He had that scourge of youth, acne, and was rather conscious of it.

"Don't worry about it lad," consoled Campbell after seeing the latter looking at his reflection in a mess tin. "A good woman is what you need." For his part, Findlay endeared himself to the big Highlander by admiring Campbell's tattoos from India, especially the dirk on his calf, which revealed the handle just above the hose top.

There were quite a few grumbles when the battalion practised trench bombing in the rain. Because the real things were in short supply, bomb-throwing training was done with large stones. They spent time on the firing ranges practising machine gun drills and rapid rifle fire. With little time for rest, bayonet practice and route marches were the order of the day.

On the day Sir John French visited the battalion it had been raining since early morning, turning the parade ground into a bog. Although the companies had been drawn up since 9.00am, it was still cascading down when the Commander-in-Chief, together with a brace of staff officers, finally arrived two hours later.

When Regimental Sergeant Major Macrae gave the order to shoulder arms prior to inspection, Donna, in a rear rank, fumbled the arms drill in the atrocious conditions and allowed the butt of his rifle to slip from his grasp in the rain. Recovering quickly, he hoped nobody had noticed.

Declining the parody of an inspection in such conditions, the diminutive general, from the shelter of a parasol of an aide, extolled the battalion for its recent action in the trenches. It was, he said, in keeping with the tradition of a regiment noted for its tenacity and fighting qualities. He had no doubt, he went on, that victory would be theirs if these virtues were maintained, adding he had every confidence they would be. It was a grand speech, the general finishing with 'God Save The King'. However, the soaking-wet hungry troops were glad when he was ushered off surrounded by his staff officers.

The smell of drying tunics met the sad-looking Sergeant Cooper that evening as he pushed open the makeshift door to the cottage. The toe of his boot skimmed the top of a puddle on the stone floor, causing a fine spray to radiate inside the room.

"Watch yer fucking feet sergeant," grumbled Campbell.

"Sorry lads," said Cooper. He looked about the interior, various items of dress hung from lines criss-crossed about the room, obscuring his view from the billeted men.

"I'm looking for Donna," he said after working his head from side to side like a spectator at a tennis match.

James was on his knees persuading the fire to accept chips of wet wood.

"Over here Sergeant."

"You're on company orders tomorrow Donna. 9.00am."

"What for?"

Cooper shrugged. "I dunno son. Lieutenant Roylance reported you."

There were a few hisses at the latter's name.

"He'll get one through the head one of these days," intoned the usually silent Harper after the N.C.O. had left.

The R.S.M. marched Donna into Colonel Richie's office the following morning, then took his place by the side of the commanding officer's desk.

Roylance's piggy eyes avoided Donna as he said, "I saw this man drop his rifle while on parade, Sir."

Richie looked from the lieutenant to the accused.

"Anything to say?"

"No, Sir."

"About six weeks ago," said the colonel looking at his Sergeant Major, then at Donna, "ye were charged with dumb insolence while on a similar parade. Tell me Private Donna, have ye something against generals?"

"No, Sir."

"Mister Macrae tells me in Agra ye broke the battalion record for target hits with the machine gun," said the Commanding Officer attempting to mitigate, "and I'm told you're a first-class shot with a rifle."

"Yes, Sir," came Donna's tacit reply.

Colonel Richie possessed a quality essential for all good Commanders, he understood men. He suspected there was some kind of undercurrent between the accuser and the accused.

"Would ye be better in another company?"

Donna shook his head. "No, Sir."

"Right," sighed the colonel, "extra duties until ye go back in the line."

"Aboot turn, quick march, left right, left right," barked Macrae to Donna.

The guard awakened Donna well before dawn. He didn't have much to put on, because of the cold he'd slept in shirt, singlet, socks and puttees, with his kilt used as an extra cover. Instinctively he upturned his boots before lacing them up, wound himself into the kilt, tied the apron, but left his tunic unbuttoned. Before leaving to go out into the darkness, he picked up rifle and hat with one hand and threw a lump of wood on the almost dead fire with the other.

His boots echoed on the cobbles as he passed the still sleeping billets. Donna's boots must have disturbed an owl, for it floated across the road just ahead of him like a white handkerchief. He was making towards the Richbourg/Bethune crossroads, where the cooks had erected a field kitchen under canvas. Somebody was there ahead of him, the lamps were lit. Sensibly he did up his tunic buttons.

"'Ello mate, what's new?" said Andy Conroy, the cook.

"Fuck all," retorted Donna miserably.

Conroy smiled, guessing what the latecomer's reply was likely to be. As usual he offered Donna his tobacco and papers.

Donna shook his head, not because he was anti-social, he liked the southerner, but he wasn't at his best early in the morning.

"What are you so happy about?" he asked grumpily.

"Bollock brains has gone on leave." He was referring to his sergeant, Mullins.

Donna nodded. Apart from 'A' Company, a lot of the N.C.O.s and officers from the other companies had been granted five days Blighty leave. "You never know, he might bring you a present back," said Donna.

"Like fuck. Anyway, how come you're back on fatigues?" asked the cook in a tone more in keeping with his friend's mood.

"I'm after a good conduct stripe," said Donna dryly.

Conroy laughed out loud. "Yer a dry bastard Donna." He flicked the end of his cigarette away. "We'd better get cracking mate. Can you sort the fires out?"

Without another word, Donna cleaned out the dead embers beneath the huge dixies. It wasn't long before he had two fires going strongly, one heating up water. It was getting lighter by the minute. The first birds were beginning to sing, but interruption came with the rumble of distant shellfire from the direction of La Bassee in the east, heralding the day's hostilities. By now Conroy had a small pot of water boiling on the metal range. There would soon be tea for both.

The battalion's field kitchens commanded an uninterrupted view of all four roads, which began awakening as the light improved. A battery of French artillery trundled towards Festubert and minutes later a troop of British cavalry clattered by, causing sparks to fly from some of the horses' hooves on the cobbles.

An officer and half a dozen men of the Lincolnshire regiment escorting a prisoner quietly marched past. They turned left towards Richbourg.

Donna frowned, nudging Conroy. "What's going on there? One of them was carrying a folded stretcher on his shoulder."

The officer halted the firing party by a derelict farmhouse just off the deserted, pock-marked Richbourg road.

"Fall out, assemble at the rear of the cottage," he ordered.

The condemned man looked bewildered, hardly believing what was happening to him. His legs moved of their own accord. He glanced fearfully at the rear wall of the dwelling. He was about 20 years old.

"I wasn't deserting Sir, I got lost, couldn't find my way back," he pleaded, protesting his innocence to the last.

The firing squad stood about silent and grim-faced.

"Be quiet," said the officer, proffering a cigarette and looking up at the sky. "Listen, when you've smoked that I'm not going to have you put against the wall, I'm going to let you go." He pointed across the open flat farmland behind the cottage. "I want you to go that way and keep off the roads, otherwise you will be arrested again. Try to make for the coast."

The relief transformed the young man's face.

"Oh thank you, thank you, Sir," he cried.

The officer glanced skywards once more; it was full daylight by now.

"Right, off you go."

The prisoner took to his heels, stumbling as fast as he was able across the muddy, churned-up field. He'd covered perhaps thirty yards when the officer spoke quietly to the group of men.

"Squad, take up the prone firing position." The firing squad lay down. "Take aim...Fire!"

The bullets struck the fugitive in the back, but not all together, with the effect of knocking him forward, then forward again. He fell with arms outstretched face downwards in the mud.

"Clear breaches, retrieve the body," ordered the officer, rubbing his hands to keep warm.

****

They were issued with greatcoats prior to going back into the line. 'About fucking time too' was the general comment after months of seeing the red-banded staff officers, who rarely went in the trenches, strutting about in fur-lined overcoats and knee-length boots.

George Campbell, hot iron in hand, was stooped half-naked killing lice which had colonised the folds of his kilt.

"Why we no get trews instead of these fucking things?"

Jimmy Robb, who'd replaced the wounded Littler as lance corporal, was playing cards but wasn't too engrossed in the game not to answer.

"Och, well ye see George, the German prisoners taken after Givenchy and Festubert kept on calling us 'die damen von holle'."

Campbell, having replaced his kilt, was now doing the same killing act with his shirt. "What the fuck does that mean?"

"'Die damen von holle' means 'the ladies from hell' in German," replied Robb a mite smugly.

"Oh," said George, "what does 'I'm sick and tired of the fucking place' mean in German?"

"Nee idea," said the card player.

The padre held an open air service on the day the battalion left Le Touret. There was a sprinkling of snow on the parade ground and the cold frosty air made his breath into vapour as he delivered the sermon. They marched towards Richbourg St. Vaast along a road whose fringes were littered with the debris of war; frost-covered dud shells, broken wheels, discarded limbers and the rotting carcasses of mules and horses.

An hour later the leading columns halted before a row of grand looking two-storied houses, no doubt the residences in peacetime of the professional classes. Now the buildings were used as billets. Further along the street on the opposite side stood half a dozen shell-damaged shops, some of whose contents scattered the pavements. The Seaforths were to relieve the 2/3 Gurkhas of the Garhwal Brigade that night in trenches to the east of Richbourg.

"What's bothering you mon?" whispered Jimmy Robb. He'd covertly watched the Englishman go casually to the door of the house, peer up and down the darkened street, then return to sit and fidget on his pack in the bitterly cold room. He'd gone to the doorway twice in the last twenty minutes, while the other occupants huddled up trying to keep warm.

"What time is it?" asked Donna by way of an answer.

"Twenty after nine," said Robb looking at his watch.

"Why do we always have to wait? They tell us nothing. An infantryman waits for everything," grumbled Donna. "We wait for hours on parade, we wait to get fed, we wait for hours and days to go into the trenches." He rubbed his hands vigorously. "What time are we due to leave here?"

Jimmy Robb shook his head. "Ah dinna ken."

The Englishman grimaced, got to his feet and went to the doorway, but this time, instead of returning to his seat, he disappeared into the night. In the street he darted quickly across the road and, keeping off the pavements, worked his way down to the derelict shops and in the darkness, crept into a milliner's shop. He goose-stepped slowly in the interior; his feet making contact with what felt like bobbins of cotton or rolls of ribbon. He struck a match, then extinguished it quickly, not wanting to be charged with looting. The last thing he wished was to be discovered by some battalion patrol or M.P.

Donna located a few rolls of fabric and, mainly by touch, cut off two lengths and wrapped a piece around each leg from ankle to thigh, securing the cloth with ribbon. He began to feel warmer already 'At least now I won't freeze when in the line,' he thought.

The Seaforths relieved the tough little soldiers from India at 1.00am the following morning. Recent shelling had obliterated parapets and dugouts were non-existent, but the worst aspect for the men about to occupy the positions was to discover the trenches were waterlogged, in some places almost waist high. They worked all night fortifying the parapets or filling sandbags to reconstruct the smashed dugouts, but however hard they worked there was no escaping the calf and thigh-deep ice cold water.

After he'd helped position and supply the machine gun, Donna waded through the water in the darkness to where Campbell and Robb crouched.

"Ahoy there," he growled, "I'm thinking of transferring to the fucking navy."

"Dinna cause waves, tha water's going up ma arse," said Campbell.

With his entrenching tool, Donna began hacking out the rear side of the trench above the water line; they watched him in silence. It was only after he'd been working for ten minutes that the purpose of his toil became obvious, then they joined in, making the ledge in the clay of such proportions as to allow them to sit on and pull their legs clear of the icy liquid. However, they were back into it a few hours later when the order to "stand-to" was given.

In the daylight the trench ran parallel with the near Estaires Road. The German positions 150 yards in front were quiet. Donna was perched with drawn up knees trying to snatch a few minutes sleep when sudden shouts and a spate of rifle shots made him open his eyes.

"What's up?"

A soldier on the submerged firestep pointed skywards. The Germans had put up an observation balloon behind their lines. As the firing intensified Donna watched the balloon being hurriedly winched down again on its cable, to the loud cheers from the soldiers in the canal-like trench.

He closed his eyes, then opened them again glancing down at his knees. He smiled. The cloth he'd wrapped around his legs the previous night was of different colours, one was red, the other blue.

By way of retaliation, the trench was dive-bombed in the afternoon, a black painted Fokker Wolf biplane sneaked from out of the clouds and dropped spike bombs, which didn't explode but would have killed instantly any infantryman unfortunate to be hit by one. The pilot and his bomb aimer could clearly be seen smiling at what they thought was panic below them. They flew the length of the trench dropping the lethal darts, but the missiles scored no hits, just buried themselves in the soft clay.

Its surprise attack over, the aircraft banked and flew off with a wave, pursued by volleys of rifle shots from below.

TEN

Farewell RAMC

Matron Alice Grey ran the medical wards at Mill Hill, Colchester like a sergeant major. She was a short plump woman in her late thirties. She wore a long navy blue uniform with a starched white apron and cuffs, and on her head she carried a stiff white bonnet tied under a severe chin. The pained expression on her face would have, some said, caused a clock to stop had she gazed at it long enough. She hovered continually about the wards and corridors looking for things to complain about. The staff disliked her, not least because of her habit of standing over them while they changed dressings or administered medicines, tut tutting, making even the most able and efficient of her orderlies nervous. She seemed to take pleasure in reprimanding her staff in the presence of the patients. The sight of her approach was enough to create dread in the breasts of her staff. Some tried to be charitable and explain her vindictiveness by saying that she was so dedicated to nursing that any hospital work done less than perfect was something she couldn't bear. Donna, however, had met her kind before, particularly as a pupil at St. Oswald's school. He knew her for what she was, a bully.

Work on the wards began at 6.00am for the day orderlies; they recorded the pulse and temperatures of each patient. After serving breakfast, they cleaned and polished the ward. Patients fit enough usually helped, and just prior to the doctor's first tour the matron sailed in to inspect and criticise. A ward sister and senior orderly accompanied the officer doctor on his rounds. 'Up' patients, those inmates allowed out of bed, were made to lie in the attention position on their beds during the medical inspections. The rest of the day's work was taken up with treatments and operating theatre work. General duties included kitchen, laundry and cleaning work, which never ceased for a moment, Matron Grey saw to that. The day shift finished at 6.00pm, with the night staff taking over.

The military hospital was built on high acreage with an excellent view of the rural countryside. It stood in its own grounds with a narrow 50-yard approach path from the main road on which were built a handful of cottages and The Mill public house. There were stables for the cavalry horses that romped and grazed in the surrounding fields out of sight of the hospital.

Donna shared a room at the hospital with two others, Fred Renalls, a slim lad from East London who he'd known from training at Aldershot, and John Clare, a tall gangling man with spiky hair and big owl-like eyes. He came from Sunderland. Donna usually had trouble understanding Clare, especially when he got excited.

As far as the Manchester man could see, John's only interests were darts and improving his physique. He kept a pair of Indian clubs in his locker and practised with them or did press-ups by the side of his bunk, usually first thing in the morning and last thing at night. Despite his diligent efforts, Clare's arms and shoulders didn't appear to get any more muscular.

"Turn it in mate, I've seen better bodies in butchers' shops," said Renalls after Clare had puffed and panted through one of his club-swinging sessions. The Londoner was lying on his bed reading. He smiled and looked at Donna for approval, but he ignored him. Instead he concentrated on writing up some lecture notes given that day by Sergeant Nicholas. Renalls pulled a face and went back to the local paper. Clare began doing press-ups. Donna became stuck on a word given that day in the lecture room. It was 'bistoury'. He tried to think back to what the fat sergeant had said, but to no avail. He looked around at his two room mates but decided not to ask either of them. Since his experience at York with Quither, Donna had become more insular. He sighed, closed his notebook, left the room and made his way down the corridor towards one of the wards. As he came level with the laundry room the door opened and out stepped a short rotund orderly with spectacles.

"Excuse me Corporal, what's a 'bistoury'?" asked Donna.

Corporal Alf Bennett, arms full of bed sheets, blinked up at Donna.

"You're new here aren't you?"

Donna nodded. "Yes, I've just been posted from York."

"Do you play football."

"Yes, I can kick a case ball," replied Donna a little intrigued.

"Are you any good?"

Donna shrugged.

"Good, we've got a practice game Wednesday night, 7.00pm. What's your name?" he asked, giving Donna the sheets to hold while he wrote his name in a book.

Donna tried again. "What's a 'bistoury' Corporal?"

"Oh, a bistoury is a long slender surgical knife. See you Wednesday," Bennett said and walked off down the corridor.

Donna watched him go past the entrance to the kitchen, then vanish down a side ward. There was something about Bennett he liked.

The following Wednesday, attired in PT singlet and shorts, Donna performed well in the football game despite his lack of match practice. He displayed quickness and skill, augmented by a few 'Scots tricks' he'd picked up as a boy on the croft behind The Grapes inn in Collyhurst.

Later that night, back in his room, he realised that sport in the army was the one place where rank counted for nothing. Every participant was equal, subject only to the natural skill each individual possessed. Donna was picked to play against the Royal Artillery the following week; the hospital team won 3-1, largely due to Donna's pace on the right wing, which continually confused the gunners' defence. As he left the field at the end of the game, he noticed there were officers from both units amongst the spectators.

As weeks passed and the year headed into summer, the Essex countryside attained great beauty, trees and hedges blossomed into pinks and lilacs, the fields were seas of greens and golds, the long summer days produced warm perfumed nights. For the man from Manchester to be able to share these atmospheric splendours and the wild life was sublime. He found out that to be a member of the hospital football team meant you were given time off to train, which amounted to being excused the mundane duties of guard and fire picket. Donna's favourite method was to go for a five mile or so run, thus allowing him the dual benefits of keeping fit and savouring the glorious vistas.

Clare sat next to Donna in the lecture room. Written on the blackboard in white chalk was: 'Poisons and their effects and counter measures on the body'. There were eight others in the classroom grouped together. Sitting at the rear and apart from the orderlies was Matron Grey.

The warm beams of the sunlight streamed through the open windows, causing minute specs of pollen and dust to rise through the rays.

"Now," exclaimed the corpulent, bald-headed Sergeant Nicholas, calling for attention, "a patient has mistakenly drunk some disinfectant; shall we say creosote. There is no doctor or senior sister about. What's the first thing one should do?"

Nicholas appealed to the class for the answer. Someone at the front put up a hand.

"Yes."

"Make him sick."

"That's right," said the sergeant.

He looked towards Donna and Clare.

"Private Clare, how do we do that?"

It startled Clare to be suddenly picked out and he began to speak without thinking.

"Er, stick ye…"

Donna gave him a nudge. Clare was about to say 'stick your fingers down his throat'. "Salt and water," whispered Donna out of the side of his mouth.

"Er, make the patient drink a solution of salt and water, Sergeant," answered Private Clare.

"Very good." The sergeant walked towards the window and looked out. The sun reflected from his bald pate, creating a halo of light on the ceiling. Donna spotted the phenomenon and smiled.

"Private Donna, what if the patient is unconscious?" asked the lecturer, his back still to the class.

Donna shifted in his seat. "In that case, the patient's stomach should be pumped and artificial respiration may have to be given, Sergeant."

"Good," said the N.C.O. moving away from the window. However, his bald head still cast a halo above.

"You there," snapped the matron to Donna, "pay attention. Report to my office tomorrow morning." As always, Grey's outburst cast a shadow over the rest of the lecture period.

The next morning Donna found he wasn't the only one standing to attention outside the Matron's office. There was another chap, a well-built man with fair hair called Morris. The latter looked at Donna. "Hadn't one of us better knock and tell the old crow we've arrived?" he enquired.

Before he could answer, the office door opened and Matron emerged into the corridor. With a pained look she stood before the two, her hands clasped behind her back inspecting them. She took a small pair of spectacles from her apron and squeezed them onto her nose.

"Show me your hands," she snapped. She scrutinised Morris's hands, examining them back and front. When it was Donna's turn, he allowed an amused, condescending expression to creep across his eyes. 'Why is it,' he thought, 'that some people who have even the minimum of authority seem so intent on making the lives of others so miserable.' He'd experienced it as a small boy and in the prison at York, now it was here at Mill Hill. Why? Fear and intimidation didn't make one a better pupil or inmate. It created in the Manchester man feelings of resentment.

She removed her spectacles and fixed Donna with the same pained expression.

"What's your name?" She asked abruptly.

"Donna ma'am."

"Oh yes," she replied with quiet menace, "you're the sullen one from Yorkshire."

"Begging your pardon ma'am, I'm the sullen one from Lancashire," he replied dryly.

Donna's companion saved himself from laughing out loud by coughing and moving his feet.

Grey's eyes flashed. "Stand to attention or I'll report the two of you to your commanding officer," she fumed. "Now report to Corporal Bennett in the mortuary."

The two men turned smartly and headed for the rear of the hospital where the 'dead house', as the orderlies referred to it, was situated.

"Have you ever seen a dead person before?" asked Bennett, bedecked in a white hospital gown. They stood in the mortuary. A few feet away on a table lay a covered corpse.

"Yes," said Donna. "How about you?" he asked Morris. Morris shook his head.

Corporal Bennett grinned and said: "Don't worry, the dead can't hurt you, it's only the living that can inflict pain."

He turned to Donna. "Are you fit for Thursday?"

Donna nodded.

"Good. We're playing the Engineers. They've not lost a game. We got walloped 6-2 the last time we played them, but with Jock McConnell in defence and you in the forward line Mill Hill's team is stronger now. It should be more of an even match. I'm looking forward to it."

"Me too," agreed Donna.

Although Bennett didn't play in the team, he selected and managed the players. Football was an obsession of his. Nothing gave him greater pleasure than to see his team play well or, better still, win. After each match he'd discuss it over and over, even if it was only a practice game. He constantly worried about the health of his players, especially if they'd taken a knock on the knee or ankle. At times it amazed Donna how someone not a participant could be so besotted by the game of football.

The corporal continued to enthuse about his favourite subject until Donna, patiently waiting for a pause in the conversation, steered Bennett back to the job in hand.

"Alf, what do you want us two to do here?"

The N.C.O. shrugged, collecting his thoughts, a little fretful at having to interrupt his passion. He nodded towards the table. "Right, I'll show you."

Morris stayed where he was, a little away from the table.

The corporal lifted the sheet from the dead man's head. "He was a cavalry officer found shot in his quarters. Apparently he shot himself in the mouth."

"Why?" asked Donna quietly, gazing down at the waxen bloodstained face of a young man not much older than himself.

Bennett shook his head. "Who knows." He was silent for a moment, then went on: "Tomorrow some of his relations, possibly his father and brother, are coming to take him home for burial, so do you think you could clean him up a bit? Get him into his dress uniform. It shouldn't be too difficult, rigor mortis has passed off him."

"Where is his dress uniform?" enquired Donna

"In the cupboard over there. Oh, there's also some women's make-up to liven him up a bit," added the corporal with a macabre grin.

Before leaving, he studied Morris through his spectacles. "Don't tell me you're scared of a stiff," he said with a grin

Morris nodded sheepishly, then spoke for the first time: "When the matron told us to report here, I thought it would be to clean windows or polish the floor, not to wrestle with a fucking dead man," he moaned.

Bennett, with a twinkle in his eye, looked Morris up and down, then trying hard to keep his face straight said, "You look a big strong lad, if the dead man attacks you while you're dressing him grab his balls, he'll soon stop."

After the N.C.O. had gone, Donna found a couple of gowns in a cupboard and threw one to Morris, who hovered well away from the corpse. Donna, now clad in white, uncovered the corpse and stood by the table waiting.

"Look, just give me a lift to dress him and if you're squeamish, I'll clean up his face and head."

Morris nodded and fetched the gold-braided uniform and laid it on top of the discarded shroud by the table. Morris was glad the dead man still wore his long white underwear. It meant he didn't have to touch the dead flesh. Nevertheless, Donna did most of the pulling and tugging to fit the trousers and cavalry boots. Next came the tunic. Donna achieved this by placing one arm of the corpse into the sleeve of the jacket and then pushed the garment beneath the body, doing the same with the other arm. Morris didn't attempt to assist; instead he crept around keeping close to his companion.

After buttoning up the tunic and laying the dead officer's arms by his side, Donna bent down and took a closer look at the face. The eyes were sunken and closed and the nose was pinched, dark dried blood covered the lower half of the face. He studied the lower mandible; it appeared out of line to the upper jaw. As he straightened up from the table, he bumped into Morris, who had crept up behind him and had been peering over Donna's shoulder.

"For Jesus sake, there's nothing to be scared of," exclaimed the former, a little irritated.

"Sorry," mumbled Morris.

"Look," said Donna, "if you get me some warm water and a few cotton swabs from one of the wards, I'll clean the stiff's mug myself. You can stay well away from him if it makes you feel better."

"Right," said Morris, darting out of the mortuary.

Five minutes later Morris returned with wool and a bowl of warm water, which Donna placed on the dead man's chest. Morris positioned himself near the mortuary door, as though he was standing guard or ready to bolt out of the place.

Beginning at the forehead, Donna swabbed the corpse's face with warm water and began working towards the dried blood of the jaw. As he progressed he noticed Morris had left the doorway and was standing watching him with a kind of hypnotic fascination. Ignoring him, Donna mopped away the blood from the cheeks and around the mouth. Then, as he discarded one bloodstained swab and reached in the bowl for a fresh one, the warm water caused the corpse to open one eye and almost simultaneously the mouth slowly opened and the lower jaw fell to one side, partly revealing the upper teeth, producing a grotesque grinning appearance.

There was a sudden yell, so loud it made even Donna jump. Morris fled, but he didn't travel very far. In his haste to gain the sanctuary of the corridor, he ran full tilt into the door jamb. There was the sound of a dull thud; Morris lay stretched full length on the floor, unconscious on the mortuary floor.

Donna sighed and examined him where he lay. A gash pumped blood near his temple but his breathing was regular. So he loosened Morris's collar and left him to recover in his own time.

Without further interruptions, he returned to the task of trying to make the dead officer a little more presentable. He gently closed the eye and mouth using collodion from the ward's dispensary. Next he powdered the cheeks and reddened the lips with material he found in the make-up box. His final touch was to part the deceased's hair in the middle, leaving a quiff above the right eyebrow. 'Hmm,' thought Donna as he removed his gown, 'at least he looks a little less mortified than before.'

The following day Donna was back working on the medical wards. Morris's injury had proved more serious than was first thought. Apart from a wound that needed four stitches, he was suffering from concussion.

Also, they discovered a nerve near the eye had been damaged. He was confined to bed on M1 ward where Donna worked.

"How do you feel?" asked Donna. "You must have had the mother and father of a headache."

Morris, his head swathed in bandages, nodded. "I can't remember anything," he said feebly.

"You can remember your name can't you?" asked Donna, concerned.

"Oh yes, I can remember that, but I can't remember how I knocked myself out."

"Don't worry," consoled Donna, "it'll all come back."

Their conversation was interrupted by a mild squabble between two 'up' patients further down the ward. Donna left Morris and moved to where the duo were playing draughts across a bed.

"Keep your voices down lads," said Donna reasonably.

"Who says so?" demanded one of them, a sergeant of artillery. Donna felt himself getting angry, but he kept his voice even.

"I say so, Sergeant. You're disturbing the other patients and you know as well as anyone no games are allowed until after 6.00pm."

Sergeant Trenchem was a dark-complexioned man of about 30. He had narrow slanted eyes and a black drooping moustache. Since being admitted with a minor foot complaint, his off-hand obstreperous manner had made him unpopular with the orderlies and the other patients. He was a big-head in every sense of the word.

"Who do you think you're ordering about?" said Trenchem, his face distorted. "If you were in my battery I'd have your guts for garters."

Donna felt his face blanch with anger. "But I'm not in your battery Sergeant, and as a man with stripes you're expected to set an example."

The sergeant leaned back on one elbow and leered up at the mild-looking Donna. "Listen kid, if I didn't have this bad foot I'd take you out in the corridor and knock three kinds of shit out of you."

Donna was furious. He could see that some of the other patients were listening. It was with quite an effort that he didn't smash Trenchem there and then. Instead he leaned forward towards him, his face a mask of hatred.

"Listen, when that foot gets better come back any time you like. I'll be here ready for you, you loud-mouthed bastard," hissed Donna before walking away shaking with anger.

Almost all of the hospital's staff not needed for duty, officers and other ranks, turned up to watch the anticipated prodigious clash between the football teams of Mill Hill and the Royal Engineers. They were not disappointed. As usual, before the game Corporal Bennett busied himself with advice and tactics. Once the whistle went to start the match it was a mixture of robust and skilful football, with neither team dominating the play for very long. At half time the score stood at Mill Hill 0, Royal Engineers 0. With only 15 minutes to go, Donna's flying feet on the right wing outpaced the tiring Engineers' defenders. He crossed the ball into the opponent's goalmouth where big Geordie Jones, Mill Hill's centre forward, headed past the opponent's goalkeeper to give the hospital the lead.

In the last minute of the game, Donna, going like an express train in an effort to make the score 2-0, collided with the Engineers' goalkeeper and had to be carried from the field with a badly wrenched left hip. However, the hospital had won the game and the victory helped to nullify the pain of injury for Donna.

Corporal Bennett, ecstatic with joy, fussed over his injured player like a mother hen. "How do you feel, Donna? You there," he ordered someone, "get him a drink."

"I'll be alright Alf," said Donna.

The corporal dismissed his assurances with a wave of the hand. "Nonsense," he said, organising helpers to carry Donna back to his room and getting Captain Robinson, who had been a spectator, to examine him.

Donna was given two days bed rest and light duties for a week. He was something of a sporting hero. Most of the other members of the football team came to visit during his days in bed, but one evening after he'd been allowed up, Renalls, who'd been sprucing himself up in the mirror, said to Donna, "Me and Hercules are going for a pint in The Mill. Why don't you join us."

Donna would have preferred to spend his evenings in the countryside, not being much of a drinker, but now his mobility was impaired he reasoned a visit to the pub could be a welcome diversion for once. "Right, I'll meet you about nine."

There were other men from the hospital in the low-ceilinged Mill pub that night, and a few nodded as he limped into the saloon. His two friends were standing at the bar talking to the landlord. As Donna approached, the latter vanished from sight.

"What'll it be mate?" asked Renalls, going to his pocket.

"Pint of dark."

Renalls called the barmaid. "Lillian, a pint of your finest dark for the gentleman." The barmaid was a woman of around forty, and although her figure had begun to thicken, she possessed large expressive eyes and fine features. The soft lights of the bar enhanced her pale skin against the frame of her long dark hair. Donna stared at her face and the way her dress bulged at the front.

She watched him covertly. "One penny my dear," she said to Renalls, proffering a small well-shaped hand for payment.

"Cheers, Fred," acknowledged Donna, drinking the froth off his beer.

The woman left the group to serve someone else. The landlord reappeared carrying a crateful of soda water He was red-faced and sweating. He wheezed for breath as he began stacking the bottles behind the bar. Donna caught the barmaid glancing in their direction.

"Is she his missus?" he wanted to know, nodding towards the landlord.

Renalls wiped his mouth after taking a drink. "No, Lillian's a widow. She works here a few nights just to help out."

John Clare, who had been itching for a game of darts since entering the place, finally managed to persuade Renalls to partake. Declining the invitation to watch the game, Donna stayed at the saloon bar while his two friends played in the taproom.

The barmaid drifted over to where Donna stood. "I've not seen you in here before," she said as she collected a couple of empty glasses from a nearby table.

"No, I don't drink much," answered Donna.

"Spill most of it do you?" she replied, trying to keep her face straight but the humour in her eyes betraying her.

Donna liked her sense of humour. He smiled and shook his head.

She spoke again. "You don't talk much either do you. Where do you come from?"

Instead of replying with words, he made signs with his fingers as though communicating in the language of the deaf. She laughed, showing even white teeth.

"Quick, aren't you?" she said. Still smiling, she moved away to serve another customer.

Donna sighed a little and wished she'd stayed. The game over, the three took their drinks over to a table that was more comfortable. Donna chose a chair that gave him a view of the bar and the woman. In this cosy informal atmosphere, they talked and laughed, enjoying the euphoria of getting slightly drunk.

Then, half an hour before closing time, Renalls suggested having a drink in The Haystack, which was another pub at the crossroads. Clare was game but Donna declined.

"No thanks, not with my hip."

"Alright, see you later mate," said Renalls before hurrying off with the gangling Clare in tow.

Donna sat for a moment staring at the dregs in his glass, then at the two empty ones of his departed friends. He debated with himself whether to have another drink or not, deciding he would. He limped to the bar. Lillian the barmaid, ignoring a prior plea for service, was there to meet him.

"Yes my dear."

"Same again, please," said Donna, placing his empty glass on the counter.

She looked at him as she pulled a refill. "What's wrong with your leg?"

"I was injured playing football a few days ago."

She stared at him for a long moment, then said pointedly, "Your name's Connor or something isn't it?"

"Donna," he corrected.

"That's it, a lot of the hospital men were in here celebrating the night Mill Hill beat the Engineers. They spoke of you as if you were Jesus Christ. Men!" she said in slight disgust.

Donna shrugged and smiled to himself as she hurried away to serve other thirsty customers.

After she'd served the last customer, Lillian left the bar to clear the tables. By the time she'd got to where Donna sat, her arms were filled with empty glasses.

"Have you enjoyed yourself?" she asked pleasantly, while reaching for Clare and Renalls' empty glasses.

He looked up at her, his head held a little to one side, his eyes wide and serious. "Yes."

She stared at him, then shook her head. "God, you do remind me of someone." There was a pause, then, not looking at him, she said, "I'll be finished here in ten minutes. Would you be a gentleman and walk me home?"

"Of course."

As they strolled side by side down Mill Hill, a slight breeze crept around them from across the fields, bringing with it the scents of freshly cut hay and honeysuckle. Donna sighed and breathed deeply, savouring the fragrance.

They had been silent up until then. "Do you like it here?" she asked gently.

"I love it. To me nights like these are almost spiritual," he said softly.

"You're a funny one Donna," she replied.

Below them a cluster of town lights came into view. "I don't live far from here now," she said. She led him left at the foot of the hill, then right below a bridge to a row of cottages. She came to a halt at one of the garden gates. "Here we are, number 18," she said. Donna was wishing the walk would never end.

She looked at him in the darkness. "Thank you for bringing me home Donna. What's your first name?"

"James."

"Oh," she said softly.

He stood looking at her, unsure of what to do next. He held out his hand for it to be shaken. She looked at him, then threw back her head and laughed, the sound musical almost.

"Oh you are lovely," she breathed, then reached up and unpinned her hat. Holding it in one hand, she gently drew Donna towards her and kissed him. He felt the warm wetness of her mouth and his body moulded to the softness of hers and her sweet fragrance.

She was breathless from his kiss. "Oh, James, you're trembling," she breathed.

He kissed her again.

****

Private Morris discovered his encounter with the mortuary door had left him with an uncontrollable wink. He'd damaged the nerve near his temple. The hospital doctors hoped his condition wouldn't be permanent, otherwise he may have to be discharged from the army, the prospect of which didn't in the least appear to bother the unfortunate orderly.

Before Donna's hip had healed completely his impulsiveness nearly caused him greater injury. One evening he caught one of the grazing cavalry horses in the nearby field. Using his trouser braces as reins he slipped onto its back intending to canter around the meadow, but the big horse had other ideas. It suddenly took flight, charging and kicking its hind legs, scattering the other horses until it finally unseated Donna and sent him head over heels into the middle of a hawthorn bush. There he hung, winded and pierced by hundreds of thorns. He dreaded to move, every slight movement brought a fresh needle prick. After gritting his teeth and painfully disentangling himself, he limped back to the hospital, his shirt torn, minus a shoe and covered in scratches. Feeling rather foolish and not wishing to be seen in such a state, Donna skirted the main entrance and entered by one of the smaller rear doors. He'd hardly taken four steps along the narrow passageway when he almost collided with the matron. She almost exploded when she saw his appearance.

"You're a disgrace to Mill Hill. You've been up to no good I'll be bound. Be outside my office tomorrow morning. In the meantime, I'm reporting you to your commanding officer. Now get out of my sight and clean yourself up," she snarled.

He slunk to his room, but just before he got there he heard his name called and the sound of hurrying feet. Reluctantly he stopped. It was Corporal Bennett.

"What the fucking hell's happened to you?"

"I've been kicked by a mad hen," muttered Donna, using a phrase from his childhood.

"Come again," said Bennett.

Donna took a deep breath. "I've been riding one of the horses," he said ruefully.

The corporal burst out laughing. "It looks like the horse has been riding you. Where's your other shoe?"

Donna shrugged. "Fuck knows."

"How's your hip?" asked Bennett, suddenly serious.

"Fine."

The corporal felt in his pocket. "Anyway, I've got something that may cheer you up." He held out a half sovereign. "This is from the father of that dead officer you attended to. He gave me a sovereign so I'll give the other half to winking Walter Morris, do you agree Donna?"

"Of course, Corporal."

Bennett nodded "Better vanish now before someone sees you."

"Bit late for that Alf," said Donna as he turned into his room. "I've got to report to Gray's office tomorrow morning."

The portly Corporal Bennett pulled a face.

"Lillian's been asking after you again," said Renalls quietly. He and Donna were off duty in their room, the latter was sitting writing a letter home. He stopped what he was doing and looked at Renalls.

"I don't want to get involved, Fred, as much as I'd like to."

"Why? She's a lovely woman, anybody in your shoes would jump at the chance. I wish it was me she was interested in," replied Renalls.

"Yes, I know, but I'm terrified of catching something. You've seen some of the syphilis cases in here yourself, the poor bastards are treated like dirt and shunned like lepers. It's only the officers who are treated differently because they are the only ones allowed to catch syph off lavatory seats," he said disgustedly.

"Yes, but she's respectable. She wouldn't go to bed with just anybody."

"Maybe not," replied Donna, "but I couldn't take the chance, not in an army town like this. If she asks for me again tell her I've gone on leave, or working late or something."

"Right you are mate," said Renalls getting to his feet. "I'm just off to the pub now. No need to ask if you're coming, then?"

Donna shook his head and went back to his writing.

He awoke in the early hours of the morning soaked in sweat. His throat was sore and he felt weak and feverish. In the darkness he could hear Renalls and Clare snoring alternately; he threw back the bed sheets and swung his feet onto the cool polished floor. His head ached. Fumbling his way he opened the door and stepped out onto the corridor. It was cooler there but his pyjamas still clung to his body. He plodded along barefooted, his feet hardly making a sound in the dimly-lit corridor. As he passed the laundry store he was certain he could hear a moan, but feeling weak he carried on walking. In the kitchen he let the water run for several minutes before filling a mug and drinking thirstily. He splashed water over his burning head and neck. He felt a little better. He filled a jug and carried it back with him along the passageway. As he came to the laundry room a second time curiosity made him open the door and peer inside. The room was in darkness but light from the corridor illuminated the interior. Matron Grey was lying on the floor with her skirt pulled high around her waist. On top of her was Sergeant Trenchem, wearing only a white singlet. The matron's fat bare legs clung to his body. She had her eyes closed and her arms around him as he rode her. A second later her piggy eyes widened in alarm as she met Donna's look.

"Quick, help me with the sergeant," she said breathlessly. "The poor man's having a fit."

Donna looked at them for a second longer, derision showing in his face. Leaving the door ajar, he went back to his room.

Not wishing to miss a leave home he kept quiet about his condition the following morning. Instead he dosed himself with linctus for his sore throat and swallowed pills for his aching head. He fell asleep on the train to London and was roused by a word and a gentle shake from a pretty girl of about twenty years of age.

"We're here ducks," she smiled.

Donna had to change stations, but before doing so he found a teashop and took a couple of the pills he'd brought with him.

He went to sleep again before the train left Euston for Manchester, but an hour and a half later, as the train approached Rugby, he came to his senses and felt somewhat better.

It was dark by the time he got to Brydenvilla Street; his mother, who'd been expecting him, opened the door.

"Oh, it's our Jim," she squealed in delight. "Come in son," she said, smiling and grasping his hand in both of hers as she always did on greeting him. "Are you hungry?" she asked.

"Not really. I'd like a drink, though," he answered wearily.

She looked more closely at him in the gaslight, concern showing in her eyes.

"Jim, what's wrong with your face?"

She let go of his hands so he could look in the wall mirror. His face and neck were covered in red spots. He had measles. At his age!

Returning to Mill Hill he found he was on the move again.

"We're sending you to the military hospital at Great Yarmouth on the East Coast," informed his Commanding Officer.

"Anyone else going beside myself, Sir?"

"No, Donna."

"Can I ask why, Sir?"

The Officer coughed. "Well, yes. I'm sending you because they are short of experienced nursing staff there. Now you've done very well here, your work is good, you've got on splendidly with the other chaps and you're a fine sportsman. I've written all this in your report, so keep up the good work and good luck to you."

"Thank you, Sir," said Donna saluting, but not convinced all the officer said was true. The matron, he felt, was instrumental in him being moved on. He was sorry to leave Colchester and the friends he had made there.

The hospital at Great Yarmouth was built on the cobbled coast road facing the sea. Separating one from the other was half a mile of hilly, grass-topped sand dunes, which formed the beach, a favourite haunt in the evenings of lovers and courting couples. Yarmouth was in complete contrast to Colchester, with its tall boarding houses, pubs and sideshows. Donna nevertheless enjoyed his saunters around the harbours and shorelines. He liked to watch the fishing boats returning with their 'fruit of the sea' as the French call fish, or the tall sailing ships riding the huge swells as they came into port.

After settling in at his new surroundings he studied hard and sat the advanced medical examination, which he passed without much difficulty.

In October the murder of a soubrette actress from one of the theatres was front-page news. The town's newspapers reported the grisly death of actress Dolly Grey; she was found strangled and violated amongst the sand dunes. The article went on to say that the police had little to go on. Donna, like everyone else, was appalled by the young woman's death, but after reading the account he thought no more about it.

A few days later, after finishing work on the ward, he returned to his room to find his neatly folded civilian clothes and the contents of his locker had been disturbed. He thought he'd been the victim of a thief at first, but even though his money and letters from home had been gone through, apparently the only thing missing were his shoes. He slumped down on his bed mystified. Who would steal shoes and yet leave money? Still trying to puzzle it out, he went in search of the guard commander.

"Right," said the sergeant in charge of the guard, "let's have your name." He was sat at a table in the guardroom and carefully wrote down Donna's name in the report book. "You say you've had something stolen?"

"Yes, a pair of shoes, civilian. But that's not all, my lockers have been gone through as well."

"Anything else missing?"

"It's hard to say," replied Donna, perplexed. "I can't understand it. I don't think so."

The N.C.O. felt in his tunic pocket for cigarettes and matches. He proffered one. "Smoke?"

Donna shook his head. The sergeant blew smoke to one side, then indicated a chair. "Sit down a minute lad." He stared at Donna for a moment. "Now then, lad," he began, as though searching for the right words. "Now then, I'm sure you've read in the papers about the terrible crime done to this poor girl?"

Donna looked at him for a moment, unclear what the guard commander was getting at. Then realisation dawned. He started to rise from the chair. "You load of bastards." He felt insulted, unclean, angry.

"Steady there, watch yer language or yew'll be on a charge," warned the Sergeant. With an effort Donna controlled himself.

"The local Constabulary said they were only borrowing yer footwear to check some footprints found near the woman. Yer should have 'em back tomorrer. We thought you wouldn't miss 'em fer one night."

"Who's we?" asked Donna angrily.

The N.C.O. waved his hand. "The Adjutant and others," he replied vaguely.

The following morning Donna asked to see his Commanding Officer. "I want a transfer, Sir, overseas if possible. If not, anywhere away from here as soon as possible."

A few weeks later he stood swaying in the carriage doorway as the train drew slowly into Shorncliffe railway station. In his tunic pocket was his posting authorisation papers for Shorncliffe Military Hospital. Getting off at the same station was a group of kilted Scottish soldiers.

The red-bricked hospital was situated on the high ground next to a Royal Artillery barracks. The elevated position gave an excellent view of the English Channel and the constant movement of ships. Below the cliffs, hugging the narrow pebble beach, nestled the little coastal village of Sandgate. Across the water was France. On fine days the coast was visible. At night the Cape Griz Nez lighthouse seemed tantalisingly near.

Having passed the advanced nursing examination, Donna was allowed to work in the operating theatre, which he found fascinating, and was soon in charge of an infection ward. However, although he now had greater responsibility, he remained introvert. Inwardly he felt it was because of his army record, especially his prison term. It seemed to confirm his fears when he was passed over for promotion for others he considered less deserving and less qualified.

Shortly afterwards, the C.O. sent for Donna.

"Ah, come in Private Donna," said his Commanding Officer. "I see by your record you've passed the class 2 nursing exam and wish to go overseas."

"Yes, Sir."

"Well, I've some good news for you. We feel you're the ideal man to go to Germany to train in a new treatment for venereal disease."

"Am I correct, Sir, that this treatment... does it involve the use of mercury?"

The C.O. looked a little surprised at Donna's knowledge.

"Why, yes."

"Is it not a fact, Sir, that prolonged use, especially for the nursing staff, can result in the loss of hair and teeth?"

The officer tried to laugh away Donna's concerns.

"There are some side effects, but I think they've been grossly exaggerated. Don't worry."

Donna wasn't convinced, but at that moment another matter bothered him.

"Sir, in army regulations it states a soldier volunteering for service abroad has the right to request that all crimes be removed from his record. If I go to Germany would my record be wiped clean?"

His C.O. Shook his head.

"'Fraid not. Germany isn't one of our possessions, it's a country in its own right."

"Then I have no wish to go, Sir," he said emphatically.

"Now, come come man," said the Officer, "that's not the attitude to take. Think of the corps, think of the help you'd be to others."

"No thank you, Sir," said Donna stubbornly.

"Are you saying that you don't want to be in the Medical Corps?"

"Not exactly, Sir. I just don't want to know how to treat venereal patients."

"But you'd be willing to go to Germany if it would clean your record?"

"Yes, Sir, but only on that condition."

The C.O.'s face reddened. "That's a selfish attitude to take. Dismiss," he snapped.

That wasn't the end of the matter. Some time later he was sent for by the adjutant, who tried to persuade him to change his mind, but Donna was adamant. Then, on his day off, fate took a hand. Thumbing through a magazine in search of day trips to France, he came to a picture of a piper in full Highland dress leading a squad of kilted soldiers. They looked fearless and charismatic; it was a recruiting advert. Beneath the picture were the words:

WANTED
Men to make up Battalion strength.
Shortly sailing for India.
Serving soldiers of other regiments given priority.
Join First Seaforth Highlanders At Shorncliffe Barracks.

Donna read the captions through twice. Without a word to anyone, and with no more thoughts of France, he left the hospital and signed on.

ELEVEN

Blighty

'A' Company got home leave after struggling from the trenches at Richbourg. Numb from exposure, they were given baths and a change of clothing and then helped like drunken men into horse-drawn cars which took them to the railway station at Bethune. They had to wait two hours to board; the station platform was filled with wounded soldiers, mostly stretcher cases. When eventually the Seaforths did board the train, in straw-strewn cattle trucks, most of them just sprawled about the floor and went to sleep.

The sudden lurch and clanking as the troop train jerked forward aroused Donna from cramped unconsciousness. He threw off a man's booted foot which lay across him. A lantern hung from one of the wooden walls and he could see shiny condensation beginning to form on the truck's side. He felt hungry and ached all over. Easing his shoulders, he fumbled in his tunic for a cigarette. There was no talk from the heaps of recumbent men bathed in the soft yellow lamplight; the only sounds were the groans and rattles of the wheels as the train moved slowly forward into the darkness.

He stubbed out his fag but kept the butt. His mouth felt like the inside of a horsebox. Altering his position on the hard floor, he tried sleeping, but to no avail. Then, sounds from the next truck made him listen intently. He was sure he could hear singing and, inclining his head, he listened once more, trying to differentiate between the sounds of track and what he was sure were human voices. When he realised what the 'singing' was he lay back again. "Poor bastards," he muttered. The voices he could hear were the moans and wails of the wounded next door. One and a half hours later the train shuddered to a halt at Hazebrook. Outside on the platform came the sound of many boots and orders being shouted. It was obvious that more men were entraining. Somebody slid open the door of Donna's truck, letting in the cold air. The soldier was met with grunts and curses from the weary Highlanders, after which the truck lapsed into silence once more.

At last, and with much blowing of whistles, the train grumbled and ambled into motion. It seemed to the Englishman to be going little more than walking pace and, in what seemed to be an age later, they arrived at the Boulogne rail terminal. They were still tired and hungry, but the brisk march through the chill night air to the teeming dockside soon awakened the men. It was in the early hours of the morning by the time the packed rusty old ferry steamed towards Dover, closely shadowed by a dazzle-painted destroyer.

The boat train from Dover arrived one hour late into London's Victoria Station, but the stationmaster had held back the northbound connection to allow the soldiers to board. The station was a cauldron of steam, noise and crowds of khaki figures with packs and rifles. In the melee Donna became separated from his friends and, as he threaded his way through the masses towards the northbound express, a small rat-faced civilian approached him.

"'Er' Jock, fancy a drop o' whisky?" he said, producing a half bottle of amber coloured liquid from his pocket.

"How much?" asked Donna. As he spoke he could hear the calls to board.

"Fifteen bob."

"Try again," said Donna walking away.

"Go on then, arfa quid."

Donna bought the whisky and had to run to catch the train. A sailor already aboard helped him on.

"Thanks, mate," panted Donna. The compartment was filled with servicemen standing or sitting on packs. Of Campbell and the others there was no sign. Unable to move more than a few inches from the carriage door, Donna loosened his tunic collar and took a swig of the whisky and almost immediately spat it out. It was cold tea. His anger was such that at that moment he would have gladly strangled the spiv who sold it to him.

As the train sped through the midlands, then on towards the suburbs of his native town, he reflected on his three years absence. He'd experienced much, sailed on the great seas and oceans, touched the soils of foreign lands, watched men die and others blown to pieces. Now he was coming home and wondered whether he would appear or act differently to his family. He knew Bob Brady, his childhood friend, had died. Mussel poisoning his mother had said in her letter; childhood seemed to pass so quickly.

It was raining as he trudged passed a line of horse-drawn cabs outside Manchester's London Road Station. He smiled wryly to himself; rain and Manchester were synonymous. As his hobnailed boots clumped down the approach incline, he observed two searchlight beams probing the rain-laden sky. The city was in blackout. Mute black figures passed him on the glistening pavements. At Market Street he bought a newspaper from an urchin crowing, 'Extra, Extra'.

'ZEPPELIN RAID IN LINCOLN' said the headline. He stuffed the paper in his pocket and, adjusting his pack, made his way to Oldham Street. At the tram stop he joined half a dozen other sodden Mancunians. The lights from the nearby Kings Arms glowed welcomingly. He waited like the rest, becoming wetter by the minute, but no tram came. Opposite the tram stop on the other side of the street was the deep doorway of the Central Hall. He nipped quickly across the tram tracks and took shelter in the Hall's deep doorway. If a tram appeared he'd have plenty of time to re-cross the rain-lashed almost deserted street.

From inside the Hall he could hear music. He tried the door and it was open. In front was a flight of stairs leading upwards. On an impulse he entered and climbed towards the sound. At the top of the stairs he found himself at the rear of a hall, where sat an audience of dignitaries in evening dress listening attentively to an orchestra playing the most exquisite music Donna had ever heard. As he listened a tall grey-haired attendant approached him.

"Have you a ticket?"

Donna shook his head. "No, I'm waiting for a tram, but whose music is this?"

"It's a concert by the French composer Debussy."

"It's beautiful," said Donna almost reverently.

The attendant looked at Donna's kilt and uniform, noticing where the yellow mud of the trenches still clung to his greatcoat.

"I can't let you in son, not dressed like that or without a ticket, but if I get you a folding chair you could listen out of sight at the back if you like," he said quietly.

Donna nodded, taking off his pack. He took the chair and listened out of sight to the most delicate, beautiful music he had ever heard. He felt for a cigarette, then changing his mind he closed his eyes and just listened, letting the soft, haunting sound surround him. It seemed to touch his very spirit in a way he couldn't explain. Its beauty touched him so intently because it was in complete contrast to the carnage and brutality of the trenches. He couldn't help himself, so he let his head sink onto his chest and tears came to his eyes.

****

Tizzie's eyes opened wide as she answered his knock. "It's Jim!" she proclaimed in her husky voice. He hardly recognised this beautiful red-haired woman. She'd blossomed in the three years he'd been away. He could smell her gentle scent as she kissed him on the cheek.

His mother's face appeared behind her, looking pale with large worried eyes. "Oh, what a lovely surprise," she sighed, clasping his hand. "Tizzie, be a good girl and make us all a drink before you go."

Donna, starved of affection for so long, felt a little embarrassed with the fuss they were making of him. He unslung his rifle and propped his pack by the drawer where his father's account books were still kept.

"Here James, let me take your coat," said his mother. The house seemed smaller than Donna remembered. It also had a smell all its own that he had forgotten. His mother sat with him on the couch by the coal fire.

"When are you going back?"

He looked at her sideways with mock disapproval.

"Mother, I've only just stepped through the door."

They could hear Tizzie laughing in the kitchen.

"You know what I mean luv," said his mother.

He nodded. "I've got five days leave."

His mother stared into the fire. "Not long Jim," she said absently.

As the three of them drank tea he suddenly remembered something which his mother had said that had puzzled him. It concerned asking Tizzie to make tea before she left. Left to go where?

"I'm married now Jim," explained Tizzie.

"Who to?"

"George Ward."

"Is he the man you worked for on the markets?" asked Donna.

"That's right."

"Are you happy?"

"Yes. We've got a nice little house in Sebina Street near St. James Church."

"Dick's courting too," said their mother.

"Yes, I know, Eliza Jones is her name," said Donna. "She's a nice girl. I met her brother Joe in France. He told me."

When it was time for Tizzie to leave, Donna insisted on walking her home. "I'm not tired," he said, "a little fresh air will do me good."

The rain had stopped as she took his arm up the steep dark Bridenvilla Street.

"When are you going to get yourself a girl?" she asked.

He laughed and shrugged his shoulders. "God knows, nothing is certain with this war."

They walked along in silence, skirting puddles of water in the darkness. Then, from the railway viaduct behind them came the sudden roar and hiss of an express train as it thundered into the night. Donna instinctively tensed and pulled Tizzie half double.

"Oh, I'm sorry Tizzie," he said somewhat embarrassed, and tried to laugh it off. But Tizzie didn't laugh; instead she clung tighter to his arm.

"What's it like out there Jim?" she asked softly.

Donna shook his head and sighed. "A bit rough, but never mind, let's hope it's over soon. Don't worry, they won't get me Tizz."

At her door he said, "No, I won't come in. It's late and I'm tired now. I'll meet your husband before I go back. Goodnight, God bless."

She kissed him again on the cheek. "Goodnight, God bless Jim."

He lit a cigarette as he walked home, a habit he'd acquired in the trenches to stave off hunger. In the dark streets he pondered the complexities of the opposite sex.

He and his sister were never close growing up. Tizzie was a few years older than he was and, being so, either bossed or ignored her younger brother. Now she was married she had become more affectionate and warm. Women were strange! Richard was home by the time Donna returned to Bridenvilla Street, but because of the hour their reunion was brief.

Donna had a dream that night in his old room. He was in a railway station waiting for a train to take him to he didn't know where. Then, a train arrived filled with people dressed in white. They beckoned him through the window to get on, but there was something sinister about their faces and he refused. They became angry and left the train and tried to pull him aboard. He fended them off and swore, but they became more determined and many hands grabbed hold of him and tried to drag him onto the train. He swore at them vehemently and, struggling free, fixed the bayonet to his rifle. His would-be abductors backed off, but then, from nearby, he heard James Robb calling fearfully, "Donna, they've got me." In his dream he thrust at the men in white who were holding his friend, but the bayonet just seemed to pass through their bodies with little effect as though they were made of vapour.

He awoke early the following morning but stayed in bed with his eyes closed listening to Richard getting ready to go to work. He knew his mother, who always rose early, would be up first preparing to remake the fire. He could hear the two voices below him, together with a series of dull thuds coming from the living room.

The noise puzzled him at first, then he remembered Dick's peculiar habit of hopping about to keep warm while the fire got going. Donna smiled to himself; he'd been so long away he'd forgotten such things.

After his brother had left the house he heard his mother's tread climbing the stairs.

"Oh, so you're awake Jim." He smiled up at her and nodded by way of a reply. She straightened Richard's bed and picked articles of clothing from off the floor. "He's an untidy so and so," she said, half to herself.

"Where's Joe these days?" he asked

"He still lives in Smedley Lane," said his mother. "Oh Jim, could you fix the clothes rack, it's coming loose from the ceiling?"

"Of course."

"Would you like me to bring you up a cup of tea Jim?"

"No thanks, mam. I'll be getting up shortly and I'll fix that clothes rack for you."

After breakfast, and unable to settle, he wandered about the rooms to see if they were as he remembered them. Then, to avoid his mother's awkward questions, he went for a walk down Collyhurst Road, up Bob's Brow behind the Grapes Pub, up the steps of the small railway bridge to Gorton Street past the school, then onto Rochdale Road. He wandered aimlessly along the pavements, stopping sometimes to gaze into the shops. Women and young girls with men not in uniform smiled at him. There were posters urging men to enlist and details of German atrocities in Belgium.

There was much traffic on the road, trams and horse-drawn cabs competed with brass bands leading squads of marching men dressed in a variety of civilian wear, spats and smart suits, contrasting with scarves and shabby overcoats. Sudden noises and the cracks of whips made Donna tense involuntarily. He came to the Frankenberg shop where Tizzie used to work to find the windows boarded up. Next door was a tobacconist. He went in to buy some cigarettes.

"What's happened to the milliner's shop next door?" he asked the elderly grey-haired woman who served him.

She shook her head, her expression grave. "It was terrible. They had to leave. A crowd came one night and broke all their shop windows; they were German you know." said the woman sorrowfully.

"Yes," protested Donna, "but they'd left Germany years ago. My sister worked for them and she considered them to be very nice people."

"I agree, I got on very well with Mr and Mrs Frankenberg, but what the Germans are doing to women and children in Belgium is bestial," she said and shivered, unable to look him in the eye.

"Why, what are they doing?"

She looked at his uniform and said, "Have you been to France?"

"Since last October," he answered.

She twisted her fingers in embarrassment and looked away from him. "Well, you must have seen the women being raped and babies bayoneted."

He waited for her eyes to meet his and said quietly, "Missus, I've been in action six times and I've never witnessed anything like that."

Outside the shop the traffic and bustle of people got on his nerves. He needed a drink. He made for The Crescent public house near St. Oswald's Church. It was a little more select than The Hedge or The Swan. There were only two people in the saloon bar. They looked like businessmen; they wore pinstriped suits and bowler hats. Before ordering Donna went to the big coal fire and rubbed some warmth into his cold hands. He could feel the two men watching him.

"Whisky," said Donna to the barman. He felt in need of something stronger than beer, something that would act quickly and nullify this inner tension that gripped him.

"Tuppence," said the barman delivering the drink.

Donna felt in his tunic for the money.

"I'll pay for that," said one of the men, indicating Donna's drink.

Donna thanked him, then took a gulp of the fiery liquid, closing his eyes as the whisky burned his throat.

"Are you alright?" asked the man.

"Yes," he nodded.

The man wanted to talk. "What's it like out there?"

Donna looked at him. He was tempted to say, 'Why don't you fucking well get out there and find out for yourself', but, after all, he had bought Donna a whisky. Instead, he shrugged and mumbled, "Pretty bad."

He ordered another whisky, inviting the man to join him this time, but the man politely refused.

"No, thank you, we must be getting back to the office," he said, scrutinising the stripes and badges on Donna's sleeves. The man pointed to a shoulder badge with a Roman number III on it.

"What does that mean?"

"It means I belong to the 3rd division 1st Indian Army.

The civilian pointed to a stripe on Donna's sleeve. "What's that for?"

"Good conduct," said Donna.

The office worker pointed to another. "What's that badge for?"

Donna was getting a little irritated by the man's questions.

"Fucking patience," he answered tersely and, finishing his drink, started to leave the bar for the peace of the fire, but from outside came the sound of a band and marching feet.

"More potential fucking landowners," muttered Donna bitterly.

" Pardon?" enquired the man.

Donna fixed him unblinkingly from his seat by the fire.

"Aren't you due back at the office?" he replied quietly, but with a voice loaded with menace.

The two men drank up and left without another word.

****

"You were shouting out in your sleep last night," said Richard that evening when they were sitting eating in the kitchen.

"What was I saying?" asked Donna.

"Don't know, but your language was colourful," laughed his brother. They ate in silence for a while, then Richard spoke again. "Another two lads joined up today from where I work."

"Well," said Donna, "let 'em all fucking join up if they want to, it doesn't mean that you have to join up!"

They had a visitor at this point.

"Oh, come in John," they heard their mother say from the other room. It was Johnny Foggaty, her brother's son, in uniform.

"I hope I'm not intruding," he said politely, cap in hand, "only I have to go back to camp later tonight and I wanted to see James and say goodbye before I left."

"You haven't intruded, you're always welcome. You know that John," said Donna, shaking hands and remembering his father's last Christmas party and the impromptu singing.

Mrs. Donna gave him a cup of tea.

"I can't stay long," he said apologetically. "My train leaves at 10.00 o'clock."

"Who's going to see you off?" asked Richard.

"My brother," said Foggaty.

Donna sat studying his uniform and said, "I thought you were in the Manchesters John?"

Foggaty smiled and pointed at Donna. "You're the first one to notice. You're right. I was in the Manchesters but I've transferred to the Machine Gun Corps, but I'm not sure I've done the right thing," he answered doubtfully.

There followed a discourse between Donna and his cousin on the merits of the Vickers and Maxim machine guns, which included weight, rate of fire, what to do in the event of jams and so on, until Mrs. Donna interrupted them and said, "No more you two, I don't like this talk of guns, especially with a war on."

167

She smiled as she spoke, but this hardly masked the concern in her face.

"Sorry Auntie," said John, rising to his feet, "I'd better be going. I'll visit you on my next leave."

The two lads shook hands with him again.

"Keep your head down Cousin," said Donna.

His mother echoed this. "Yes, take care of yourself John," she said, and following him to the door took both his hands in hers and kissed him on the cheek. Returning to the living room she sniffed and wiped her eyes on her pinny. "Damn all wars," she said bitterly.

Her sons pretended not to notice. In the kitchen she fiddled with things on shelves, her usual practice whilst composing herself. But tonight she took longer than usual, emerging finally to announce: "I've made your sandwiches for work Dick. Now I think I'll go to bed. Goodnight, God bless."

Donna found it hard to settle at home during the day, the quietness of the house with just the crackle of the fire and the ticking of the clock made him restless. He was unable to cope with the looks of admiration and naive questions from his mother's friends who called; he had to get away from them.

He left the house and walked aimlessly under a cold heavy sky to places he frequented as a lad; to the redhills, now appearing pitifully small and insignificant. It seems memories forged in childhood made large hills of what were in reality rather small sandstone mounds. Leaving the redhills fields he headed towards Collyhurst Road. As he approached the huge red-bricked viaducts some small boys were playing football with bricks for goalposts. As he grew nearer the game, the ball was kicked erratically towards him, pursued intently by a freckled-faced lad of about eight. Donna nimbly stepped forward and with his right boot volleyed the ball back towards the players. Then, fearful that the boy would collide with him, caught the youngster in his arms. Smiling slightly he set the lad down on his feet, and looking more closely at the tousled brown hair and familiar impish face asked, "What's your name son?"

"Robert Brady," replied the boy, looking up at him with a puzzled expression.

"I thought so," said Donna gravely.

Feeling inside his pocket, he gave the lad a copper

Mystified, the lad carefully put the money away in his trousers, then ran back to the game.

By the time he reached Collyhurst Road it had begun to snow. He took shelter in The Grapes pub, a Boddingtons house built at the foot of, but sufficiently far away from, the huge corporation tip. The smokey taproom was crowded with navvies and mill workers, evident by the cotton fibres which clung to their jackets and caps. He didn't recognise any of the faces turned in his direction, so, brushing the snow from his tunic, he ordered a pint of beer at the bar and took it to an empty chair by the fire. He nodded to an elderly man sitting nearby, who returned the nod.

"In France are you lad?" asked the old-timer.

Donna nodded. "Yes."

"Rough is it?"

Donna, not really wanting to talk, just nodded. Above the cigarette smoke and babble of voices someone nearby dropped a bottle of beer onto the sawdust-covered floor. It smashed into fragments, spraying ale in all directions. The sudden noise made Donna flinch and cower. Everyone else cheered. He felt like screaming profanities at the drunken oaf, but instead he fumbled for a cigarette and searched his tunic irritably for a match. He'd have to do something about his nerves. His hands shook as he tried to light his fag. The old man had been watching him

"Here, have a light from me," he said, proffering the lighted bowl of his clay pipe.

"Thanks," said Donna. The man reminded him of his father.

The noise and the clamour began to irritate him and he regretted entering the place. Just as he was draining his glass and about to leave, he felt a tap on his shoulder. The smiling face he looked into was vaguely familiar.

"Don't you recognise me?"

Donna stared at the dark-haired young man for a few moments, then realisation dawned. "You're Willie Stringer, aren't you?"

The young man nodded. "What are you having?" he asked, indicating Donna's glass.

Donna shrugged. "I was just about to leave," he said.

"No Jim, we must have a drink together. It's been years since we last met," insisted Willie.

Donna shrugged. "Right, let's go somewhere less noisy where we can talk," he said.

The old chap shook hands with Donna and wished him good luck before he and Willie left to go into a less crowded room of the pub. The room they chose was the select bar, whose only occupants were two youngish women with rouged faces.

"Have you lost your way?" asked one, smiling and nudging her companion.

Willie smiled but didn't reply. The other woman, who appeared slightly drunk, smiled at Donna but gave Willie a look that would have frozen fire.

"At least one of you isn't afraid to fight," she said insultingly. Her friend shushed her.

Willie said nothing except to order two pints at the bar, but Donna could feel his anger rising.

"Take no notice, the woman's drunk."

"I'm going to join up though," said Willie with a determined shake of the head.

Donna supped the froth off his glass.

"Don't be a fool, stay out of it, these people here have no idea what it's like. They think it's all marching bands and glory. I've seen men blown to bits by shells and parts of their bodies kill other men," he said bitterly. Donna shook his head and went on. "Even death isn't dignified. When a man dies he evacuates his bowels and if a corpse can't be buried because of enemy fire, the body's colour turns from white to green, then black, and the smell can make you vomit. That's providing the rats haven't eaten the corpses or made a nest in the dead man's ribs."

Willie didn't say anything.

"Anyway," continued Donna trying for a more optimistic note, "let's hope there'll be an armistice or something soon so there'll be no need to send more men out there."

"I'll drink to that," said Willie quietly, more like his old self.

The sound of chairs being moved announced that the women were leaving. The drunken one paused as she passed the bar where the two men stood. She rummaged in her handbag trying to find something. After apparently locating it, she handed the object to Willie, then walked unsteadily out of the pub. The object was a white feather.

"What does it mean?" asked Donna.

"It means," said Willie gloomily, "that I'm a coward for not being in uniform."

"Don't talk wet," snapped Donna.

Willie just shrugged.

Before going home that evening Donna called on Helen Kirk, Bob Brady's widow, and gave her a half a sovereign. He asked about young Robert, the lad he'd watched playing football and had given a copper to earlier, but he had long since gone to bed.

In a strange way Donna was glad when his leave was up, though he hated to leave family and friends after such a brief spell. He didn't relish the thought of returning to a life where the best he could hope for was that he might survive in conditions of abject misery, but nevertheless he was going back to men who understood what it was like to be frightened and under fire. That was what people at home could never imagine.

TWELVE

Neuve Chapelle

The cold dark morning air turned the men's breath to vapour. Eighty yards diagonally to the silent machine gun team came the sound of rifle and flash bomb fire. The team crouched red-eyed and half-frozen as groups of figures stumbled, most of them in the mud, across no-man's-land towards 'B' Company's trench to the machine gunner's right.

Lieutenant Roylance strained his eyes trying to penetrate the smoke and pre-dawn mist; he was nervous and despite the cold, sweat beaded his forehead as he saw the figures getting nearer 'B' Company's position, with no apparent defence from that part of the line.

"Why don't they fire?" he muttered in desperation. "What's wrong with them?"

Then, when they were less than 60 yards off the second company's barbed wire, he suddenly screamed, "Open up! open up!"

Donna instinctively sent a short burst into the nearest shadowy group and saw three or four fall, but there was something not quite right about the figures. For one thing, some of them appeared to be bent double and fleeing from the German trench and he wondered why 'B' Company were apparently asleep to the danger?

Of the 'attackers' nothing could be seen. They were lying doggo in the mud. Donna concentrated his fire at the German trenches until ordered to cease firing. Then, as the sporadic noise and flashes of rifle fire died away over the black and grey countryside, it was replaced by shouts and swear words from the churned-up ground in front of 'B' Company's position. There was a murmur of voices in the trench where the machine gun team had sandbagged its position, and the figure of Captain Shornberg, recently returned to the battalion after being wounded, stood bristling with anger, accompanied by Sergeant Cooper. Even in the gloom the machine gun team could feel the fury the officer felt.

"Who in God's name fired those fucking shots?"

Roylance, desperate to apportion blame, looked around, first at Donna and then at the other members of the machine gun team, but there were too many witnesses to his order.

"Er, we, er thought they were Germans, Captain," he stuttered.

"Those men were Leicesters. They were our own men!" roared Captain Shornberg. "Were you not at company briefings?"

Roylance was silent, his piggy eyes downcast.

The calls to 'stand-to' echoed along the trench as German rifle fire became more intense, putting an end to the altercation. Pointing his finger at Roylance to emphasise his words, Shornberg snarled, "I want a word with you later Lieutenant."

Still fuming, he threaded his way along the trench, which rapidly began filling with figures appearing from holes in the trench sides. They manned the firestep in one continuous line in readiness for any attack from the Germans. But this morning, as the light improved and the rifle fire from the enemy ceased, it became relatively calm. Except for the songs of a pair of small birds, all was quiet. The only indication that other humans shared these tortured acres was the thin smoke of the trench fires of the German infantrymen 180 yards away.

During the lull the dead and wounded of the Leicesters were brought in from no-man's-land and taken away to the rear.

Sergeant Cooper brought the rum ration around, dishing out the measure into men's mess tins. It was Gurkha rum, dark thick liquid which when swallowed bit the throat and chest and spread out like fire to all parts of the anatomy. Breakfast was bread and jam and disinfectant-tasting tea, after which Donna, not on guard, went to sleep sitting up on an ammunition box. It didn't seem any time at all before he felt himself being shaken.

"Fuck off," grunted Donna.

Lance Corporal Robb smiled. "Come on hot shot, we've a job to do. Ye're to come with me and Campbell. It's just the job to clear your heed."

"I'm not with you lot. I'm a member of the Vickers gun team," replied Donna.

"Not any more, ye're ta come with us."

They dug latrines, yet Donna was glad to be away from Roylance; he made his skin creep.

In the afternoon the cold gave way to snow, but the rise in temperature made the slush in the trenches appear like porridge, submerging even the duckboards. However, these trenches were a lot more luxurious than the Givenchy or Festubert lines. For here there were dugouts fashioned from corrugated iron, timber and sacking, and as usual the previous occupants had given them names. 'The Grand Hotel', 'The Ritz' and one more aptly named 'The Dirt Box'.

The grey sky produced more snow, which covered no-man's-land and the German positions with a soft white brightness, which was even more deadly to the careless. 'C' Company lost two men in as many days, both with head wounds.

On the eve of the Seaforths being relieved, Campbell was puzzled by a mysterious noise which appeared to come from the side of the forward Sap trench while he was doing guard duty.

"What is it George?" asked Robb

The big Highlander shook his head. "Ahm no sure."

Robb took his bayonet and rammed it about nine inches into the clay of the trench wall, then put his ear to the handle. It was surprising what could be heard by this simple device. He could hear the sound of men of 'B' Company to his right moving about in one of the dugouts. To his left the clear sounds of footsteps on duckboards and the sound of shovels, but these he knew and understood. It was something else that had aroused Campbell. Then Robb heard it. It was the sound of a motor or some kind or drill. That was it, he thought, the bastards are drilling a tunnel.

They were relieved about six hours later by the Second Gurkha Battalion and left the line down the communicating trenches to emerge on cobbled roads, which hurt the feet and made a few stumble and fall with a clatter of pans and equipment in the blackness. There were more than a few grunts and curses from tired coughing men. Though dirty and lice-ridden, and most of them nearly at the end of their tether, nevertheless they were happy knowing that for the present at least they had survived another stint in the line.

The weary columns of men trudged through the cold darkness for over an hour, then halted in a hamlet by large wooden huts which had fires and three huge steaming square tanks filled with hot water. The village the battalion had halted in was Le Touret, three miles west of the British trenches. Many camp orderlies helped strip the aching, bone-weary soldiers of their equipment, kilts and lice-ridden tunics. Naked, the shivering Seaforths climbed into the huge vats of hot water, where the hot steaming liquid began to revive these half-alive men. Fifteen minutes of immersion and they were hauled out, rolled into blankets, given a large measure of rum and allowed to sleep by one of the many fires.

It was three days before Donna felt sufficiently recovered to venture into Bethune, the nearest town. He, like his comrades, had spent the time mostly sleeping. As soon as he felt sufficiently recovered, Donna joined a half a dozen men from 'A' Company going to Bethune for a few hours leave. The group got a lift on one of the ration wagons.

174

The journey took over an hour due to the unusually heavy traffic on the cobbled roads. Heavy guns and shells pulled by teams of steaming horses passed them going the other way. The roads into Bethune were the same.

"There must be some big push about to start," muttered Donna to one of the other men.

"Aye, it certainly looks like it," agreed his companion.

Bethune was full of uniforms of all kinds. Donna left the others and went in search of Army Service Corps men. He was hoping to find 'Gedder' Jones, the friend from Collyhurst, to talk and have a drink with. The few Service Corps men he enquired of said they were new men recently drafted into the area and didn't know anyone by that name. Then his luck changed. As he stood in the city square crowded with motorised and horse-drawn vehicles of every description, a cart filled with coal bags drew up and stopped where he stood. The driver, a Service Corps man, took one of the bags of coal into a building opposite. When he returned with the empty bag, Donna questioned him. The man was older than Donna, in his forties, thin, with grey hair, and said that, yes, he knew driver Joe Jones. In fact, he was a pal of his, but Joe, unfortunately, had been found drunk on duty and had been sentenced, amongst other things, to three days field punishment and loss of pay.

"Where is he now?" asked Donna.

"At the Dor'enc depot, near the railway station."

"Will they let me see him?"

The man shrugged. "You can try. Say you're a relative, then they might let you."

"Thanks. Which way is the railway station?"

Donna arrived at the sandbagged makeshift depot office.

"What can I do for you Jock?" asked the sergeant. He was a rather corpulent, balding man with a droopy black moustache and watery blue eyes.

"I've come to see one of your men sergeant, name of Jones. He's my cousin and I've got a personal message from his mother."

The sergeant looked Donna up and down, shaking his head slightly but making no sound. Donna realised that if he was going to have any chance at all of seeing his friend it was going to have to be a battle of wits with this N.C.O. Noticing that the sergeant had the Mons ribbon on his tunic, Donna tried another ploy. He suddenly became very concerned. "Sergeant, my cousin was one of the brave few who took part in the terrible retreat from Mons. I hope you're not telling me he's ill or something, are you?"

The sergeant seemed to like what Donna said about the terrible retreat and for a moment his thoughts were elsewhere.

"No. no lad, he's not ill or anything," soothed the Service Corps sergeant. "He's doing punishment – three days field to be exact."

"Oh, I didn't know," lied Donna, "and I've come all the way from Le Touret, special leave. I go back in the line tomorrow."

The sergeant's watery eyes looked Donna up and down, shaking his head slightly. "I don't think the prisoner is allowed visitors," he said. Then he shrugged. "I'll get someone to take you to him. Don't stay longer than a couple of minutes, though."

"Thanks, Sergeant."

A guard took Donna to where his friend was sat on the ground with both arms tied across the wheel of a supply wagon. Joe looked a bit pale and miserable, but his eyes widened to a smile when he saw Donna.

"Well, I'll be damned, if it isn't Jim Chadd. Ya know Jim, you could have knocked me down with a feather when I saw you in that bar in Bethune. I thought you were in India. Now here you are again. How did you manage it?"

"Oh, a little bit of soft soap cousin." He smiled and pulled out a packet of Woodbines and looked at the nearby guard enquiringly. The guard nodded. Donna gave a cigarette to Joe and lit one himself, stuffing the rest of the packet into Joe's tunic pocket.

"We haven't got much time Joe. I told the sergeant that I was your cousin and had a message from your mother."

Joe was thoughtful for a minute, then said quietly, "There's a big push coming soon Jim. For weeks we've been unloading ammunition and stores and delivering them behind the lines from Festubert to Aubers 24 hours a day."

Joe's eyes suddenly brightened. "I saw your real cousin last week, Jim. Johnny Fogerty. Johnny's 3rd Machine Gun Company passed me on the La Bassee Road. I waved to him but I don't think he recognised me. We were going in opposite directions. Where's your battalion entrenched?"

"Near Neuve Chapelle," replied Donna.

"When do you go back in the line?" asked Joe.

"In a couple of days," replied Donna.

Donna changed the subject; he wanted to know how the mild-mannered Joe came to be drunk on duty.

His friend's face wrinkled wryly in recollection. "I'd been bringing stuff up from before dawn from the railway sidings and driving them up to supply dumps at Lacouture and Richbourg. The weather was bitterly cold, so I kept taking a swig of whisky to keep the cold out. In the early hours of the following morning, when returning my umpteenth load, I thought I'd just close my eyes for a few seconds and rest them. The next thing I knew I was roughly awakened by a guard here. He had an officer with him who smelled the whisky on me. The horses had found their own way back here instead of going to the railway sidings."

****

3.00am and the battalion was already assembled on La Bassee Road. Each man wore a greatcoat and carried a small pack with mess tins and iron rations, as well as 250 rounds of .303 ammunition and two empty sandbags to be filled when they took up positions in the trenches. Carts followed behind the columns of soldiers, loaded with barbed wire, picks and shovels and extra ammunition. In the pitch-blackness before dawn they took up positions in the trenches near the crossroads, during which time it began to snow lightly, tracing out lines and wire. To the left of the Seaforths were trenches packed with Indian soldiers; to their right were the lst Leicesters and troops of the 1/39 Garwal Rifles. Behind the British front line were more troops in reserve. These now took any position of cover from the German trenches facing them. Situated out of sight along the La Bassee Estaires Road was the British artillery, together with a few French 75s.

During the night the barbed wire in front of the lines was cut and laid flat and, in various places along the snaking trench ladders, boards and planks were placed against the trench walls to allow reserve troops behind the front line easier access in support of an attack.

At 7.30am the road behind Donna erupted as the allied guns opened up in unison. Their targets were the three lines of German trenches and the village just beyond. The troops could feel the air above being displaced as the shells roared over to burst cimson and black on the German positions. The tremendous tumult lasted thirty-five minutes, sending echoes rolling away over the churned and pockmarked farmland. To Donna's left, from trenches and brest works, rose lines of British and Indian soldiers with fixed bayonets, yelling with all their pent-up nervous adrenaline as they charged towards the enemy trenches. The Germans replied with trench mortars, which whistled and exploded in the air with showers of white hot metal and black smoke. He watched soldiers hit and lie still, the rest crashing on into German rifle and machine gun fire, which knocked down more.

Donna's trench was a salient, which always drew more fire from the German lines opposite because it bulged out nearer their trenches.

"Right my lucky lads," said Sergeant Cooper dry-mouthed, "it's our turn next."

Captain Shornberg held a Webley revolver in one hand and a watch in the other hand. "Ten seconds to go," he shouted, which was relayed by the N.C.O.s up and the down the trench. "Get ready." He counted off the seconds as bullets, dirt and debris showered the crouching, tense men. Then, with whistles blowing, the First Battalion Seaforths scrambled over the top into no-man's-land.

Donna was one of the first men to go over into the killing ground. He kept his head down and bent double, skirmishing forward, never keeping in a straight line. He came upon men dead and some badly wounded. In a shell hole he saw an Indian soldier, dead and lying on his back with outstretched arms.

Despite his khaki uniform, the long hair and black beard reminded Donna of Jesus on the cross. Despite the carnage, noise and the stench of explosives, his adrenaline made him feel unbalanced. He was oblivious to the inferno; he just felt a tremendous vitality. During the hours of darkness before the guns had blasted the village and the German lines, he'd felt cold and dog-tired, but now there was this surge of energy that banished cold and weariness and replaced it with feelings of almost mad elation. He was just in front of the German trench. There were grey German uniforms all around him, some with their hands up, some firing and others covered in blood. He fired from the hip at a group of Germans running from him towards their second support trench. He watched a German thrust a bayonet towards a badly wounded lad in the Leicester regiment. The youth lay crouched, trying to hold his intestines in with one hand while the other still gripped his rifle. As the German came to finish him off, the lad raised his head, and with what must have been his last ounce of strength, shot the German in the chest before he, himself, jerked in death.

The British and Indian troops overran the first line of German trenches and at the second Donna could see Germans falling back. There were pockets still fighting, but mortars which had claimed many of the attackers were now silent. It wasn't long before the men in the second support trenches were soon overwhelmed and began surrendering. Others ran towards the third lines of defence and re-grouped, but resistance here didn't last long in the face of lines of British and Indian infantry with fixed bayonets.

Across the battlefield the lines of German defenders crumbled once the British came within 50 yards and the Germans took to their heels and headed towards the wooded area half a mile or so to the rear. Donna, covered in dirt and eyes red-rimmed, stood looking down into a German trench at the dead and cowed German prisoners with their hands in the air. They looked dirty and sorry for themselves. He stood with other members of 'A' Company not really knowing what to do next, whether to pursue the retreating enemy towards the village of Aubers in the distance or others making for the wooded area. He sought Sergeant Cooper out.

"What do we do now, Sergeant?"

Cooper, minus hat and looking the worse for wear, shrugged. "Just cover these bastards," he said, indicating the captive Germans, "until further orders." He moved off, leaving Donna to gaze down at the grey-uniformed prisoners, a few of whom were wounded, with one or two supported by their comrades. Then, as if watching a film, Donna saw a small rat-faced German with a flat grey field cap slowly lower his hands, pick up a rifle from the many discarded on the top of the trench and aim the weapon at Campbell, whose attention, like most of the others, was drawn to the retreating enemy and the conflict in the village. The shot was easily lost in the tumult of noise and spent bullets and the big red-headed Highlander slumped dead on top of the trench. The German, his work done, quickly dropped the rifle and raised his hands again, his rat-like eyes darting about to see if his deed had been noticed.

Donna could hardly believe his eyes. He was speechless and appalled by this blatant act. He grabbed the first officer he could find; it was a lieutenant in the London Regiment.

"Sir," he stuttered, pointing towards the group of prisoners, "that rat-faced bastard has just shot one of my Company."

The officer, startled to be suddenly grabbed by the arm by this dirty wild-eyed Scotsman, muttered, "What? Don't tell me. Report it to one of your own officers man!"

Donna had a better idea: He made sure he had a bullet up the spout and tried to pick out the rat-faced bastard in the group. Before he could avenge Campbell however, 'A' Company was ordered forward to the village. As he ran forward he regretted bitterly his slowness in not taking the law into his own hands. He felt guilty for not having shot the German and faced whatever consequences later. But for now there was the village to take care of. Yet the guilt of not having avenged Campbell stayed with Donna for days.

All across the wide expanse of the battlefield he could see prisoners and wounded being brought back. He trudged forward, rifle and bayonet at the ready. Harper and other members of 'A' Company appeared next to him. The village seemed to be on fire from end to end, with smoke billowing high into the air. The shelling from the British had stopped now; it was the infantry's turn to go in and clear it. The Seaforths entered the badly shattered blazing buildings from the Eastern side, while the Black Watch and 3rd London Regiment attacked from the west. But the Germans had gone, leaving scattered about arms, ammunition, dead men and horses. They could be seen taking up new positions on high ground roughly half a mile distant. Some had dug in on the edge of a wood and were trying for targets in and around the village with rifle and machine gun fire.

Donna took cover behind a wall and lit a cigarette. He suddenly felt extremely tired and looked at his watch. At first he thought it had stopped. It was no use him putting it to his ear because he was deaf from the noise of battle. The watch said 12.30pm. He could hardly believe the battle had been raging for five hours. Time seemed to have stood still since the British 28-pounder and the French 75s had opened up in the darkness of the morning.

An officer sent up three green coloured Very Lights to let operation headquarters know the good news that the Germans had been routed and the village of Neuve Chapelle was in British hands. The men of 'A' Company milled around, unsure of what to do. However, their immediate actions were decided for them when the Germans began to hit back with mortars and rifle fire from a line of trees to the north.

Donna and Harper took refuge in what appeared to have been the village school. On the shattered walls were children's drawings and pictures. Donna took a swig from his water bottle and chewed the cheese he'd saved from his pack. He decided not to bother trying to gnaw on the hard tack biscuit each man was issued with. Instead, from a hole in the School wall he observed the Germans still retreating to the west. The taciturn Harper was trying to soften the rock-hard biscuit with water from his bottle. As the two men crouched, one in one corner, one in the other, trying to escape the explosions and flying debris, the cold overcast clouds parted for a few minutes and a shaft of sunlight illuminated the village. The sudden warmth on his coat and webbing made Donna turn his head to the wall and close his heavy eyes. He was oblivious to his surroundings for a couple of minutes, but the slumber refreshed him. He closed his eyes again to rest them this time.

"Come on Donna," said Harper, shaking him. "We're moving out."

He ached as he got to his feet and scrambled out of the derelict building, but he felt better for his brief shut-eye. 'A' Company, together with some Leicesters and a platoon of Indian Garwal rifles, ghosted through the smoke of the village and took any cover or ditch that faced the German line, now hastily regrouped and some 150 yards distant. The shelling from the forest stopped. Probably the Germans were out of mortar shells, such was their haste in retreating. Their response now was rifle and bursts of machine gun fire. The firing eased as the day moved into the afternoon and the encroaching darkness.

Donna started collecting bits of wood, lit them, and placed his billy can, half full of water from his bottle, on top and waited for it to boil. Still keeping the German positions under observation, he carefully nursed the fire, keeping it alive several times with bits of straw shavings just when he thought it would go out, until his patience was rewarded with a whiff of steam from the vessel. With his water boiling, he removed it from the fire and carefully placed it on top of a wall while he searched through his greatcoat pockets for a small packet of dry tea. Just as he located it there came a distant crack of a rifle and the silver mess tin was sent flying with a dent in its side.

At the battalion headquarters on the Estaires La Bassee Road, Colonel Richie was speaking by telephone to divisional headquarters. Major Wright, Richie's adjutant, heard him say, "Right ye are, Sir" and then replace the handset.

"Well," enquired the Major, "do we push on or fortify what we have, Sir?"

The tired-looking Colonel Richie sighed and shook his head "I canna understand 'em," he said, glancing at the telephone. "What ground have we gained, 500, 600 yards?" He felt for his pipe. "We've got the enemy on the run, we should keep at 'em afore they have time to consolidate and dig in. HQ are full of congratulations but think it better to fortify the ground we've won." Richie was silent for a minute, then said, wistfully, "I suppose it makes sense. Anyway, any idea of our casualties Stuart?"

"Mr Macrae's rough figures are two officers and seventeen men killed and forty-nine other ranks wounded sir," said the adjutant.

"Who are the officers killed?"

"Lieutenants Scott and Hardwick, 'D' Company," said the Major.

Richie shook his head. "They've only just joined the regiment haven't they?"

Major Wright nodded.

Richie shook his head once more. "Will you write to their parents?"

"Certainly Sir," said the Major. He saluted and left the pensive Colonel Richie alone with his thoughts.

'A' Company held a ditch facing the Germans grouping in woods a quarter of a mile away. They had the 2nd Leicesters on their left flank, with the 3rd London's and 1st/3rd Garwal Indian troops on their right.

Although it was dark the enemy began mortaring with a different type of shell. They sent over salvoes on what were, until that morning, their own positions. The small shrapnel shells travelled through the air faster than sound. They usually burst above ground, then filled the air with flying curved shrapnel, producing a singing sound. The whizz of its approach was heard first, and seconds later came the boom of the distant gun that fired it. It's characteristics soon got the nickname 'whizz bangs'.

While the shelling was taking place, the Germans counter-attacked on a 200-yard front, but well aimed machine and rapid rifle fire from the British positions decimated the attack, littering the ground with dead or wounded German infantry. Some of the enemy who managed to reach the London's and Garwal trench threw their hands up in surrender.

Donna, remembering George Campbell, fired a couple of rounds towards the surrendering enemy, but it was too dark to see whether his bullets had found a target.

Thereafter, the action gradually petered out into spasmodic bursts. The Seaforths and the remnants of the 2nd Leicesters were withdrawn in the darkness back across the lunar landscape of hidden trenches, barbed wire and uncollected corpses to the Estaires La Bassee Road, their place being taken in the firing line by the 1st Battalion Black Watch.

Once formed up on the cobbled road, they were guided by spectral figures through the darkness to a further road, then across muddy country to a position in support of the Indian soldiers who were facing some new German positions 150 yards distant.

The battalion 'stood-to' in the darkness. A counter attack was expected as at this point a lot of activity had been observed just prior to nightfall. However, by 11.00pm the opposite trenches still appeared quiet. It was decided to send out two patrols, one patrol led by an officer and the other by an N.C.O. from the Seaforths. After removing all insignia and blackening their faces, they were about to slide over the parapet when the Germans began shelling the British trenches again. Flashes of white and red light erupted in the darkness as the German howitzers opened up.

Seconds later the Seaforths felt the pain of the displaced air pressure on bodies and ears as these huge shells passed overhead, with all the noisy violence of an express train, to land just behind where the soldiers crouched, heaving the ground under them. The British sent white eerie Very lights high into the black sky.

"They're coming" came a shout as groups of shadowy figures attacked the Garwal trench, some throwing bombs which fell short and stuck in the mud, only to explode harmlessly yards before their objective. The Seaforths' machine gun on the left fired in support of the Indians, causing many of the Germans to fall. The attack petered out, though the shelling continued for another ten minutes, causing little if any casualties to the British troops.

With sentries posted all along the new positions, 'A' Company was able to consolidate the new line of offense. Rations and ammunition were brought up during the lull, and under cover of darkness the dead and wounded were removed to the Field Aid Stations on the La Bassee Road.

In the early hours of the morning, Donna, who had been stood down and was trying to sleep in the bottom of the trench, felt a boot prod him. It was James Robb.

"Donna, look at this," he whispered.

"Oh, go away!" said the Englishman.

"Nay," hissed Robb.

Stirred by the urgency in his friend's voice, Donna wearily climbed to his feet and cautiously peered through a gap in the sandbags.

"Over there," whispered Robb.

Donna observed shadows moving about no-man's-land. These brave men were in twos. No shots were fired from the British lines. This unofficial truce was to allow the enemy to remove their dead and wounded from the battlefield.

Two days later, the Germans counter-attacked with at least fifteen battalions spread out along a wide front. The British stood firm and repulsed the massed ranks, cutting the attackers to pieces and leaving heaps of corpses. In the afternoon it was the British infantry's turn to advance. The whole line rose with fixed bayonets, but the little extra ground gained was at a heavy cost in Indian and British casualties.

As the light faded the 1st Seaforth Battalion dug in. Then it began to snow again. It was as if nature and the elements had become so sickened by the mutilation and bloodshed of the battle it wanted to cover it from sight with a blanket of pure white. Although it had been bought with considerable losses, the ground gained at Neuve Chapelle had been a dent in the German front line 1000 yards deep and one and a quarter miles wide.

It was the first major British success of the First World War. Six days after forming the new front line, a German balloon was seen observing the British supply lines and the crossroads called Port

Arthur. Two days later the battalion marched at 9.15pm to billets in Veille Chapelle and L'epinette.

POSTSCRIPT

Adolf Hitler took part in the battle of Neuve Chapelle. He was a company runner in the 6th Bavarian Reserve Regiment.

THIRTEEN

Belgium – 2nd Battle of Ypres

At 9.15am the battalion marched through blustery light snow to billets in Vieille Chapelle. It was a cold black night, but the men were glad to be out of the line and the inactivity of the waterlogged trenches to feel the cobbled La Basse Road under their feet.

Their stay at Vieille Chapelle would only be for a few hours, however, to allow the men to recover. At 3.45pm the battalion continued northwards to barns and farm buildings amongst leafless skeletal trees. By the time the columns of men halted before the buildings, the snow had given way to rain. After a few days' rest the men practised bomb throwing and bayonet drill. Equipment was replaced, boots replaced or repaired, and then it was on the move again in the rain to Voormetzeele and in billets once more on the Ypres road.

On 22nd April, news reached the battalion headquarters that the Germans had used a new and terrible weapon – poison gas. In the early morning of that day, as the mist rose, the Germans released 168 tons of chlorine gas from 5,000 cylinders against two French African divisions at Longemarck in the Ypres salient. The Germans released the six-foot high creeping horror in the morning after sending off a heavy artillery barrage in the hope the French Colonial Zouaves in trenches opposite would be caught unaware.

The African soldiers had no time or means to protect themselves against the gas and died where they stood or crouched, fighting for breath. The effect of the gas was devastating. The African troops who were able to fled, leaving a gap in the line over half a mile wide. The Germans, wearing rubber gas masks, overran the allied trenches and captured 3060 prisoners and over 50 field guns.

The next day it was the Canadians in trenches near Longemarck who suffered the same fate. Despite heroic defence they succumbed and were overrun by a mass of German infantry, protected again by respirator face masks. Some of the Canadians had tried to nullify the gas with urine-soaked handkerchiefs over their mouths. The trenches were littered with corpses, while others not yet dead lay foaming at the mouth trying to breathe, but it was a slow, agonising end. The eyes and throat felt on fire and the death came as a relief.

On the Menin Road troops of the Indian Army, including 1st Seaforth, Meerut and Lahore Battalions, were poised to help fill in what was now a two-mile gap in the allied line in front of the city of Ypres. Before they moved off the Seaforth Commanding Officer, Colonel Richie, looking pale and drawn, spoke with his men. Earlier that day a German balloon and aeroplane had bombed and strafed the trenches. The Colonel spoke quietly: "Against all the rules of the Hague Convention on Warfare, and so intent on capturing the town of Ypres and thereby the channel ports, they're using poison gas. They've broken through at Longemarck!"

At this there were a few murmurs from the soldiers. As Richie continued, a German shell exploded nearby and shook the wooden farm building they were in. Realising the danger of a direct hit, the Colonel concluded with, "That's all I have to say for now, good luck," and to R.S.M. Macrae, "Fall the men in, Sergeant Major."

The Menin Road that led to the town of Ypres was crowded with horses and vehicles of all kinds, all going towards the trenches. Set off the road either side in scrub trees lining the thoroughfare were field aid stations, ration stores and shell and ammunition dumps. Moving away from the conflict were lines of horse-drawn ambulances stacked with wounded and weary-looking prisoners. The battalion waited until dark in what had once been a wood before taking up positions near Zillebeke. The shelling had died down by 10.00pm, but the soldiers worked continuously at trying to fill sandbags in the wet sandy soil to make some sort of parapet in trenches that were little more than shell holes three feet deep. Before them, no-mans-land as far as the eye could see was filled with shell holes, corpses and military equipment.

The Seaforths were on the right of the Lahore Division in this mainly Flemish area. The Germans had a higher ridge opposite, which overlooked the allies' positions. Harper and Donna worked together building up the leading edge of the crater they were in. Behind them on the road they could hear the artillerymen coaxing the horses as they dug new positions for their field guns.

Sergeant Cooper and Lieutenant Roylance made their way along the trench and stopped where the two men toiled. Roylance pointed to Harper and Donna. "You two away to the Q.M. Stores on the Menin Road."

The two made their way back along the trench, down the slope that led to the road, then slipping and sliding to the area known as 'shell box dump'. Most of the traffic on the road was horse-drawn army service wagons bringing supplies of shells, ammunition, wood and rations, each illuminated by paraffin lamps hung on the wagons, red at the rear, white at the front. There were other men from 'A' Company at the shell box road dump collecting rations and various items. Donna and Slim Harper joined the queue and when it was Donna's turn he was given a box two foot square.

"What's inside? Tea? Sugar?" he asked, shaking the box.

The storeman shook his head. "No, gas masks."

On the way back Donna heard his name called. A slight, khaki-clad figure tending one of his horses beckoned to him. It was Gedder Jones. They shook hands.

"We're a long way from home Jim," said Gedder.

"Aye," said Donna, "I could think of better places to run into each other."

Gedder nodded. "I had a letter recently from our Elysa as well as one from me dad. You know your brother Dick is courting our Elysa don't you?"

Donna nodded. "Yes, I had a letter off him."

"Well, Dick's in the King's Lancaster Regiment. He couldn't get in the Manchesters as they already had 50 battalions, so they advised him to go to Lancaster barracks and join the King's instead."

Donna nodded again. "Yes, I heard," he muttered soberly.

Gedder carried on: "Well, Morecambe being near Lancaster, Elysa went to Lancaster and Dick managed to get leave and they spent the day at the seaside together. Elysa says if I run into you to tell you your mam's well and that she and Tizzie wrote to you over a month ago but they've not had a reply."

"Yes, I know. I'll write tonight if I get the chance."

It started to rain, big blotchy drops of rain.

"We'd better go," said Donna.

Before the two moved off, Gedder dived into his wagon and brought out a French loaf and a tin of 'Tommy Ticklers' jam.

"Put these out of sight. Good luck Jim."

"Good luck to you too, and God bless," called Donna, hiding his gifts.

Back in the trenches the gas masks turned out to be made of wads of cotton wool to go over the mouth, but first the masks had to be soaked in a solution of bicarbonate – one pound of powder to two gallons of water. The mask was tied on with two tapes, with goggles protecting the eyes.

The men remained alert throughout the night. The shelling from the German trenches had lessened with the rain and darkness, so much so that pinpoints of light could be seen all the way along the enemy's positions.

Donna stared across no-mans-land until his eyes ached. Once or twice he thought he saw movement in the dark heaps of dead. He stiffened several times.

"What's the matter?" asked Jimmy Robb, who was next to him.

The Englishman didn't answer at first, his feet were wet and he was weary. Along with the rest of the infantrymen in 'A' Company, he didn't get enough sleep. Even when out of the line they were always practising something, bayonet drill or marching. He thought to himself, 'I can put up with poor food, inadequate equipment and pointless orders, but I'd give anything for a few hours kip.'

Rob nudged him. "What have you seen?"

Donna shrugged. "Oh, I think it was just rats."

"Do you think any of 'em are still alive oot there?"

Donna shook his head. "Not from the smell."

The terrain the Seaforths held was on the edge of a wood, with the remains of stark stunted trees to the right and left. The ground undulated and the men either made the shell craters deeper or dug into the sides of the humps and stacked sandbags on the forward edge to give more protection. However, there was a limit of a couple of feet down before the low water table began to appear, making the bottom of the trench muddy, then wet with the heavy rain running with water a foot deep.

The Germans were 300 yards opposite, dug into the high rise of the Belgium plain. The ground they now claimed was some of the two miles of allied territory they gained when they used chlorine gas on the African and Canadian lines a few days before.

During the night the men in the trenches snatched whatever sleep they could. Every fifth man took two-hour turns in watching the German positions for any movement. In the early hours of the morning the rain ceased and the moon appeared from behind angry black clouds, illuminating the vast expanse of no-mans-land. The moon's reflection shone in some of the water-filled shell craters, an abused pock-marked earth stretching as far as the eye could see, cold and forbidding.

"What a fuckin' place," muttered the normally taciturn Harper.

Donna nodded in agreement. "It's like the arse-end of the fucking world." He was leaning next to Harper staring into no-mans-land, hands inside his kilt to keep warm, his rifle placed before him in a gap in the sandbags, ready in case of a night raid or ordered to go 'over the top'.

At first light the German artillery opened up all the way along the front, the crashing and blasting of shells throwing earth and shrapnel in all directions.

"Fix gas masks" came the shouts all along the trench. The shells were 'Jack Johnsons', huge, like meteors from space that addled the brains with a high-pitched scream, then exploded in an orange flash, emitting clouds of thick black smoke. The first salvo fell short, throwing earth and parts of corpses high into the air. The second and third salvos passed over and exploded in a wood behind the Menin Road, setting fire to trees and destroying a field gun. Every one of the six-man team dug in off the road.

The German gunners were finding their range and their accuracy improved. One shell exploded in the Indians' trench to the rear, killing four sepoys outright and wounding another four. The noise made Donna stuff some of the wool from his mask in his ears. He felt himself lifted and thrown into the back of the trench by a couple of nearby detonations. Some of the earth and objects blown skywards took many seconds to come down. The head of a Sikh, complete with beard and turban, dropped on the parapet in front of Harper. Without a word the laconic Lancastrian poked it over the top into no-man's-land with his bayonet.

The shelling from the Germans continued for about an hour, with an increase in the use of the smaller whizz-bangs fired from trench mortars. From behind the Menin Road the allied artillery, French 75s and British 28-pounders, sought to silence the guns opposite.

As daylight improved, greenish-yellow clouds began to issue from the German trenches in elongated banks of swirling mist. They were propelled rapidly at first across no-mans-land, but because the prevailing early morning breeze had disappeared, as had the inertia from the chlorine gas cylinders, the deadly gas slowed down and was hardly moving after about 150 yards

Behind the gas the German machine guns kept up an a withering rate of fire into the allied lines. Then, with the gas hardly moving, lines of grey-clad battalions of German Jäger infantry came moving rapidly towards the allied positions. They came clad in gas masks and fixed bayonets, like aliens from another world. They picked their way across no-man's-land, but the pale mud slowed them down.

"Steady Seaforths" came the order to the waiting men, who were mesmerised by the advancing enemy.

Then came the order. "Fire at will!"

The machine guns and the fifteen rounds a minute enfilade from the soldiers, firing into massed ranks of the attackers, decimated the front ranks, but there were many more behind to take their places. As the bodies began to pile up the gas quickened pace and began drifting nearer the allied lines. The Germans took advantage of this and many, obscured by the yellowy-green chloride, followed the gas towards the Seaforths' positions.

With the frantic loading and reloading of the Seaforths' musketry, the noise was deafening, spent cartridge cases littered the trenches and the smell of cordite choked the air. It got into the soldiers' eyes and lungs, but there was something more sinister creeping towards them now, less than 50 yards away. Donna, unable to see clear targets with the smoke and the creeping chlorine, emptied magazine after magazine into the gas until his rifle barrel blistered his hands. Because the breeze had dropped, nullifying the effectiveness of the poison gas, the Germans quickly resumed the bombardment with whizz-bangs on the Seaforths' trenches, cutting the barbed wire and destroying the parapets and causing casualties all along the trenches. However, the positions held and the attack was beaten back, leaving heaps of dead and wounded in the stinking yellow mud.

"Ceasefire!" came the order. Then "stand-to".

They stood to for the rest of the morning whilst the dead in the trenches were covered with groundsheets and the wounded were attended to. As the day moved into afternoon the usual hurried re-building of the trench work was carried out while every fifth man stayed on guard on the parapet.

By now the poison gas had become predominantly static or begun to dissipate back towards the German trenches. Although the rifle fire had become spasmodic, the Germans continued to lay down a frequent bombardment of trench mortars all along the allied front. There were casualties of the whizz-bangs. The seeping stream of water in the bottom of the trench was often stained red from the higher reaches. To the Seaforth's left the Germans increased the intensity of the shelling by sending over their biggest howitzer shells, whose aim was not only at the soldiers opposite, but also to destroy the support lines, field stores and aid stations.

Some of the Indian soldiers who were sent to fight in this alien climate, constantly cold and wet, poorly fed and subject to the rigours of trench warfare, simply lost the will to live. After reciting passages from the Koran many were found dead at 'stand-to' in the pre-dawn hours, wrapped curled up in their groundsheets.

As the daylight waned the German trench mortars and hiss of flying shrapnel relented. Usually an attack was signalled by heavy shelling at first light. Now it was dark and bitterly cold, light snow beginning to fall. Lanterns were lit at various points below the parapets. Although the attack had been repulsed, work in the trenches didn't cease. The dead and wounded were cleared to the rear areas, parapets repaired, sap heads and listening posts were dug out, rifles cleaned and boxes of ammunition and rations re-stocked from the support lines.

Donna and Harper were busy clearing shattered wood and branches blown into the trench from the shelling. When the rations came along the trench Harper uttered a surprised expletive. "Well, fuck me! Look who's here."

It was Macfedris, the obsequious friend of Lieutenant Roylance, back after being wounded. Macfedris had taken the credit when Donna's marksmanship had silenced the German sniper responsible for killing several of 'A' Company's men at Givency in March. Was it only a month ago? It seemed an age. Macfedris was in the ration party, carrying tea, potato soup and bread. In a sandbag were strips of bacon.

"I thought you'd be in Blighty by now, tucked up in a warm bed, being fed by some pretty nurse," said Donna.

Macfedris shook his head. "Nay such luck. After ah was hit an' couldne walk, the stretcher bearers carried me until one of them was hit through the heed. Then I was taken to a field aid station where the doctor thought ah done it ma'sel. After they'd bandaged ma legs they kept saying things to each other like S.I.W. and askin' me over an over how ah'd come by them. The aid station soon became crowded and they had ta leave badly injured men ootside on stretchers in the rain. They sent me an' twenty others to the field hospital in Bethune. It was there that a mon in the next bed told me what S.I.W. meant."

Donna nodded, saying nothing.

Macfedris continued. "I said ta the mon in the next bed, what the fuck is S.I.W.? The mon told me it meant self-inflicted wounds. Ah went off ma heed. Ah was wild, ah called everybody bastards. Ah got oot of bed, but the holes in my legs started to bleed."

This caused quite a quite a bit of laughter, one man saying, "But ya'll be sure o' a couple of wound stripes though, Mac!"

After the ration party moved off, Donna broke the gas mask box up with his feet and made a small fire. Using his bayonet he managed to saw a few chunks off the cast iron hard tack biscuit into his potato soup, reheating it in the flames. The bacon he cooked over the fire on the end of his bayonet. The food made him not just tired but weary. He lit a cigarette and struggled to keep his eyes open. Leaving the warmth of the fire, he shuffled to the small corrugated-covered ammunition store. It held half a dozen boxes of .303 bullets. He climbed in alongside the boxes and, with his back resting against the trench wall, he fell instantly asleep, the cigarette dropping from his hand, his feet the only visible sign.

Donna hadn't been asleep long when Colonel Richie and Macrae paid a visit to 'A' Company's trench. "Stand easy," he said to Lieutenant Roylance and Sergeant Cooper, returning their salutes.

"Wake these men up," snapped Roylance to Cooper and Corporal Robb, indicating two other men, who like Donna crouched in holes in the trench walls.

However, Colonel Richie, himself looking tired and hollow-eyed in the pale light from the trench lamp, stopped Roylance. "No, don't wake them up, leave them be Lieutenant, until it's their time to stand-to." Then, as he passed down the trench, he added to no-one in particular, "I've an idea sleep is something we'll all be needin'."

Some time later someone awakened Donna in the darkness by kicking the underside of his boot.

"Time to wake up. We've a job to do." It was Lance Corporal Robb. He was carrying leather gloves and wire cutters.

"Don't tell me, let me guess," said Donna. His muscles were stiff and his left leg had gone to sleep because of the way he had been lying, but he felt better for having slept.

"We've to cut the wire in front of the parapets before first light."

"Then that can only mean one thing," said Donna quietly.

"Aye, afraid so."

Donna followed Robb along the sap trench into no-mans-land, but there were already shadowy figures there, cutting the barbed wire and laying it flat. Each section of trench was responsible for clearing any obstruction that might impede men going over.

At 11.00pm the Seaforths were joined in the trenches by 200 Scots Grays. After midnight the soldiers in the trenches were given a rum ration to keep out the damp and cold conditions. Bodies of the dead still lay out in no-mans-land, which was quiet now but for the scurrying and squeaking of scores of huge rats banqueting on the corpses. Knowing that they would be going over the top in the morning, men not on guard tried to escape the reality of trench life with a few priceless hours of sleep.

Most men were nervous and apprehensive about what they would face at first light, but pride would not let them show fear. As for the sassenachs in this tough highland regiment, they felt they had to appear nonchalant, otherwise they felt they would be letting their country down.

There was little talk; each man was occupied with his own thoughts. As for Donna, he hadn't felt his feet for the last couple of days. He knew the dangers of feet continually immersed in water. While visiting Laidlaw in hospital, he and Robb witnessed men with bandaged stumps where their feet should have been.

Donna hadn't felt good for the last couple of months. It was a malaise that had manifested itself in feelings of weakness, then shivering. Could it be, he thought, malaria? It had got gradually worse over the last couple of months. He'd had headaches, a rash and pains in his legs. He dismissed the idea of malaria, remembering that while in India the soldiers had been ordered to take quinine to prevent the disease. He recalled that prolonged use of quinine yellowed the teeth and skin in some soldiers, but nevertheless controlled the malaria. He wasn't to know at the time but what he was suffering from already had a name. It was called trench fever and was caused by the blood-sucking body lice that the infantry soldiers in the trenches were never free from.

At 7.30am the French and British artillery opened fire on the German trenches. They sent salvo after salvo, attempting to smash the German front line and cut the barbed wire barricades. While this was going on every man fixed bayonets, knowing that for some awaiting the order to advance this would be their last day on earth.

Mercifully the rain had relented and Roylance, revolver in hand, stood behind the lines of men. Donna eased the safety catch off his rifle and adjusted his ammunition belt. An hour before the bombardment he'd chewed a lump of hard cheese. He'd done so in every attack he'd been involved in since coming to France, believing that the cheese would seal the stomach wall in the event of an abdominal wound, so reducing the bleeding. He doubted whether there was any truth in this as he'd seen more than one casualty shot through the stomach. The last one was a German soldier, shot in the guts in front of the Seaforths' barbed wire. He died after an hour where he lay, calling for his mutter. When faced with danger quite a few men had superstitious good luck rituals, some making the sign of the cross, or saying a little silent prayer, or carrying some token of good luck, such as a religious medal. Donna's was to chew cheese.

Donna could hear Roylance's breathing becoming short and rapid. "Ten seconds to go," he screeched. "Anyone refusing to go will be shot." He counted the seconds off, then blew a long blast on the whistle.

The lines of soldiers rose from the trenches, yelling and howling as if in torment, only to flounder in the quagmire of the lunar landscape of no-mans-land. Donna had gone over the top from the forward sap trench dug at right angles to the main line and used at night as a listening post or a jump-off trench for night raids. With two other men of his company, he skirmished forward as best he could, slithering from one shell hole to the next shell hole, or corpse, for cover. To his right and left he could see, through the smoke and flying dirt of battle, men being hit and dropping. Others, crouching like himself and his two companions, waited for the German machine guns to relent before wading through pools of stinking mud, then dropping into the ooze once more before timing their next move forward.

To his left he saw some Scots Greys struggling forward through the mire; they were being cut to ribbons by the crossfire of the German gunners. One of the soldiers lying doggo next to Donna was shot in the chest. Donna felt the wind of the bullet as it passed. The force of it knocked the man on his back where he started to cough up blood.

"Are you all right?" asked Donna.

The man nodded, his face ashen trying to breathe. Donna felt in the soldier's side pocket for the big shell dressing they all carried. He stuffed the dressing inside the man's tunic in an attempt to stem the bleeding. The wounded man mouthed the word 'thanks', then, coughing up more blood, he rolled his eyes and died still clutching his rifle. Even in this hell-on-earth, where the noise of explosions hurt your eardrums and ahead were hundreds of the enemy trying to end your life, Donna mentally saluted this man for not letting go of his rifle. He was a soldier to the end.

The Germans began shelling by sending over triples of trench mortars on the advancing Indian soldiers, causing dirt and metal to spatter down. During a brief lull in the shelling, Donna pushed himself up into a crouch and, moving as quickly as he could, lurched forward half a dozen yards, diving into another crater. A few seconds later he felt Jimmy Robb land next to him.

"Why don't you find your own fucking hole?" Donna shouted above the carnage.

Lance Corporal Robb smiled. "Ahm jes makin' sure ya nay get inter bother, ye English cunt."

On the Seaforths' left the Indian soldiers from the Meerut and the Lahore Battalions were pinned down by the German shell and machine gun fire. They had hardly advanced more than a few yards past their own barbed wire; only on the extreme right and left did they make any progress.

A bullet went through Robb's epaulettes; another creased his glengarry. "Come on," said Robb "it's gettin' tay hot here fer ma likin'." He pointed towards a raised hump in the earth. "When I shout 1, 2, 3, head fer tha' bank."

Donna nodded.

After three Robb took off for the little hump of cover. Donna quickly tried to follow him but felt something trip him up as he crouched and began to move forward. The leather apron that protected and covered the kilt had come loose, slowing him down. He remembered wrenching the apron free from his waist, then finding himself flat on his back with no rifle and a throbbing pain in his temple. He was shaking. He gingerly felt the side of his head above the ear; it was wet with blood. Not knowing how long he'd been unconscious, he looked for his rifle. But the ground around him was piled with dead, highlanders sprawled one on top of the other. Donna rolled onto his stomach, then realised he was nearer the German trench than he thought. Faking death he watched a blond-haired German machine gunner sending short bursts across the battlefield. Donna could see another Maxim machine gunner a few yards from the German. 'They must have machine guns every few yards,' he thought. Although weak, he eased a rifle from under a corpse and, after making sure there was a round up the spout, he lay watching his adversary, determined to kill him should the blond German swing the machine gun in his direction.

Mercifully, it was late afternoon and it started to get dark. With no further attacks by the British, he decided to wait for darkness and gather strength before trying to get back.

As the gloom of dusk crept over the slaughter, the firing became sporadic. He felt the bloody groove the bullet had left above his ear. 'You've not got me yet, yer bastards,' he thought.

He took a closer look at his surroundings. Bodies covered the ground as far as he could see. It was like an abattoir; there were corpses and parts of bodies everywhere. Even in the gloom he could tell some these men were from 'A' Company by their shoulder emblems. The right side of his head felt numb. His hand came away wet and sticky. However, the three-inch ridge didn't feel too deep. He tried to move but he felt very weak.

He knew if he stayed in no-mans-land there was a chance he could die. Many wounded men had died after being left in the open because they couldn't be collected as the enemy fire was too great. He started to crawl forward towards his own lines through the stinking mud and shell holes and was instantly sick. When the nausea had passed somewhat, he pressed on. It took him an hour and a half to cover the 70 yards back to his own trenches. On the way he came across a wounded man, who kept saying, over and over, "Ah canna move ma legs." Donna tried to reassure him, saying that someone would come for him soon. In the blackness Donna was near enough to hear the man's shallow breathing.

"What's your name?" asked Donna.

"Ma name's Alex, Alex Gordon from Inverness."

"What company are you from?"

"'B' Company."

"Don't worry your head, someone will come soon."

The man didn't reply. Then he started to snore, softly at first, then loudly, until after a few moments there was silence.

Donna knew what that meant. He'd heard the so-called death rattle more than once during the last few months. With the last of his strength and ten yards out from the sap trench, he shouted, "Hold your fire!"

"Who are ye," came a voice from the darkness.

"Donna, 'A' Company."

Harper and another man helped him in. Too weak to stand he slumped onto the firestep. He was covered in dirt and dried blood layered one side of his face.

"Here, take a dram of this," said Robb, and held a bottle to Donna's lips.

The whisky made him cough, but it warmed his innards.

"Ah thought ye'd fucking had it Donna when ya didne come back," said Robb solemnly.

Donna looked about him in the oil lamp's soft light.

"Where's 'A' Company's men?"

Robb nodded towards no-mans-land. "Most of 'em are still oot there, as are 'B' and 'C' Companies, plus the poor fucking Greys," he said bitterly.

What Robb didn't know was at 12.00 noon the same day, at another part of the Salient, two companies of Black Watch, leading the Barailly Brigade, had been annihilated almost to a man.

At 4.00pm the Garwal Brigade and the Leicester Regiment were due to carry on the attack, but, mercifully, this was stopped.

Although the shelling had stopped for the night, sporadic sniping went on, hindering the search for wounded by the stretcher-bearers. Ordered to go for treatment, Donna made his way to a field aid station in a cluster of trees off the Menin Road. Leg-weary, he stumbled in the darkness across holes and debris towards the lighted station. The road was mainly busy with men loading horse-drawn ambulances with the wounded.

As Donna trudged across the road he approached a small group of officers watching the proceedings. Donna recognised Captain Wright and Colonel Richie, but not the staff officer with a red armband and polished leather boots. Donna stopped to avoid stretcher-bearers and was about to pass the officers when the Colonel stopped him. He peered searchingly into Donna's blood-encrusted face. The officer's eyes were hollow and there was foam on his mouth.

"Can ye speak lad?" he asked.

Donna saluted and nodded. "Yes, Sir."

"What's yer name?"

"Donna, Sir, 'A' Company."

Richie patted his shoulder. "Ye'll be all right son."

As Donna stepped off the cobbles and into the trees he looked back and could see his C.O. shaking his head in anguish. "Ma soldiers," he kept saying, "ma men, they're all dead." The two other officers could be heard speaking softly, trying to console and pacify Richie, who suddenly sat down by the side of the road with his head in his hands.

Donna recognised from his medical training that his C.O. was under a great strain, which was causing in him a great mental imbalance.

The aid station was packed with the wounded, some on stretchers, others beyond help lay side by side next to the wooden structure. The blood on Donna's face looked more serious than it was. An orderly found him a seat next to an artilleryman with the humerus bone of his upper arm broken and sticking out at right angles. He sat there without a word, an improvised tourniquet made of a lanyard and a stick had stopped the bleeding.

Although crammed with men with every type of bullet and shell wound, some severe, there was no moaning or crying out. They just sat or lay waiting to be attended to. A harassed orderly wearily took Donna's name, unit and extent of his wounds, after which a Royal Army Medical Doctor briefly examined his head wound and, staring into Donna's eyes and holding up two, then three, fingers, muttered to the orderly, "Concussion, Merville."

Donna had to wait until the more seriously injured had been loaded onto ambulances before he was helped onto the horse-drawn vehicle. Despite his hunger and the irritating body lice, once on board he fell asleep to the motion of the ambulance. It was breaking daylight when he arrived at the Merville field hospital.

The hospital had been a large grain barn before the war; now it had two rows of beds, all of them occupied. Down one side was a corridor with a dispensary and linen rooms plus two operating theatres. The outside wall had a big red cross painted on it. The place reeked of carbolic and urine. Donna sat on a stretcher near the entrance. The sleep in the ambulance had refreshed him and he began to feel better. He grabbed a passing orderly by the sleeve.

"Could I have something to drink mate?"

The orderly looked down at him. "Are you suffering with a chest or stomach wound?" he asked.

"No."

The orderly returned a little later with some water, which took away some of the hunger in his stomach and, despite the noise and bustle of the place, he dozed off again in the foetal position. He was awakened by a nurse with beautiful blue eyes wearing a face mask.

"Are you all right?"

He nodded.

A middle-aged moustachioed doctor was with the nurse. He examined Donna's head; the pressing and squeezing hurt.

"You were lucky there," said the Doctor. "Can you stand up?"

Helped by the nurse, he managed to get unsteadily to his feet.

"Any pain?"

"Not much, but I keep feeling dizzy," said Donna laconically.

"Right then, a dressing and number 9 pills for the head and I think we'll admit him for 24 hours," he said to the nurse, who scribbled it down.

"Thank you, Sir," said Donna.

A bed was found for Donna next to a thin, pale-faced man with bright eyes who coughed and wheezed continually. By the side of his bed the man had a sputum pot, which he spat into after a coughing bout. Donna, being dead tired, soon fell asleep.

He awoke three hours later wondering where he was. Although half-awake he watched the man in the next bed press the point of a penknife into his palm and squeeze a few drops of blood into the pot. During the night he covertly observed him doing the same thing again until, finally intrigued, the Englishman blurted out.

"Why the fuck do you do that?"

The thin-faced man jumped at Donna's sudden outburst, then winked in an attempt at being friendly now he'd been found out.

"Don't say anything will you," he whined. "I want them to think I've got TB or something so they'll send me back to Blighty. Please don't say anything." Donna looked at him in disgust.

"Look, I'll make a deal with you. Stop fucking coughing so that I can get a few hours sleep and I'll keep my mouth shut. Agreed?"

"Agreed."

Donna was discharged the following day and given a pass to rejoin the regiment, who, he was informed, were no longer in the line but had been relieved by the 2nd Leicester Regiment and were now in billets at Lacouture, south of Ypres.

When he limped into the camp he was struck by how the battalion was shrinking in personnel. After reporting to 'A' Company's office, he caught up with Private Conroy making his way to the mobile kitchen.

"Fuck me!" exclaimed Conroy after recognising him for the first time, despite the bandaged head. "We thought you'd been seen off."

Donna didn't answer, he just shuffled off in search of a bath and somewhere to sleep.

The following day, having heard that Donna was back with the regiment, his friend Lance Corporal Robb sought him out. From him he learned that the Germans had released a second gas attack on the French Senegalese troops on the allied trenches at Ypres. However, the Africans became terrified and fled, shooting their officers who had threatened to shoot them if they left their positions. Hurrying back through their own supply lines, they looted supply dumps and raped nurses at casualty clearing stations. The French military asked the British to help. The British sent a brigade of cavalry to round up the deserters and put down the revolt.

As for the Seaforths, the recent slaughter at Ypres meant that the battalion almost ceased to exist. Although boosted by the addition of 200 Scots Greys in the attack, making a total of 1,100 men, 1,050 were killed. Donna was one of only 50 who had survived when the roll was called.

However, Roylance had survived and was promoted to Captain. But better news as far as Donna was concerned was that Roylance would be going to 'B' Company. More good news was that some of the men, including Lance Corporal Littler, would be back from hospital any day. During the five-day rest period at Lacouture, the depleted Seaforths gathered strength from sleep, adequate food and delousing. Although they had no bombs to practice with as yet, they utilised stones of a similar weight and size.

The odd German shell became more frequent on the billets at Lacouture, but a sudden thunderstorm and heavy rain brought a cessation to the shelling.

By the end of the week a patched-up regiment with two machine guns marched to relieve the Gurkhas in trenches to the right of the La Basse Road, opposite the high ground of Aubers Village and a wooded ridge 500 yards distant.

FOURTEEN

Aubers Ridge

The trenches near the small town of La Basse were not new to the men of 'A' Company. It was from this area two months previously that the British and Indian soldiers had attacked and taken Neuve Chapelle. However, the village of Aubers on the high ground had been denied them, despite concerted attacks.

On the morning of 9th May, the British artillery opened fire on the German brest works 400 yards distant. The aim was to destroy the trenches and the barbed wire. It seemed to the British and Indian soldiers waiting to attack with fixed bayonets that most of the shells sent over were 18-pounders; few were the high explosive rounds needed to sever the wire or destroy the enemy's positions. Compared with the huge German 'Jack Johnsons', high velocity shells that killed men by just the concussion, the British bombardment was puny. The British artillery barrage lasted less than an hour and was almost totally ineffective. The German wire had hardly been touched, with most of the rounds landing short of their objectives.

The Company commander, Captain Shornberg, who had recently returned from hospital leave, counted the seconds off to giving the order, by whistle, to go over the top. Kilted Highlanders, British and khaki-clad Indian soldiers rose and dashed forward, yelling as though possessed by devils. They ploughed towards the German trenches, not knowing whether they would be cut down or blown to pieces. Their bodies were fuelled by fear and masses of adrenaline that made men charging into a maelstrom of death temporarily unhinged. There was also the element of national pride between the men in the regiment.

Donna preferred to be one of the first 'over the top'. He believed the first few who showed would catch the German machine gunners by surprise.

For the past couple of days Donna had been suffering once more with what the medical officer described as neuritis. But now the feelings of malaise were swept away as Donna jumped shoulder to shoulder with his comrades into the inferno of noise, thick black smoke and the acrid smell of cordite that made the eyes and nose sore and stained the ground.

The air was thick with dirt. Usually nervous before going into action, once in no-man's-land Donna's nerves left him. He'd picked his way forward for perhaps 30 yards when a shell like an express roared above him. He'd heard it coming. It started in the distance, the noise increasing as it got nearer until, with a deafening whoosh, it passed overhead, the disturbance of the air throwing him about and nearly sucking out his eyeballs. He rolled onto his feet and carried on forward abreast of others with rifle and bayonets at the charge. There was smoke everywhere.

At 300 yards from the German trenches, and with the smoke clearing, the enemy's machine guns began slicing into the British and Indian soldiers. It was obvious even at that distance that the British artillery had failed to damage the German wire or earthworks. Donna could see it was hopeless and dived into a shell hole and watched as men from the East Lancashire Regiment on the right pressed forward, only to be cut down in the crossfire from the German trenches. The dead and wounded began to cover the ground.

A German officer wrote after the battle: 'After the British bombardment had lifted and the smoke cleared, there were rows and rows of British and Indian troops side by side. There was only one possible order – fire until the barrels burst.' It was also discovered later that a lot of the shells fired by the British artillery were duds and didn't explode. Some shells were filled with dirt or sawdust instead of explosives. The crossfire from the German trenches continued as more lines of men took the place of the fallen and were dealt with the same way, falling dead and wounded in heaps.

Donna's only hope was to drive on in skirmishing order, moving forward then dropping and lying doggo in the brown grass and potholed-earth, taking advantage of shell holes or a corpse for cover. While the thick waves of bullets hissed and pinged around him, he expected to be hit, but his luck held. He waited until he felt the German machine gunners had switched from his area to another before rising to a crouch and dashing forward to cover a few yards. In the 30 minutes since the attack had first started, Donna reckoned his battalion and the rest of the 19 brigades had advanced only 100 yards. 'A hundred fucking yards,' he thought. In the most extreme circumstances, the thoughts of men often turn away from reality in an attempt to escape it.

'I can do the 100 yards in even time,' he kept repeating to himself, remembering the battalion sports day in Agra when he clocked the fastest time. 'No one got anywhere near me.'

Rifle and bayonet at the charge, he went forward again through the smoke and the noise, through the falling earth and flying metal. From the rear he could hear the British artillery start up again.

The men going forward were fewer now, but behind him he glimpsed more lines of men leaving the trenches. They were not Seaforths or Indian troops, but with their peaked hats and khaki uniforms they looked like Sherwood Foresters, the eager volunteers who had responded to Lord Kitchener's appeal.

'Poor cunts,' thought Donna as they began to fall in threes and fours before they'd covered less than 50 yards. Shells whistled overhead and buried themselves in the earth 20 feet away. 'Duds,' thought the Englishman, diving to earth as they burst sending outsize splinters whirring through the air. Scrambling forward he found Robb in a shell hole taking cover; he was agitated, his blackened face accentuating the whiteness of his teeth. He kept mouthing words to Donna, but the latter couldn't hear him because of the noise. He just spread his hands and shook his head.

The shelling continued, smashing into the advancing men. Robb became more agitated with every shell burst. He began jerking his thumb towards his own lines and screaming, "Those are our shells killing our men."

The pattern of the bombardment was familiar to Donna. 'They are like ours,' he thought. 'Fucking hell, they aren't ours, are they?' The two watched helplessly as the killing and maiming went on for nearly an hour before it mercifully ceased, leaving heaps of dead and wounded in its wake. It was obvious the day's attack had failed. It had been a fiasco from the beginning.

As Donna crouched preparing to move forward, he felt a blow very like being punched in the hip that knocked him flat. He lay there dreading to look down at his leg. Although his thigh felt numb, he could move his toes and shake his foot. Forgetting the pain he managed to make it to a forward shell crater.

Against all the odds some soldiers had managed to reach a German forward sap trench and had taken a number of prisoners. However, when the men in the British trenches saw these prisoners running towards them, they assumed it was a German counter-attack and mowed down the lot, killing most of their own men as well.

Seeing that the allied offensive had been stopped all across the front, the soldiers began falling back to their own lines. The Germans fired fierce volleys of rifle and machine gun fire into the retreating British. Some in the German trenches could be seen rattling their steel helmets on their bayonets and jeering as the British made for the safety of their own lines. It took Donna an hour before he slid back into the safety of the trench he'd left in the morning.

He was caked in the filth; he was hatless and had holes in his tunic and kilt apron. He was exhausted and couldn't feel his left leg; the scab on his head was bleeding again. And he didn't recognise any of the faces he'd stood shoulder to shoulder with earlier. Instead, the trench contained about a dozen soldiers of the Black Watch. Donna swayed as his bad leg buckled and he slumped down on the firestep. He noticed that the trench had been hit since the morning. The dugout where he'd snatched a few hours sleep when not on guard had been demolished, the roof was just a mess of earth and blackened timber which was still smoking. More ominous were the two covered bodies.

Captain Shornberg appeared in the trench. He looked beat, his tunic torn. He spotted Donna and came over. Donna arched himself but saluted the captain, who waved him to remain seated. His moustachioed face was grim.

"Donna, isn't it?" he asked.

"Yes, Sir."

He pointed to the blood running down Donna's face, "Yer'd better get that seen to later," he muttered.

"I think I've stopped one in the leg too, Sir."

Shornberg nodded, then was gone.

Donna didn't move. He was irritated with lice, but he felt too weak to scratch. Instead he took a swig from his water bottle as more Black Watch began filling the trench.

One gave Donna a cigarette. Smoking was something the Englishman had rarely indulged in, but in the eight months he'd been in the trenches he found tobacco helped to dull the ever-present hunger pangs.

In the packed lines the Black Watch got ready, together with the Garwal Brigade, to attack the German positions where earlier in the morning the Seaforths and men from the Dehra Dun Brigade had failed to make a breakthrough.

Just after 2pm, the Highlanders from Stirling lined up to the skirl of the pipes, every man tense. Donna was mistaken for a Black Watch soldier and ordered to take his place on the firestep. It was only at the last minute that the young Lieutenant Robinson, who had replaced Roylance, stood him down from the attack. With fixed bayonets the Black Watch, together with the sepoys of the Garwal Brigade, launched themselves towards the enemy trenches.

The Germans responded with the flashes from hundreds of rifles and the rat,tat,tat, of many machine guns. The soldiers made easy targets. Without adequate artillery to support them, they were soon wiped out.

Hardly any of the men made it to halfway. Some were hit near their own barbed wire. Donna, watching grimly through a gap in the sandbags, heard rather than saw the piper go down, signalled by a discordant wail which trailed to silence.

Donna had listened silently an hour before as the Black Watch officers had told their men that a personal message had come from Field Marshall Haig (himself a Scot) that the attack must succeed and be pushed in with the bayonet.

"The wee bastard should come here an' show us then," said one Highlander with two wound stripes and the South African ribbon.

At 3.00pm the Leicester Regiment moved from the support trenches to the front line. They were to continue the attack at 4.00pm, but when they saw the carnage in no-man's-land they mutinied. "If that's the best Officers can do, who needs 'em? We'll go over by ourselves and fuck 'em!"

It was only when two machine guns were placed at each end of the trench that the Leicesters were stopped from going over the top alone.

Donna, his face set, watched as the leading men tried to skirmish forward from any cover, be it a shell crater, hollow or human remains. The bullets were flying all around no-man's-land like sparks from a thousand blacksmiths' hammers. Intent on the events before him, the man from Manchester hardly felt someone grip his arm from behind. It was Sergeant Cooper.

"What the fuck do you want?" asked Donna belligerently.

Cooper ignored Donna's insubordination. "I want you as Number Two with me on the machine gun. Numbers One and Two have been hit."

"How bad?" asked Donna.

"One killed, one wounded." said Cooper.

"How?"

"By a shell?"

"What, by our own fucking artillery sergeant?"

"Don't ask me, I just take orders," he said resignedly.

"Don't we all," replied Donna sarcastically.

Donna nodded towards the sentry spy-hole. "So do these poor cunts," he said grimly, at the same time feeling the swelling and blood where he'd been shot in the hip.

Donna hobbled after the sergeant along the trench. On the way he looked for men he'd gone over the top with that morning, especially Robb, Harper and Corporal Littler, but of them there was no sign. The knocked-out Vickers machine gun pit was being repaired when he and

204

Cooper arrived, and it was almost dark. By it lay two bodies in the bottom of the trench. One with head and shoulders covered and just the legs protruding was obviously dead, the other was still alive and conscious.

"Here," said Donna to one of the men, "give me a hand with this one."

The man just stared at Donna as though he'd not heard him.

The wounded man mumbled, "Water, water."

"Don't stand there, do as you're fucking told!" roared Cooper at the soldier.

With the sergeant's help the three lifted the man and laid him on boxes of belted Vickers ammunition. Squinting along his body, Donna saw his tunic was ripped and covered in blood. Uncertain whether the man was conscious or not, and remembering his medical corps training, he reassured him and gently opened his uniform. His stomach was just a mass of red and yellow bile tissue, which kept welling up. The wounded man groaned and whispered something. Donna had to bend down to catch the words.

"What did he say?" asked Cooper.

"He wants a drink."

Just then, a R.A.M.C. corporal came up and had a look at the wounded man. From his white satchel he took a big shell dressing of tincture of iodine and placed it over his mangled abdomen, tying a bandage around the outside of his uniform to keep it in place. Then, placing his hand on his shoulder, he said, "We'll soon get you fixed up." Before moving off he looked at Donna and Cooper and shook his head.

Donna kept quiet about his leg. Because of the high incidence of gangrene he preferred to see a doctor. He dreaded being one the hundreds of amputees he'd seen of the dreaded gas gangrene.

Cooper started to undo his water bottle, but then another member of the machine gun team who had saved his rum ration gave it to the badly wounded man.

Before dying he called out for "Jamie".

"It's his son," muttered one of the men in answer to Donna's inquiring look.

Once the machine gun had been sandbagged and was ready for action, Sergeant Cooper cocked the weapon by pulling back the crank handle twice, but there was no response when he thumbed the buttons with both hands to fire.

Donna, as his Number Two, freed the jam by striking the magazine twice with the heel of his hand. Once free, Cooper directed the fire in five and ten second bursts on the German front lines. Donna then fed the belts of .303 ammunition into the breech while the other members of the machine gun team kept him supplied.

The Germans, as always, claimed the high ground, and without heavy artillery similar to the enemy's it was obvious that the afternoon attack would be like the earlier ones and come to nothing.

The Leicesters' casualties began to pile up. Only in a few places was there any movement. In a way they were luckier than the earlier attackers; dusk began shrouding them. But their momentum had long petered out. They waited hopefully for the cover of darkness in order to get back to their own lines.

By 8.30pm, the shelling and rifle fire became sporadic. There were shouts and curses as men began dropping, exhausted, back into the comparative safety of their own trenches. The numbers returning were much depleted and many wounded still lay in the battlefield. However, as the Germans were expected to counter attack, as they had done so often, the men 'stood-to'. As the hours dragged by Sergeant Cooper and Donna stayed with the machine gun team. Though hungry and deafened they were ready for any movement from across the blackness.

At 10.00pm, stretcher-bearers removed the two corpses in the trench, but not before Cooper had removed both men's identity discs and pay books from their breast pockets. He also took cigarettes from the dead men and shared them out with Donna and the machine gun team.

By 11.30pm the quagmire that had been the killing field was relatively quiet. The man from Manchester, through extreme tiredness, thought he was hallucinating as he perceived spectral shadows appearing in no-man's-land, but then realised it was the battalion's stretcher-bearers looking for wounded.

Lieutenant Robinson, with his right arm in a sling, appeared, accompanied by Lance Corporal Robb.

"Everything in order, Sergeant?"

Cooper saluted him. "Yes, Sir."

"Seen anything suspicious?"

"No, Sir."

"Good."

As the officer turned to move on, Donna caught his eye and went to speak, but before he could the Lieutenant looked at Donna more closely.

"Ye're the man who nearly joined the Black Watch today aren't you?" he said with a smile.

"That's right, Sir, but I suppose I can't help being popular," said Donna, smiling to himself.

Robinson nodded. "What's yer name?"

"Donna, Sir."

"Ye're English?"

"Yes, Sir."

"Well, nay one's perfect," he said, and smiled back. "Anyway, what's yer question Donna?"

"I've taken a slug in my leg. Permission to go to the F.A.S.?"

"We should be relieved soon. Can ye wait? Then we can both go, you with your leg an' me with ma arm."

He moved off down the trench with Robb in his wake. Although it was the first time he'd spoken with this new officer, Donna liked his easy manner.

At 2.00am the Seaforths were relieved by soldiers from the 3rd Battalion Gurkha Regiment. As they stumbled down the communication trench and onto the La Basse Road, two military policemen tried to hurry them up by using verbal abuse, until Captain Shornberg stopped them.

'Bastards,' thought Donna, 'they're too frightened to go into the line so they become army policemen, safe and out of harm's way.'

The remnants of 'A' Company lined up just off the road. Donna looked uncomprehendingly at first at dirty, hollow-eyed soldiers. His fuddled brain wanted to know where the rest were? At roll call, only 33 men answered their names.

"Aren't you going to get the bullet out?" asked Donna.

The doctor shook his head. "No, better left where it is. The entry wound is small. You were lucky, it's missed the bone and all the vital blood vessels. In 24 hours your body will cover that foreign object with a membrane to allow it to move freely about your muscles. Had it been a dumdum bullet that the German snipers sometimes use, the entry hole would have been three or more inches wide with a great risk of infection!"

"Thank you, doctor," said Donna, who left the field aid station with an iodine dressing on his thigh.

It was nearly dawn when the survivors trudged off to billets. After a couple of days of delousing baths, sleep and more food than usual due to the extra rations of the missing men, Donna was summoned to 'A' Company's office to see Major Wright. After the sergeant major announced him, Donna came to attention and saluted the seated officer.

"Stand at ease," said Wright. "How's the leg wound?"

Donna shrugged his shoulders.

"I suppose you're wondering why I've sent for you Private Donna?"

"Yes, Sir."

The Major looked down at his notes. "Mr. Macrae tells me you speak Urdu."

"Yes, Sir. I speak some. Learnt it while the regiment was in India."

"Hmm, that's very good. You were two years in the medical corps. Why did you leave?"

"I wanted to see other parts of the world, Sir."

"While in Agra you were also awarded the stick for being the smartest soldier on parade on one occasion."

"Yes, Sir."

"You are also a good shot, and as I remember you got that troublesome sniper at Givency."

"Yes, Sir."

"Tell me Donna, why haven't you tried for promotion?"

"Well, Sir, I was one of the last to join the battalion and I felt that all these men were senior to me. Some had even served in South Africa."

"That may have been the case then, but that is irrelevant now. I called you in today to ask whether you'd like to try for a commission in one of the Indian regiments?"

"No, Sir."

Wright raised his eyebrows. "Why not? Have you anything against officers?"

"Not our officers, Sir, but after the last action..." As he said this his hand went involuntarily to the scab on his head. "I have to be candid and repeat what some of the Leicesters said after seeing our dead piled up four feet high, Sir."

"Oh, and what was that?"

"They said that if that's the best that officers can do, we don't need them and we'll go over the top without them."

Major Wright nodded. "Yes, I know it was a poor show. We were let down by our artillery."

"Then why didn't we postpone the attack until we had enough heavy guns and not pea shooters that fired duds?"

The officer nodded in agreement, but said nothing.

Donna stood at ease, beginning to feel weak again.

"Anyway, Sir, I hardly feel fit enough to look after myself, let alone 50 or so others. I have what the M.O. says is trench fever that I can't get rid of."

The officer looked at Donna's pale, drawn face and nodded. "Right, you can go," he said resignedly.

They saluted each other and Donna limped out of 'A' Company's office.

Jimmy Robb was outside waiting to go in.

"How did ye go on?" he asked from the side of his mouth.

Donna just shook his head.

While at Lacouture Donna got a letter and a parcel with two pairs of woollen socks inside. The letter and the socks were both from his sister Tizzie but had been sent at different times. The letter was the most recent and in it she asked whether he'd received the socks. She said the socks were from the Frankenberg's shop where she used to work. Coppul, the son, had come to the house with four pairs, so it was two pairs each for him and Richard.

She went on to say that more women were doing men's work now because most able-bodied men had joined up. Apart from working in factories and munitions, women now drove trams and ambulances. Of the Stringer family who lived near them, Sarah, Katherine and Margaret all worked on the railway, while Willie Stringer, his friend, was in the army.

She told him that a Zeppelin was observed over Cheadle, then it flew on and dropped a bomb in Buxton town centre, and that beerhouses weren't allowed to open all day now, just two hours at dinner time and three hours at night. She closed her letter saying that she and mam prayed for him and Richard every night, and asked if he would be getting leave soon.

The body lice that infested the soldiers in the trenches were as a result of not being able to wash for weeks on end. The lice lived on the blood of the host, causing rashes and debility. Body hair was the lice's favourite place, crotch, armpits, head, even eyebrows and beards. In the rest camps the treatment for lice infestation was to boil the garments in hot water or to use a hot iron. But although it killed the adult lice, it rarely killed the eggs, which had been laid in the seams of the clothing and the pleats of the kilts. The soldiers whose clothing had been treated would probably have a few days of peace until the eggs of the lice hatched with the warmth of the host's body.

Away from the front lines and areas of conflict, the country in Northern France was mainly farmland and forest. It reminded Donna of the countryside in Collyhurst, where farms and woods spread in all directions from Crumpsall to Blackley. Whilst he was near Lacouture the weather became sunny and turned the trees and hedgerows that lined the cobbled Richbourg into a myriad of greens. There were wild bluebells and daisies and little yellow flowers he didn't know the name of. There was birdsong, and as he walked further he spied a heron fishing motionless on the La Bassee Canal. There was, he thought, a fragrance about all flora. It was not only the trees and blossoms but the grass and the earth as well. Although there was the thud, thud of shells being fired in the distance, it didn't spoil his idyll. Donna sat down and lit a cigarette. He wanted to make the moment last as long as possible. Making his way back to the camp, he felt better and more relaxed; in a strange way, savouring nature like this was like having been to church, he thought.

Because of the renewed heavy shelling of the British positions along the Lacouture/Richbourg road, the return to the trenches for the Seaforths began at night at 8.15pm. The depleted 'B', 'C', 'D' and 'A' companies marched from billets in single file at quarter hour intervals to relieve Gurkha troops in the trenches. 'B' Company took the two machine guns into the line, with 'C' and 'D' Companies in support. As 'A' Company alone had held the same position and had taken the brunt of the casualties in leading the last attack, it was ordered into the reserve trenches, which weren't a great distance from the front line. Therefore the soldiers holding the reserve positions were in almost as much danger from shelling and enemy rifle fire as the front line. Even with the limited illumination from the paraffin lamps, the damage to the reserve trenches stood out. The dugouts had what looked like recent direct hits.

Donna worked with Harper, who had miraculously survived the previous attack, sandbagging the sides. One held the bag while the other filled it up two-thirds full with earth, the regulation amount. At 1.00am Conroy and Sergeant Cooper brought the rum ration, one small tot in a silver measure per man. The thick black rum was always welcome at night.

First light revealed the battlefield of no-man's-land. To Donna it looked little different to when he and 'A' Company had tried to attack the lines of German fortifications a week before, only to be met by withering rifle and machine gun fire. What made things even worse, however, were the casualties caused by the poor quality of artillery shells, which accounted for the killing of many allied lives.

"Fucking dulali artillery officers," said Donna, bitterly. "They couldn't hit a barn door from three paces."

The many bodies of soldiers from British and Indian regiments lay between the two opposing armies. The detritus of the battle was everywhere, rifles, coils of barbed wire, shell holes, soldiers' packs, splintered wood.

Harper wanted to know if all of 'A' Company's wounded had been brought in or managed to get back. He learned from Robb, now a full Corporal, that two stretcher-bearers had been killed attempting to look for the wounded at night, and after lying for two days near the German barbed wire, two men from 'A' Company had managed to crawl back to the British front line, but their wounds had become gangrenous.

As the weeks passed the weather suddenly improved. It was warm with bright sunshine. Life in the trenches was almost pleasant. These young men were always hungry as they didn't get enough to eat, but as long as they kept their heads down and dodged the whizz-bangs and 'Jack Johnsons', their existence was bearable.

Trench work for the men was digging and extending the dugouts, heightening the trench walls and creating spy holes. For the men in the reserve trenches it was the same, but when not on guard they brought up supplies of ammunition, water and rations from the supply dumps or the field kitchens behind the lines.

There were no further mass attacks by the allies at Aubers Ridge. It had proved too costly. Now the question in the minds of the generals was whether the Germans would retaliate with a mass attack of their own, knowing now that British artillery was of poor quality. Surveillance and observation of the German brest works opposite had observed clandestine activity during the hours of darkness. During the day, whatever it was had been covered over and camouflaged with earth and clay. Was it the footings for a new type of trench mortar? Or was it the entrance to a tunnel being dug under the British front line?

At Givency in December the Germans had exploded a mine under the trench of 'E' Company, the Lahore Indian Regiment, and none of the soldiers were ever found

It was decided that a trench raid would be carried out on the first moonless night. At 2.00am, an N.C.O., a Private from 'C' Company and two Indian soldiers were ordered to get as near as possible and find out what the enemy were up to. Stripped of tell-tale noisy webbing and ammunition pouches, minus cap badges and divisional identification insignia, and armed only with a Webley pistol and a wooden cosh, the four men slipped as silently as shadows along the narrow listening trench and dropped into no-man's-land. Avoiding the masses of tangled barbed wire, and shielded by the heaps of waste and the rotting dead, they began moving towards their objective, sometimes on all fours. Earlier, a pinprick of light had winked briefly, betraying activity in the earthwork.

At Divisional Headquarters, General Willcocks and his staff officers had little or no faith in the success of the raid, but this was nothing new. (Field Marshall Haig, when first seeing the machine gun, believed it had little use in the army). Something needed to be done, however. Telephone communication was scant and with little or no reliable intelligence, the British General Staff relied on information from aircraft or from the observation balloons.

Misinformation had led Haig and his staff to believe the Germans had moved forces from the Aubers Ridge to reinforce soldiers on the Russian Front. This was untrue. The result was that the allied mass attack was stopped dead in its tracks with devastating results.

Against all the odds the night trench raid was successful. The Germans didn't expect the British to be so audacious after they had made no-man's-land resemble a slaughterhouse. But using the stealth learned fighting the Pathans in the North West Frontier of India, they accomplished their mission and returned with a terrified prisoner. He was taken to Battalion Headquarters on the Richebourg Road. He wasn't very tall and had a thin face and frightened eyes. He was agitated and on edge. His head was bloody and his grey uniform was filthy where his captors had dragged him through the clay.

Captain Shornberg, who could speak German, interrogated Stabsunter Offizier Hans Kleeva. He didn't need much persuading to talk. He said he was a corporal in the 12th Jägers Infanterie and had been in charge of a digging party excavating a sap trench 40 yards out from his own brestworks. He'd been alone in the trench, having sent the two other men to shore some timber, and was having a piss when he was suddenly hit over the head and yanked out of the hole by a black devil with a beard.

Questioned by Shornberg, he said his commanding officer was Oberoberst Franz Keitel. Apart from his regiment, there were Bavarian reserve units and perhaps Austrian militia regiments. He shrugged his shoulders when asked how many guns they had. He began to sweat when asked if the Germans were about to counter-attack. He said he didn't think so. When asked what they thought of the Seaforths as soldiers, he replied that all German troops hated the kilted soldiers, calling them 'ladies from hell' who never took prisoners. But then, quickly adding, that he and his comrades thought the Seaforths were good soldiers. When he realised he wasn't going to be shot he produced a picture of his wife and children and fell on his knees clasping the picture.

When the time approached for men to be relieved from the misery of the trenches, and a few days or so of relaxation beckoned, it wasn't surprising that spirits rose and outlooks brightened. They were more tolerant with one another as the weather turned fine and hot. Because of the sudden shelling and shrapnel fire, the Seaforths' eagerly-awaited relief was delayed. The relieving soldiers were men from the Connaught Rangers, who had collected a few casualties even before they got into the line. However, by 2.30am the changeover had taken place and the battalion was on its way to billets. A couple of days later the sunny weather tempted the men to go swimming in the La Bassee Canal, taking it in turns in case a sudden call to action was ordered. On the opposite bank, broad-faced French women working in the fields giggled behind their hands and made suggestive gestures to the bathers.

A few of the recovered wounded returned, but men from other units were needed to go some way to making up battalion strength. The battalion was hardly recognisable from the one that had landed in France barely eight months before.

The re-named Kings Road was busy with horse and motorised traffic travelling slowly behind columns of the bearded French Poilus infantry. The beard was a status symbol, denoting taking part in active service. The French military authorities didn't insist on the infantry shaving whilst engaged in front line action; they were excused the razor.

The lethargy that had plagued Donna for the last couple of months appeared to have lessened. He was standing outside 'A' Company's office having just received his pay. He waited for Corporal Robb to appear from inside.

"Full corporal now I see," said Donna with a smile. "More pay eh?"

"Aye," said Robb, "and more being fucked aboot."

Donna, still smiling, said, "Do you fancy a drink?"

Robb nodded. "Aye, there's a bordello in Lacouture where ah'v seen men queuing up, so we could have a few drams, then have a fuck," he said, his eyes twinkling.

The Englishman didn't reply. He was still haunted by the cases of venereal disease he'd seen and treated in the Great Yarmouth and Aldershot hospitals. The two started off, one walking, the other limping, towards Lacouture a mile distant. They hadn't covered more than a few yards when they heard a shout and rapid footsteps behind them

"D'ya mind if ah join ye?"

Alec Love was one of the replacements who had recently joined the battalion. Love was a cheery 20-year old youth who had enlisted in the Seaforths in preference to their twin regiment, the Cameron Highlanders. He signed on in Elgin in the north of Scotland, just as Robb had done years before. Love had decided to join up, he had said, because everywhere you went, in shops, in the pubs, everywhere, there were notices urging you to join the army!

"Ah was fed up with farm labour anyway," he said.

Robb nodded sagely but declined to say the reason why he'd joined the ranks nine years before.

The truth was Robb came from quite a good family who lived near Nairn. As a boy he got into trouble with two of his friends. The magistrate in Inverness sent him to a borstal near Edinburgh. After his release, his parents threatened to disown him unless he joined the army and redeemed himself. Tall and handsome, he soon took to a soldier's life, but occasionally he'd reflect on the borstal as "a bastard of a place". Donna could empathise with his friend after his treatment in York Castle. Since that time he'd hated all Red Caps.

As the trio continued to walk down the Kings Road towards Lacouture, they came upon a burial service taking place in a small cemetery amongst the trees. The cemetery was a small cluster of wooden crosses behind a field aid station. Two freshly dug graves lay side by side. A solemn-faced padre looked over the crosses and two men with shovels stood to attention with heads bowed. The three newcomers stopped and paid their respects.

In Lacouture the estaminet was typical of the drinking, sawdust-strewn cafes of northern France. The place was noisy and filled with soldiers. Behind the bar a fat man in shirtsleeves and braces and two thin women with grey-lined faces fought to keep up with their thirsty clients. A notice said in English, 'Beer 2 sous per glass. Vin rouge, 1. F75 la bouteille'.

Private Love, with the exuberance of youth, wanted to buy the drinks for the three of them, but Robb would have none of it. He pulled rank and told him to save his money and be guided by Donna and himself. However, the young man insisted. "Ahm no' short of money," he protested, diving into his khaki tunic. He had to shout above a babble of conversation to make himself heard. "Ma parents gave it ta me for my birthday afore ah left home."

"When's yer birthday?"

" July," replied Love.

"Still a wee way off," said Robb.

When it was their turn to be served, Corporal Robb took command. He bought a bottle each for Donna and himself and a glass of beer for the new recruit. There were no empty chairs, so Robb led them over to the broad window ledges where they could sit down, and not only were they able to drink in comparative comfort but they could be seen from outside by passers by.

It wasn't long before two prostitutes stopped and smiled; one of them cheekily pulling down the front of her blouse, pleased to be ogled by the men inside.

Since the war, Lacouture had grown to twice its size due to the wealth and business that wars sometimes generate. Donna, who was shy and uncomfortable where women were concerned, was becoming a little embarrassed with Robb, who, ever the ladies man, winked and smiled at the two businesswomen outside. The Englishman was glad when the two tarts walked off arm in arm with two men from the Sherwood Foresters.

A little Frenchman with a black moustache and a woollen chapeau pushed his way around the tables selling postcards with patriotic and religious scenes, as well as pictures of naked women with huge black pubic hair. There were also humorous ones showing naked soldiers jumping into hot baths and the lice jumping out.

After a few refills, Love was beginning to get glassy-eyed. He hadn't been in the front line yet, he'd just been company runner. He was very interested in the wound stripe Donna had on his sleeve. However, the Englishman, although becoming a little euphoric himself, smiled at his young companion and shook his head, saying, "It would take too long to tell." The youth pulled a face, a little disappointed. Donna, taking another swig from the bottle, said, "I'll give you some simple yet priceless advice though. Always keep your head down when in the line."

Colonel Richie was never seen again. After spending all his life in the regiment it was rumoured he was sent to Netley, a psychiatric hospital in the south of England. The needless slaughter of his men at Ypres had been too much for him. As a commanding officer. the rank and file greatly respected him. He was someone who considered that the welfare of his soldiers was paramount. He had quickly seen that the brogue shoes and lightweight tropical topcoats would be inadequate for the rigours of a northern winter and had the shoes replaced with ammunition boots and puttees.

It was said that Colonel Richie refused to order his battalion into the line until warm greatcoats and boots had been issued. His soldiers considered Colonel Richie, as the French say, *sans egal*.

FIFTEEN

Festubert again

After an early evening thunderstorm, the battalion relieved the Gurkhas to the north of the La Bassee Road. Before going into the trenches an extra bandoleer of 100 rounds of ammunition, biscuits and bully beef was issued to each man, plus the usual two empty sandbags folded behind their webbing straps, to be filled if needed. All that day the German front line 200-yards distant had been bombarding and sniping constantly. Evidence of this was the British and Indian bodies lying side by side just amongst the scrub trees behind the support trenches. Before going into the line, the padre held an open-air church service for all religions. Donna and Corporal Robb had attended, but the superstitious Donna had a good luck thing about cheese and made sure he carried some.

In the night, activity could be heard from the German trenches. 'A' Company stood-to, not knowing what to expect from the enemy opposite. At 2.00am, Captain Shornberg and Sergeant Cooper appeared, telling the men that when not on duty to try and get as much rest as possible. The night was quiet. After the earlier rain the sky cleared and the moon showed itself. Behind the trenches Donna recognised the quivering call of a tawny owl, answered by its mate in the distance.

Donna and Alex Love were squashed in a dugout with two others. Being new to the company Love had latched on to Robb and the Englishman. He was always ready with a question but was tactful enough to be silent when Donna had his eyes closed in sleep or just at rest. Now, however, Donna was smoking.

"D'ya think they'll attack tomorrow?" asked Love.

Donna shrugged. "Who knows?"

"In Bethune ah saw a man in the Bedfords selling a German officer's spiked hat and pistol." Donna just grunted.

The night passed without incident, but hardly anyone slept more than a few minutes. At first light the Germans began shelling the British trenches, sporadically at first, then with greater intensity, blowing the British barbed wire sky high. The thunder of these shells exploded blood red in clouds of blue and black smoke. There was little the men in the British lines could do from this airborne assault except make themselves as small a target as possible by pressing themselves into the side of the trench and covering their heads and ears. The bombardment lasted one hour, interspersed with gas shells. It was whilst these shells were falling that lines of grey and light blue-clad infantry streamed with fixed bayonets towards the Seaforths' 7th Division. Donna, tense, stood and waited in line below the parapet, the safety catch off. His short Lee Enfield could take eleven rounds, ten in the magazine and one up the spout. When the rows of German infantry began to falter crossing the many water-filled ditches and thick mud towards the British, the order came to man the firestep, then quickly following came 'Fire at will'.

The roar of the rapid fire of men stood shoulder to shoulder was ear-splitting and continuous. The British infantry's training in rapid fire was exceeded to over 20 rounds by some that morning. The rat, tat, tat of the Seaforths' machine guns, firing obliquely across the battlefield, was crowned by the enfilades from the British trenches. The Germans began falling forward; others hit in the chest were knocked off their feet and fell backwards.

As he expected, Donna's rifle barrel got so hot the wooden stock began to smoke. He used his glengarry to prevent his hands being burned. But he was impervious to the pain amidst the noise and rattle of flying cartridge cases and the smell of explosives. Nearly every bullet found a target; it was harder to miss the enemy than bring him down.

The first massed rows of Germans were stopped in the midddle of no-man's-land. The second and third lines fared little better. A few managed to get to the Sikhs' barbed wire, but they were quickly despatched. Realising the attack had failed the Germans began running back to their own barricades, leaving heaps of dead and wounded. When the order to cease fire came down the trench, Donna slumped down on the firestep and leaned his rifle and bayonet against his knees. He was joined by Love, who had stood next to him during the German attack

"Well," gasped Donna, "what d'ya think of your first time in action?"

Love, his face blackened with the smoke and dirt, shrugged.

"Ahm no sure, ah felt sick to ma stomach, not like tha other men."

"Don't you worry lad, everyone is scared the first time they go into action," explained Donna, "and some are always afraid," he added quietly.

Alec retched and coughed up black phlegm. His hands were shaking.

"Have ye ever used that?" he asked, pointing to Donna's bayonet.

"The bayonet? Yes, once," muttered Donna.

"Where was that?"

"At Givency in December." replied Donna.

The youth looked at Donna wanting more.

"The trenches were a sea of mud because of the heavy rain that never seemed to stop for weeks. The mud got everywhere, all over the uniform. It covered the magazine and filled the barrel of the rifle, making it impossible to fire."

At this point the Englishman stopped talking and stood up, not particularly wanting to be reminded of it. "I'm away for a shit," he said, shuffling off. He trudged down the line into the long communicating ditch to the latrine trench. There was a pair of a dead man's feet wearing boots protruding from one of the walls. Turning sideways to pass the feet, he looked at the stitching and the hobnails on the soles where they had worn. He smiled to himself and thought, 'I wonder what the old man would've made of the workmanship.'

That night they found a wounded German officer lying opposite the Indians' trench. His uniform was stained with earth, his breathing was shallow and rapid. He'd been shot through the chest and each breath was laboured. There was blood on his mouth and down the front of his tunic. Though gasping for breath, he kept up a continuous string of insults at the stretcher-bearers carrying him back to battalion headquarters. "Affen und untermenschen," he snarled between breaths at the four sepoys carrying him, which, in German, meant "Monkeys and sub-humans".

At battalion headquarters he was given water to drink, but it was obvious he wasn't going to last the night. His eyes began closing.

"Was ist sie name?" asked Captain Shornberg

He opened his eyes at this and said, "Major Schmitt."

When asked more questions, still with closed eyes and a heaving chest, he just shook his head, then, surprisingly and with a look of disdain, he gasped in English, "Where are all your machine guns? Every von of your men must have a Lewis machine gun."

"No, Major," said Shornberg, "it's just that my soldiers are better shots than yours."

The German officer, his sabre-scarred face twisted in hate, looked towards the captain and Macrae. "Bastard tommies," he said. "Out there is a field of von metre high corpses." Adding, "My son is von of them."

Captain Shornberg cleared his throat to change the subject. "How many divisions have you in reserve Major?" he asked.

The wounded man, again with eyes closed, just shook his head and said, "I am a German officer." He suddenly opened his eyes and said something in German. Then, in English, "I am very tired" and closed his eyes for the last time.

In the trenches the men were praised by their officers. Tea, bread and hot stew were brought up from the field kitchens, although barely warm by the time it was dished out. Nevertheless, the stew and the tea were very welcome.

After the German attacks had failed, divisional intelligence information was that the British were much stronger than the enemy, due to the heavy losses they had sustained near Arras. The German VII Corps facing them had no reserves and Headquarters was sure success would be theirs

At 7.30am over 400 guns and howitzers were fired on a wide front, aimed at the German brestwork and parapets. The 4.5-inch guns would bracket the support trenches, while 210 18-pounders firing shrapnel shells would concentrate on the German wire. However, these were not really suited for the task. What was needed were high explosive shells, but there were none available. Not only that, but as was the case at Aubers Ridge, reports came of many of the shells failing to explode and of allied guns being worn out and ineffective. Nevertheless, dud shells still fell on the German front and reserve trenches around the village of Festubert with negative effect.

By 10.00am all the attacking battalions were in position in front of the German salient. At mid-day the first lines of British soldiers scrambled their way into no-man's-land. The low lying ground was criss-crossed with water-filled drainage pools, some too wide to jump over. The Royal Berkshires, 2nd Worcesters and other units attacked the northern brestworks. They were met by deadly fire. The Welsh Fusiliers and Staffords attempted to race in support but were cut down by German shells. The Enniskillen Regiment was sent in and managed to reach the front line trenches but were beaten back.

All through the action the British guns were targeting the Germans' front line and reserve trenches. The Scots Guards, 2nd Bedfords and Cameron Highlanders attacked the southern brestworks. The men of the 7th Meerut Division were poised to make a frontal assault on the enemy. The order 'to go' was something of a relief to most of the tense, dry-mouthed soldiers packing the trenches.

At the whistle Donna dived over the parapet and under a raft of barbed wire, then dropped into no-man's-land. There was smoke and flying debris everywhere. He was hardly conscious of the noise or the reek of explosives. Ahead, to his left, he could see khaki figures trying to cross a pool about seven feet wide. 'Go fucking round, go round it,' he said to himself. He tried to jog forward with his rifle and bayonet, but it was difficult in the soft undulating ground strewn with abandoned packs and rifles.

There was the zip, then zip, zip of bullets trying to find a target, but they say you never hear the one that gets you. He was aware of being in a moving line of men to his right and left. Some suddenly fell as though they'd tripped over some invisible object. He felt himself urged forward with mostly Garwal soldiers, towards what? Eternity? All had their mouths open, yelling, yet he couldn't hear anything. Then he realised he was deaf. As the line got nearer the German front line there were fewer of them. Donna felt the wind of a couple of British artillery shrapnel shells passing overhead. But to his relief the shelling stopped. After Aubers Ridge he had little faith in the British field guns. Shelling normally is used to "soften up" the enemy before the infantry attack. But, as witnessed at "Aubers", the British artillery had had a more detrimental effect on it's own men than the enemy.

There were dead Germans lying entangled in their own barbed wire on the parapet. Inside, the trench was a heap of bodies piled one on top of each other, with a single wounded man still alive with his leg blown off. Strips of flesh hung from his knee. He'd tied his belt around his thigh as a tourniquet and he looked terrified as the Englishman slid into the trench. Then came a bang above Donna's ear and the wounded man jerked and lay still. A moment later the taciturn Harper slid into the hole behind Donna. He said one word in answer to the look Donna gave him.

"Campbell."

Donna nodded. The two climbed over the bodies and cautiously went looking for the enemy. They came upon a few more bodies and scattered weapons. When they came to the dugouts they found that they were better and deeper than anything in the British lines. There were bunk beds and wood stoves with chimneys. There were a few candles and a case on the floor stuffed with maps. But of greater importance to the two hungry infantrymen were the bottles of wine and schnapps that the enemy had left behind in their rush to flee.

Harper watched Donna open a bottle of schnapps, pour out a little on the ground and sniff the contents. After deciding it was not poisoned, he took a swig and felt the warm liquid course down to his toes and back up to his stomach. He proffered the bottle to Harper, who took a huge gulp.

"That'll put hairs on your chest," said Donna, out of breath.

They went back outside into the noise of battle, and as more British reinforcements began arriving they cautiously followed towards the German communicating trench, ever watchful for booby-trap trip wires that were often left by the retreating enemy. At the second reserve trench they came upon three German soldiers wanting to surrender. They were not from one of the Bavarian reserve regiments, they were from the elite Prince Rupprect 6th army. They all had the stains from the shelling on their uniforms. One of the spike-helmeted soldiers was wounded and unable to walk and was supported by the other two. Donna searched them for weapons and bombs. Satisfied, he motioned them towards the British lines. Ahead in the distance the Germans could be seen withdrawing towards the village of Festubert.

At almost the same time the two men realised that the booms in the distance meant that the British artillery had started up again, forcing them to duck for cover all too often. Ahead to their right the Scots Guards were coming under a lot of fire from their own guns. They withdrew and despatched a runner back with a verbal message to artillery headquarters to 'up your fucking range', or words meaning something similar.

After being ordered to take over some of the former German reserve trenches, they found the German infantry had water drainage pumps. There were stacks of duckboards and wine and supply stores in their reserve areas. On this wide farmland front there were dead cows and fearful-looking Germans wanting to give themselves up.

Although forced to retreat to the edge of the village of Festubert, the enemy made a stand near the Estaires Road and began shelling with their high velocity guns. These huge roaring monster shells blew great craters, obliterating in places their old trenches and dugouts, sending earth and splintered duckboards high into the air. The fumes and stench of explosives pervaded eyes and mouths and blackened the skin. During the bombardment Donna and 'A' Company took cover wherever they could. The terrain consisted of ditches, culverts and derelict farm buildings spread across undulating farmland.

Donna kept his head down, shielding his ears against the thunder. He waited for a lull in the shelling. When it came, and before he could move, he saw to his left the Scots Guards dash forward in an attempt to get into a small wood on the edge of the village. However, the Germans had a machine gun hidden in a pile of rubble and each time they attempted to go forward they were cut down by the crossfire. The Welsh Fusiliers tried to work their way around the Germans by taking advantage of the enemy's former trench system, hoping to get near enough to the Germans to silence the gun. Not surprisingly, the Germans knew every yard of the ground. They waited until the Fusiliers had crossed the village road and were in the open before mortaring them while a second machine gun was trained to cover anything that moved on the road.

Donna's division skirmished in support of the Fusiliers, but any attempt to charge forward was suicidal. Dusk was gathering and the light was beginning to fail. One obvious course of action was to wait for the cloak of night to consolidate the ground gained. At 7.00pm the heavens opened with a sudden thunderstorm that lasted for an hour. At least the German shelling was less frequent. During the lull, the 4th Guards Brigade was ordered up from nearby Le Touret where they had been in reserve. At 10.00pm the sky cleared and the moon appeared where the whiteness of the clouds met the dark smudge of the horizon. The scouts who had been sent out at midnight reported movement at points amongst the German positions along the two miles of front.

During the night the British artillery moved their positions forward to the rear of the besieging infantrymen. The rumblings during the night were the German guns being pulled back to target the new positions of the British more accurately.

The action at Festubert had been at the request of General Foch, who wished to relieve pressure from his hard-pressed French divisions south of the La Bassee Canal at Vimy Ridge.

There was no sleep for the men occupying the old German support lines. All they had left for rations were hard tack biscuits, hard enough to break teeth, and a water bottle. The more inventive boiled water in a mess tin, then shaved bits off the hard tack with a knife or bayonet to make a kind of soup. The biscuit was made mainly of flour and a little salt, then double baked to prevent weevils boring a home inside. The soup usually tasted like compressed wood, but it filled the stomach.

The wood left by the Germans was used to make big dixies of tea and hot water. Donna fortified his tea and hard tack soup with schnapps. Then he draped his groundsheet over his head and shoulders and fell into unconsciousness. Images came to him as he slept. There were flashes of India and his Macaque monkey

The face of George Campbell appeared speaking to him, but in his dream he couldn't understand what the big Highlander was saying. Then came the image of a man with long black hair and a beard. He lay with closed eyes and held a dagger in his left hand with the blade pointing upwards to his chin. Although not a religious man he instinctively knew the man with the dagger was Jesus Christ.

Corporal Robb shook him awake. He was with Lieutenant Robinson while two other soldiers carried a box of bombs. The bombs were the old type, round with just a fuse protruding and had to be lit before being thrown. The soldiers nicknamed these bombs 'Christmas puddings'. The trouble with these bombs was that, depending on the length of the fuse, once thrown they could easily be despatched back to the thrower. Another fault was that sometimes the fuse would come adrift and fall out. Some soldiers in the trenches made their own bombs using empty Tommy Tickler jam tins filled with nails, some cordite and a fuse. These were hardly effective, but it gave the men something to do. A new type of bomb had been promised which didn't need a fuse. It had an internal percussion cap that was activated simply by pulling a pin. However, sufficient numbers hadn't reached the front lines yet, although during the rest periods the men had practised throwing dummy bombs in anticipation of them being issued.

This new throwing grenade was called the Mills bomb. Donna stuck his Christmas pudding into a niche in the trench wall. Being metal he used it to strike matches on. He was doing this when Lieutenant Robinson and a staff officer saw him light a cigarette. The staff officer stopped and frowned at the Manchester man.

"Don't you think that's dangerous?" he asked abruptly.

Donna stared at the Captain's red armband and replied innocently. "Yes, Sir, but I've promised myself I'll stop the habit once I get out of the line."

The officer seemed about to explain before realising he was being made a fool of and controlled himself, snorted something, then moved off followed by Robinson trying hard to keep a straight face.

The Germans attacked at first light, but the British were ready and they took a terrible toll of them in the early morning gloom. Like the previous day, the first lines of German infantry had covered hardly half the distance to the British before they were knocked and flattened into the wet marshy bog. Sections of the Jägers began to push towards the centre of the lines where most of the Indian troops were concentrated, but apart from a few dogged Germans on each flank, they were either killed or beaten off. The infantrymen's rapid fire had again prevailed; the groups of brave, decimated men began running back towards their own lines, hastened by the British artillery

As the sounds of the last shells rolled across the awakening countryside, birds began singing. The air was crisp and rays of the sun began to emerge, sending golden beams earthwards onto the ground mist. It promised to be a fine warm day, and yet in no-man's-land, as the smoke and noise abated, the German dead lay sprawled all over the field, now bathed golden in the early sun's rays and rising mist.

It was this scene that made Donna remember his dream and try to make sense of it. What did it mean? One thing he did know for certain about his dream was that everyone in the dream had died – Christ, George Campbell and the monkey. Not wanting to dwell on such thoughts, he pushed them from his mind. Instead, he focused his attention on what was going on around him. Harper was examining a German standard-issue Mauser rifle he'd foraged from somewhere. In no-man's-land there were many such lying amongst the bodies. After trying the balance and squinting down the barrel, he was keen for the Manchester man's opinion. Donna thought the Mauser was a little heavier than their own short Lee Enfield. The Mauser had only a five-round magazine, so it wasn't suitable for rapid fire, unlike the British rifle. Although the Lee Enfield had superior firepower, it tended to jam in muddy conditions, whereas the nickel-plated Mauser, although heavier, was more reliable in the mud

The Canadian soldiers' weapon was the Ross rifle. It was longer and heavier than the British Lee Enfield and had a limited five-round magazine and tended to jam. It was more suited to a target range than front line trench warfare. During the first German gas attack at Ypres, when the French African troops fled in panic, the Canadian soldiers stayed and fought bravely in an attempt to hold the lines against poisonous gas and masses of German infantry. Though unsuccessful, they won two Victoria Crosses. However, many men threw down their standard issue Ross rifles and pleaded to be given the Lee Enfield.

That night 'A' and 'D' Companies, together with the 21st Brigade, were relieved and marched back to billets on the Kings Road near Richbourg. Two items of good news awaited the Manchester man. Firstly, that 'A' Company was to get home leave, and, secondly, there was a letter from his mother informing him that she'd moved back to a recently fumigated house in Fitzgeorge Street.

At noon the next day Harper and Donna were on their way by train to Boulogne. They found the busy port filled with all kinds of ships, from camouflaged frigates and destroyers to lighters, transports and fishing smacks. Their boat was the blue and black Dover Star, a converted collier. There was a queue on the quayside waiting to board. A sergeant in the military police was checking leave passes. When Donna saw him his face hardened. After his incarceration, to Donna all red caps were bastards.

In the queue next to Donna and Harper was a fresh-faced lad of about eighteen. His shoulder insignia said Lincolnshire Regiment. He seemed to get more agitated the nearer the military policeman came. Donna guessed the lad didn't have a pass.

"Show me yer pass, jock," said the flat-faced red cap to Harper. Then to Donna, "Yours."

The military policeman sniffed, then gave the warrants back to each man. Turning to the young soldier he barked, "You, your pass!"

The lad was nervous and shuffled his feet. The sergeant, his face puce, bawled, "Yer fucking pass. Where's yer camp?"

"At Le Touquet, Sergeant," stammered the lad.

The red cap now had a triumphant smirk on his face. "You ain't got a fucking pass 'ave yer? Yer tryin to desert, ain't yer?"

"No, Sergeant."

"Don't tell fucking lies. Why d'ya want to get on the boat then? You can get shot for desertion."

The young soldier's face went as white as a sheet.

"My mother's ill," he said softly.

"A likely fucking tale."

Donna felt sorry for the lad. It didn't matter to him whether the young lad was telling the truth or not, no one should be bullied and verbally abused in such a way.

The military policeman grabbed the youngster's arm, but the lad, in a state of panic, wrestled free. Then the red cap moved in to grab the young soldier by the scruff of his neck and would have succeeded but for Donna, who, as if by accident, got between the two of them, to the absolute fury of the red cap. Seizing his chance, the young soldier legged it into the crowd of khaki uniforms.

There were cheers from some men already on the ferry as the young soldier made his escape. The military policeman turned his attention to Donna now.

"You a fucking friend of his?" he snarled.

Donna shook his head. "Never set eyes on him before," he said, and made his way to the gangway.

The red cap's face was livid. He watched with suspicious eyes as the Manchester man walked away.

"I'll have the young bastard if he tries it on me again," he said.

A rare smile lit Harper's face as he followed Donna down the gangway and onto the ferry.

"I could see by yer face you didn't like that twat," said Harper.

"I hate all red caps," grunted Donna. "They're never in the front line trenches yet persecute men who get a little drunk to try to forget the horrors of being maimed or being blown to pieces."

Harper liked Donna and was always at ease in his company. It wasn't because they both came from Lancashire. Slim Harper was from the quaintly named village of Oswaldtwistle in the Lancashire hills and had a brother and a sister. He'd joined the Seaforths in 1911 in Aberdeen. The reason he'd travelled all the way to the Highlands was open to conjecture. There was a rumour that he'd done time in Wakefield prison in Yorkshire for attacking two men who had beaten up his brother Brian in a drunken brawl with an axe. Another rumour was that he'd gone to Scotland to enlist because the English police had a warrant out for his arrest. But, whatever the truth, the intense Harper was a good soldier who earned sixpence a day as a first class shot, and although he spoke little, he complained even less. Some of the men in 'A' Company thought he was dulali or a psycho, but Donna never paid any attention to the things said about Slim because during the long nights at stand-to, or when about to go over the top into no-man's-land, Donna was always glad to see the stoic Harper standing near or next to him in the line. The strange thing was, Harper felt the same about the man of few words, Donna.

The ferry took over six hours to cross from Boulogne to Folkestone and another hour before they could disembark, but the railway station was a short walk away. Quite a few trains lined up for London. Among the steam and the noise on the platforms were long-skirted ladies in fine hats handing out tea to the weary soldiers escaping the nightmare of the trenches for a few short days. The Salvation Army had a soup kitchen, which, after the hard tack and bully beef, tasted like ambrosia.

There were military policemen on the station arrogantly strutting amongst the soldiers. These men were disliked. Some of these red cap bullies would be sent to work with inexperienced raw recruits at the infamous Etaples Training Camp in France in a few months time and the bullying treatment by the military police would result in a mutiny.

They were both asleep when the train shuddered to a halt at Victoria Station. Stiff and tired, they slung their rifles and small packs and stepped out onto the crowded platform, joining the stream of soldiers going towards the exits. The two men were dying for a pint and they needed to get to Euston Station in order to travel north, but there were no likely-looking railway workers about who they could ask for directions. Donna spotted a red-bricked pub in nearby Station Road. He nodded towards the place. "Let's have a pint and ask in there," he said.

Inside, the pub was quite plush, with a long ornate bar with mirrors behind. Maroon upholstery covered the chairs where a couple of officers were seated. They both looked down their noses

226

when Donna and Harper entered. At the bar were two middle-aged men, well-dressed, wearing cravats and spats. As Donna waited at the bar to be served he noticed the man nearby making eyes at him through the mirror. Donna ignored him and ordered two pints of half-and-half from the barman. Before leaving France the two had been paid in English money, so paying wasn't a problem. It was only when the beer arrived and Donna asked the price that he was hardly able to believe his ears.

"Eleven pence," repeated the barman.

"Fucking hell," muttered Donna, "no wonder you don't get many drinkers in here."

As he felt in his tunic for the money, a voice behind him said to the barman, "I'll pay for these drinks Roger."

It was the grey-haired toff who had been eyeing Donna through the bar mirror.

Donna, pint in hand, thanked the man and said, "Where we come from a pint of beer costs a penny."

The gentleman, who's eyes never left Donna's face, said, "Really" in a flat effeminate voice, "but then I suppose everything goes up eventually."

His friend a few feet away giggled. "Now behave, Florrie," admonished his friend and continued, "or our Scottish friends will get the wrong idea."

Harper and Donna took their pints and sat down. Harper took a swig and savoured the difference between English beer and the stuff on the other side of the Channel. He lit a woodbine and nodded towards the nancies at the bar. "They're a couple of white-hatters."

"Yes, I know," said Donna. "They're probably actors. They tell me there are a lot in that profession."

Donna had come in contact with one or two homosexuals during his army service. He didn't like them, and he believed them to be abnormal. They usually kept their sexuality hidden, revealing it only at a weak moment or when they were drunk. Rumour had it that General Kitchener was a homosexual.

'Heaven help us,' thought Donna. 'What's the world coming to.' But he wasn't about to repay kindness by abusing the two queers.

Thirty minutes later they were on a tram heading for Euston Railway Station. They only just made the packed Manchester-Edinburgh train and had to sit on their packs all the way to Crewe. When eventually the train arrived at Manchester's London Road Station, it was nearly 11.00pm. Saying goodbye to Harper, who had another twenty-mile journey by train, Donna, with slung rifle and pack, was glad to get out of the station, even though it was raining as usual. He shook his head at a cab driver's invitation to board and walked instead down the station approach towards Market Street, past where the Infirmary used to be, then right into Oldham Street. What struck Donna was how dark it was, with very few gaslights lining the mostly deserted streets. There was only a young woman and a child of about five waiting at the tram stop. She had a shawl draped over her head and shoulders, with one end covering the infant's head against the cold night.

Donna felt tired and miserable and then he became aware in the darkness that the woman was watching him.

"Excuse me," she said at last, "but me and my child have no home, my husband has thrown us out." She sounded weary. "We've walked from Salford."

Donna guessed her to be no more than 20, pale with a slim figure. He guessed her next words would be to ask for money. To allay that he asked, "Where are yer going now?"

"To the women's refuge on Gaulden Street. Look," she said, "you have a kind face, do you want any business? We could go into the opposite doorway or down the entry over there."

"What about your child?" asked Donna.

"Oh, she wouldn't know what we'd be doing."

"No thanks, luv," he said, "but here's a shilling. It might help."

"God bless you," she said. "What's yer name?"

"James," he said gruffly. He was glad it was dark so that she couldn't see him blush. Women embarrassed him and he was glad when soon after a tram clanked into view from Piccadilly.

"How long are you on leave?" asked the girl.

"For a few days," said Donna.

"I'll light a candle and say a prayer fer you to keep you safe then," said the girl again.

"Thanks," said Donna.

The tram was full, but the girl found a seat near the front and sat her child on her lap. Donna stood and braced himself against the swaying of the tram, whilst at the same time clinging to one of the overhead straps. An elderly grey-haired man offered Donna his seat. Donna acknowledged his offer but declined politely, fearing he might fall asleep and miss his stop if he sat down in the warmth. Twenty minutes later the matronly conductress guided him down the metal steps at his stop on Rochdale Road.

Tizzie opened the door to him at Fitzgeorge Street and, as always, squealed with delight when she saw who it was.

"Mam," she cried, "it's our Jim. Why didn't you tell us you were coming?" she said, mildly scolding him.

"Give him a chance to get in the house Tizzie," said his mother. "Come over here and get a warm by the fire James. Are you hungry?"

He nodded.

His mother looked greyer and older than he remembered, but then, perhaps, it was the light from the gas mantle that gave her the dark-eyed wan appearance. Donna dropped his pack and propped his rifle below the living room window and did as his mother bade. Donna's mother and sister Tizzie were not the only women in the room. Tizzie's friend from work was also there sitting near the fire. She was a pretty, black-haired Irish-looking girl. She got to her feet and smiled when Donna stumbled into the living room. His sister answered his enquiring look at the slim, full-bosomed girl of about 18.

"Jim," said Tizzie, "this is Margaret Stringer from Bebbington Street. She's working with me in the railway workshops near Cornbrook."

Donna remembered the name.

"Haven't you a brother called Willie," he asked her.

"Yes," she said, nodding, "but he's joined the army now."

"Pleased to meet you," said Donna, holding out his hand.

The girl smiled, showing even white teeth, and took his hand. Her hand was small but well-shaped. He remembered her more clearly now. The last time he'd seen her was when she was about ten years old, playing on Jones's office steps with a school friend. Being more accustomed to the company of men, and soldiers in particular, he felt embarrassed and a little awkward in the presence of women that were not related to him. But, how the skinny little girl he remembered had changed. She was a real beauty now. He was reluctant to let her hand go and she sensed this and her blue eyes twinkled and the smile grew wider. He blushed a little and turned away towards the mantelpiece.

He was glad when his mother changed the subject.

"Yes," said his mother, "more and more women are doing men's jobs now because of the war. Oh, how I wish the war was over Tizz, and I pray every night for the poor men at the front."

"I'll have to go now, it's late," said Margaret.

"I'll walk you home," offered Donna.

"No, Tizzie usually walks me back and you must be tired by now, coming all the way from France," said Margaret. Then she noticed for the first time the three-inch red mark on his temple. Her eyes were full of concern. "How did you get that mark?"

"Oh," he replied, not wishing to go into details while his mother and sister were present, "it's a long story Margaret. Let's just say I was kicked by a mad hen."

This was a comical saying his mother had often used when he was a small boy and wanted to make light of something and not go into detail. After Tizzie and Margaret left the house Donna's mother, who had been busy in the kitchen making sandwiches, came and sat by him while he ate. Then, staring into the fire, she said quietly, "You look thin James, and I noticed you were limping. Tell me the truth, how did you get that mark on your face?"

"I was careless, I suppose, mam," he said. "It happened while I was breaking up wood to make a fire with my feet. A piece flew up and hit me on the temple. As for my leg, it's that old injury I got playing football when I was in Colchester."

He didn't want to worry her, but she knew he was lying. Neither of them spoke, both with their own thoughts while they waited for the kettle to boil on the hob. It was quiet in the living room, just the ticking of the wall clock and the odd crackle of the coal fire. It was Donna who broke the silence. "Have you had any word from Dick?"

His mother nodded. "We had a letter from him last week. He's still in Lancaster but he says in his letter that he's expecting to move soon with his regiment or company, or whatever they call it, but he can't say where because of security."

"I hope he doesn't go to France," said Donna quietly. He'd only seen his brother a couple of times in almost five years, and that was briefly whilst on leave from the army.

"Is he still fond of a lot of sugar in his tea?" Donna asked his mother with a smile. She smiled in return and said, "Not as much."

When Tizzie returned he said goodnight to both women and went to bed. The next day it was noon before he came downstairs. While he slept his mother had been busy and washed some of his clothes.

"What am I going to wear?" asked Donna. "I don't think my old civvies will fit!"

"Try some of Richard's," suggested his mother, giving Dick his full title. "He was always a little bit bigger than you."

The house in Fitzgeorge Street was mid-terraced and as he tucked into a big breakfast of porridge, bacon, eggs and mushrooms, the door that led into the back yard opened and a young cat, mostly white but with few ginger spots, walked into the kitchen. It looked curiously at Donna, sniffed his ankle, then strolled unhurriedly into the living room, from where came his mother's voice to the animal: "Where have you been all night?"

"What's its name?" Donna wanted to know.

"Now yer asking something," replied his mother in mock reproach. "Its name is Betsy Joe."

"Betsy Joe! What kind of a name is that for an animal?" asked Donna.

"Well yer see," explained his mother, "when it was a kitten it kept coming into our back yard and sleeping in the shed, so I took pity on it and let it keep me company in the house."

"But that doesn't explain its name."

"I know, I'm coming to that. The two Becket kids from next door were always playing with it and asking to see it. The Becket children are called Elizabeth and Joseph, so I christened the cat Betsy Joe."

Donna roared with laughter. "Well, I've never heard of a cat called that before. Is it a boy or a girl?"

"I've no idea," came his mother's voice from the other room.

"If you're right in the head, I know where there's a house full," said her son, still laughing.

Later, wanting to get out of the house for a while to see how or if any of his neighbourhood had changed since he'd been away, Donna searched upstairs for something to wear. He'd last worn his own clothes years before. He found his suit hanging next to Richard's in the front bedroom wardrobe. He knew his mother would have kept his dead father's suit and Dan's torn and bloody shirt somewhere in the house, but he didn't want to ask where.

The sun was bright as he stepped into the street. He'd forgotten how huge the red-bricked viaduct was above, spanning Fitzgeorge Street and the River Irk, that ran behind the houses. At the end of the street, on the corner, was the Star Inn, where Donna had been born when his father was landlord. Now it was under new management and was just opening for business because of the restricted licensing hours. Already there were three customers impatient to get inside. He didn't recognise any of the men and passed them without a word. He turned right onto Collyhurst Road and up the hill to the row of houses in St. Oswald Street, which ran behind the school and church of the same name.

He was going to see his half sister Janey, ten years older than him and now married. He'd not seen Janey, now called Janey Knowles, since their father had died five years before. Janey was a tall, auburn-haired, attractive woman, very much like himself in features. Recognising him, she threw her arms around his neck.

"Oh, it's good to see you Jim," she said huskily. She'd always had a soft spot for him, not because he was the youngest in the two families, but because even from a very early age Donna not only looked like his eldest sister, but also had the same serious and thoughtful demeanour, unusual in one so young. The way young Donna's hair stuck up at the crown always amused Janey. Despite all attempts to plaster it flat with soap and water, it still refused to behave. This was one of the things she found so amusing about him. Now she fussed around him.

"Come in, sit down, take yer hat off, how long are you home for? Let me see how tall you've got. It's years since I last saw you."

Smiling, he let himself be led to a chair.

She vanished into the kitchen to make tea. His eyes wandered about the living room. It smelled of furniture polish and fresh black lead in the grate. On the sideboard were wedding day photographs of Janey and her husband. In another he recognised his mother, Dick and neighbours. He reflected how she had taught him how to tell the time and helped with his reading when he was small. One of his favourite books was the Ancient Greek adventure story, 'The Iliad'. He smiled as he remembered how his mother had taught him how to tie the laces of his clogs his father had made for him and then he got told off for kicking the toes out playing football and climbing trees with his pal Bob Brady.

Janey kept wishing her husband was there to greet Donna, but, as she explained, "Jim" was on the day shift that week. Janey's husband was a policeman, a good policeman and a conscientious officer who carried out his duties not only in the interest of law and order, but also he felt his duty was to serve the public, unlike some of the bullying types the police force attracted. Because of this he wasn't very popular with some of the other constables, but this didn't bother him. In fact, he considered some of the constables he worked alongside as little better than the rogues they were employed to apprehend.

Donna had hoped he would see Jim, but after an hour he began to get restive. It was probably because, as with other front line soldiers, constant life under fire had an adverse effect on his nervous system. Even in the most mundane situations, such as travelling on a train, this syndrome would manifest itself by the sufferer continually fidgeting, or getting up from his seat to fiddle with his pack, or check the contents of his pockets agitatedly.

Cap in hand, he stood up to leave, and it was then that his sister noticed for the first time the red scar on his temple.

"Oh Jim, that looks sore," she said, and instinctively went to touch it, but he jerked his head away.

"It's nothing," he said, smiling, "it'll wash off in a couple of days."

Her eyes were troubled. "Please be careful, Jim."

He left the house saying he would return before his leave was up if time allowed. Outside it was bright sunshine. He retraced his steps down Collyhurst Road, passed the Star Inn, but instead of returning to Fitzgeorge Street he continued onto The Grapes, a Boddingtons beerhouse that stood opposite Jones's Mill and was built on the croft, overlooked by the huge corporation tip 80-yards distant. There weren't many people in the men's room of the pub apart from two grey-haired men playing cribbage in the corner, whilst at the bar two uniformed soldiers were sat with their backs to the newcomer.

Donna got served and took his pint to an empty table. He didn't particularly want to be sociable. It seemed now that there was a war, friends and strangers were much friendlier, but Donna had begun to feel weak in Janey's house and felt it must be the return of the trench fever picked up in France. He was about to leave most of his beer and get some air when one of the soldiers, a sergeant, turned around and noticed Donna for the first time. With a broad smile he came across to where Donna sat with his hand outstretched.

"Jim," exclaimed the Sergeant, "what a surprise."

It was Johnny Foggaty, Donna's cousin from his mother's side.

Donna rose from his chair and the two shook hands. The last time they'd met was in Donna's mother's house. Johnny had been uncertain if he was doing the right thing in joining the Machine Gun Corps. Now he was a sergeant and appeared to have bags of confidence.

"By fuck, it's good to see you Jim," said Foggaty, who was a couple of years older than Donna.

He called his friend over from the bar. "Here Eric, come and meet my younger brother." This wasn't strictly true, but that didn't matter. Donna's eyes lingered on the men's badges, MGC of the Machine Gun Corps. Donna knew the Germans hated the Machine Gun Corps and would shoot any prisoners captured wearing the badge. The last time they met he'd advised Foggaty of this fact.

The talk centred on how things had changed back home because of the war. Women were now doing most of the work that the men had done previously. What had struck Donna in London and Manchester were the blackout regulations, which, since the Zeppelin raids, meant showing a light could incur fines. Even the trams and cars had special shielded headlights and window blinds. There was something else new to Donna. As the clock approached 3 o'clock the landlord called from the bar for customers to order their last drinks. Although there was a shortage of most spirits, Johnny Foggaty managed to get three whiskies from the landlord, with which they toasted each other, wished each other good fortune, shook hands again, then left the pub to go their separate ways.

Donna felt somewhat out of place in the smallness of his mother's house. He felt he was under her feet and yet he could remember when the whole family filled the house.

"Why don't you go and visit Joe while you're home?" suggested his mother.

Donna's older half-brother Joe had married while Donna was in India and now lived in Smedley Lane, not far from the Irkdale Cloth Finishing Company where he worked. For something to do in the afternoon he went to Smedley Lane and found the terraced house, which overlooked the River Irk. He knocked on the door. A woman much younger than Donna expected opened it. She was plump with a round face and straight black hair.

"Who are you?" she whispered, holding a finger to her lips.

"I'm Joe's brother," said Donna, removing his cap.

"Oh, come in," she whispered again. "He's on nights, I don't want to wake him."

"Of course," said Donna.

"Can I get you a cup of tea?" she whispered.

He shook his head. "No, I'll be off, tell him I called."

"I will. What's yer name again?" she asked sheepishly.

"James."

He left the house and walked the short distance to Queens Road and stood on the bridge watching the river for a while. Then he made his way up the brow to Rochdale Road and saw columns of civilian men being harried and barked at by uniformed sergeants marching towards Heaton Park, where trenches had been dug opposite the tram sheds to give the new recruits some idea of life in France. The marchers, some looking tired, had three miles to go still.

That night he woke up to find his mother at the bottom of his bed calling his name.

"What's the matter mam?" he asked.

"You were shouting out in your sleep," she said.

"Oh, it was nothing mam, you go back to bed."

It was still dark when he left the house to return to France at 5.00am. He hadn't wanted breakfast, just a cup of tea. His uniform felt clean and smelled of carbolic soap, which hopefully would give him a few days of peace from the lice. His mother had put some sandwiches in his pack for the journey.

He was grateful to his mother for not crying. He knew what he was going back to and he knew her tears would come after he left the house.

"Oh Jim, take care of yourself out there," she opined. "Our family can't afford to lose any more."

She held him tightly and kissed him on both cheeks

"I love you," she said softly.

His last image of his mother was of her, sad-eyed, holding Betsy Jo in her arms.

SIXTEEN

Marseilles

The Folkestone ferry was delayed for four hours. Apparently, a strange object had been seen earlier in the Channel near Dover, which the harbourmaster believed was the periscope of a German U-boat.

Donna welcomed the delay. It gave him time to catch up on some sleep. However, his shut-eye was disturbed when a party of young nurses came on board and decided to sit in the quieter area aft where he'd gone to doze. When eventually the boat docked in Boulogne the light was beginning to wane. As Donna queued to go ashore he noticed an army bus waiting on the quayside. He watched the women begin loading their things on board. On an impulse he asked the driver in the Army Service Corps where he was going.

"Bapaume orspital mate," said the driver.

Donna gave him a cig."Any chance of lift?"

"It's not up to me mate." He jerked his thumb behind him. "Ask the matron."

Donna shrewdly began helping the nurses load their luggage and equipment onto the vehicle. When this was almost finished he approached the tired-looking middle-aged matron.

"Excuse me, ma'am. I need to be back in camp before nightfall. Could I have a lift in your transport as far as Richbourg on the La Bassee Road?"

The lined face of the matron lit up in a smile. Then she said, in the most beautiful of voices, "I don't see why not. Travel with the driver and tell him where to let you off. Oh, and good luck young man, wherever you are going."

"Thank you, ma'am," mumbled Donna.

Although she must easily have been twice his age, Donna found her extremely attractive as a woman. She was obviously a person from a privileged background who no doubt had volunteered, as had nearly all those pretty, courageous girls, to work in the stinking, disease-ridden abattoirs they called military hospitals.

The bus was held up by streams of ambulances and lorries arriving with wounded, attended by haggard nurses, male and female, en route to Blighty. It took 30 minutes before the bus could make headway through the traffic of the port. Once on La Côte Road, the driver picked up speed where he could over the cobbled roads. In the distance the rumble of guns could be heard, which increased as the vehicle sped northwards.

The driver cocked his head to one side and said to Donna, who was sitting beside him, "Festubert?"

Donna shook his head. "No, it seems too far. I think Neuve Chapelle."

The driver nodded. They had to queue at one of the bridges that spanned the La Bassee Canal. Through the window, apart from the laden river barges, Donna could see mallards and white and yellow narcissus growing on the banks. The weather was certainly warmer, and when the bus reached the busy dung-strewn La Bassee Road (called Kings Road by the soldiers), the bus stopped for Donna to get off. Gathering his rifle and pack, he stood and waved his thanks as the bus drove off. His thoughts, however, were of the matron.

There was enough daylight left to see that where the shelling had not stunted the trees or uprooted the hedges. The vegetation was lush with new growth. For the first time he noticed that the red and white hawthorns were in bloom and heard the tremulous song of a chaffinch.

The Kings Road and the railway system were the main supply lines used by the allies for men and materials. This was the Artois district of the Western front line. The continuous movement of men and wagons on roads and on railways went on 24 hours a day.

Keeping to the road verges for safety, Donna was passed by horse-drawn wagons, nose to tail, going northwards to the railway stock yards, to be loaded up with everything from sides of meat to shells. He could easily have got a lift from any of the transport going in his direction, but he preferred to walk the mile back to the camp. For a little while longer he wasn't subject to orders and could enjoy a degree of freedom before he reported back to the converted farm buildings at Vieille Chapelle near Richbourg.

At 'A' Company office he learned that Major Wright had been promoted to Lieutenant Colonel and was the new commanding officer of the battalion. There were new faces in the camp, men recruited in Britain and sent to France to replace men killed and missing in action. Most of the new men were usually quiet, not knowing what to expect in their new clean uniforms and boots. However, there were a few know-alls who had little respect for others. Private Kelly was one such, a big, broad-shouldered Scotsman who had been drafted in to 'A' Company and had found himself in the next bunk to Donna. Donna didn't care much for the new recruit, whose voice was unmistakable, even from a distance. The quiet Manchester man had met the odd so-called hard case like Kelly before.

One night the big man tried to steal one of Harper's blankets while Harper was on duty, but Donna, the army veteran and the only other man in the hut, spotted him.

"Put it back," said Donna quietly. Donna's voice gave Kelly a start. He thought he wasn't being observed. "Put it back," repeated Donna, "before he sees you!"

Kelly shook his head. "Ah wilne, ah'm nay feered o' that wee cunt."

Donna shrugged. "Suit yourself, but I know Harper. If he sees you with anything of his you're liable to wake up with yer head on yer chest."

Kelly thought for a moment, then slung the blanket back across Harper's neatly folded bunk.

Five days later the Seaforths marched at night to relieve men in trenches near Neuve Chapelle. The year was moving into summer, with its welcome warmth. Gone were the days of stinging rain and numbing cold that clamped into your very bones until your whole body ached. The days were now longer; the birds' dawn chorus usually began at 3.00am in the sparse trees along the Rue du Bois and no-man's-land.

The German barricades were about 300 yards in front of the battalion's line, but almost in the middle of no-man's-land, at about 150 yards distance, was a farmhouse. Although the structure had no roof, four walls were still standing. That night, Corporal Robb had orders to take two men and reconnoitre the building. He chose Donna and Harper.

Kelly wanted to know why Robb had chosen two Englishman for the job. "Because ye'd make too much clack with that fucking mouth of yours."

Lieutenant Robinson turned up in the trench just before midnight and briefed the three men on the aim of the venture. Their orders, as far as possible, were not to engage the Germans but to find out what they were up to and report back.

"Couldn't our artillery just blow the building to kingdom come, Sir?" asked Donna.

In the darkness of the trench the officer nodded. "Ah'm inclined to agree, but," Robinson shrugged, "orders are orders."

The night was warm. Minus insignia and armed with just a pistol and bayonet, the three, led by Robb, avoided the barbed wire and slid quietly into no-man's-land. Once in the field they spread out, with

Donna on the right, Harper in the middle and Corporal Robb on the left. They moved towards their objective. No-man's-land looked like a junk yard. It was only when they were in it and manoeuvring around the detritus that littered the ground that the diversity of the junk was identified. Apart from the smell, there were tin cans of all sizes, planks of wood, shell holes, broken wagon wheels and wire. It was a rat's paradise and also favoured by red foxes attracted by the swarms of rodents.

The three men crept forward in extended order, stopping every few yards or so to avoid the debris and listen, ready to dive flat at the first sign of detection. Ten yards from the building Corporal Robb signalled them to stop. They lay there amongst the bricks that had been blown out of the house and waited. The house looked deserted, but five minutes later two figures crept from the far side of the house. One appeared to be an N.C.O. showing the other man where he should stand guard before leaving him to his vigil. Then, from inside came the sound of shovelling.

Donna, wet with sweat, lay in the dark amongst large house stones. He reasoned that if the enemy could be heard digging they were not excavating a tunnel under the Seaforths' trenches. It was more likely that they were constructing the footings for one of their trench minen werfers, which, when concealed, could be fired through this roofless building.

Donna's next concern was how to get out of there without being spotted. It would begin to grow light in an hour. As if Robb had read the Englishman's thoughts, the corporal began to inch his body backwards towards their own lines followed by the other two men, but with all three revolvers trained on the dark outline of the German guard by the house wall. Surprisingly, they made it back to their own lines without any alarm being given. Robb reasoned that the German guard must have dozed off in the warm night, unaware of how lucky he'd been.

The next day the British artillery shelled the building and reduced it to rubble. Ten days later, on 15th July, after a beautiful day, Private Alec Love was shot during heavy rifle fire from the enemy. He'd been working with a digging party during the evening. It was his birthday. Donna was a little depressed to hear the bad news, but he didn't dwell on it. 'He obviously didn't keep his head down like I told him to,' he mused, 'but maybe it was a ricochet and the lad was just unlucky.' It didn't do for the men in the trenches to think too much about the demise of their pals because there was every chance that they could be the next one lying there blinded in the bottom of the trench with their brains splattering on the walls.

A week later the battalion was relieved by the 2nd Gurkha Regiment at 2.30am. Exhausted, they shuffled to billets outside Richbourg. Richbourg was a small village with a cluster of farm cottages, but the men preferred to go to Bethune or La Bassee, where there were more shops and attractions for troops trying to forget the privations of the trenches for a few hours. The French people of the region were mostly elderly farm workers. They were small of stature, due perhaps to in-breeding. The women were stout with flat features and all wore headscarves.

As for the French infantry, with their blue uniforms and red trousers, to Donna they seemed less co-ordinated than the British soldiers. However, he'd watched them at Ypres and in battles in the Artois and these bearded pipe-smoking Poilues were brave soldiers and never jibbed when ordered over the top. In addition, the French artillery were thought of by the British Tommy to be more reliable and had a greater rate of fire than their own field weapons.

It was only during rest periods out of the trenches that soldiers could visit the small towns and the hamlets that had shops and estaminets that sold beer, vin blanc and vin rouge. Although there was a war taking place on its soil, these French places never seemed to be short of any commodity.

Donna was partial to the French bread and always preferred it to the sawdust-tasting camp loaves. Two days before they were due to return to the trenches, Corporal Robb asked Donna if he fancied a trip to Bapaume, a little further away than Bethune on the Kings Road. Without enquiring the reason for the trip, Donna nodded. It was only when the two had hitched a lift on a lorry that Robb explained the reason. He'd received a letter from the mother of a school friend whose son had been wounded and was last heard of as being in Bapaume Military Hospital. The letter asked Robb, if it was not too much trouble, if he could enquire about her son and send her any news. It had been nearly five months since his last correspondence. The letter ended by her saying, 'Bless you James, sincerely Mrs Maciver.'

The journey was little over half an hour and as the lorry slowed down as it neared the Town Hall, the two men jumped off onto the cobbles, causing sparks to fly off their boots. The hospital looked as though it had been a grand chateau of some sort in peacetime. Now four orderlies were struggling up the stone steps with loaded stretchers. Donna and Robb helped them up and through the doors of the hospital. They were greeted with the familiar smells of carbolic and ether. Not wanting to interfere with the care of the two wounded men on the stretchers, the two kept in the background until they were approached by a small middle-aged sister.

"Can I help you Corporal?" she asked.

"Aye ma'am, we're enquiring about Private Rory Maciver, Cameron Highlanders."

"Are you a relation?"

Robb nodded. "Brother ma'am," he said, lying.

"I don't recall the name but let me check," she said and strode down one of the corridors.

Robb looked at Donna but said nothing. After a few minutes she returned carrying a piece of paper.

"You are correct Corporal. Private Maciver was treated here at the beginning of the month but was sent to a hospital in England."

"Which hospital?" asked Robb.

The sister looked at the sheet of paper.

"There are two hospitals written down here, Netley or Sidcup. Once they leave here we have little or no control where they finish up, but his type of injuries are treated at both these places."

"What are Maciver's injuries?"

"He had a severe shell wound to his superior maxilla."

Donna winced on hearing this.

"Where's that?" asked Robb

"It's a wound to his face," answered the sister.

"Thank yer for ye help," said Robb

Since coming to the hospital Donna had been hoping to catch a glimpse of the matron. Now, as the two men were about to leave, Donna couldn't wait any longer. "Is the matron about ma'am?" he asked.

The sister looked at him a little surprised and shook her head. "No, she's sleeping. We were very busy last night. Can I give her a message?"

Donna shook his head. "No, it doesn't matter," he said. Then he added, "I just wanted to thank her for the lift she gave me, that's all."

Outside, Robb was quiet as they walked, threading their way along the crowded street. Instinctively they were looking for a place to have a drink. The first café they came to had a few French soldiers inside, but it was by no means full. Donna bought a bottle of vin blanc, took a couple of glasses from the tray on the bar counter and found an empty table. The wine was sweet, but at least it was better than the anaemic beer sold in most drinking places.

"What's on yer mind?" Donna asked his friend, who, uncharacteristically, hadn't spoken much since leaving the hospital.

"Have ye ever seen a man's face hit by a shell fragment?"

Donna nodded. "Yes, when I was in the field hospital near Bethune I watched a nurse changing the dressings on a man in the Lincolns whose face had been torn away by a piece of a shell. There was just a hole where his nose and mouth had been. Poor devil, I heard later that he had committed suicide."

Robb spoke. "Ah think ah'd rather be deed. 'Tis nae wonder young Rory wilna gay home. Can nothing be done for these men?"

"The only thing they can do for these poor devils is to fix them up with face masks," said Donna. "There's a section of the artists' rifles, who, so I'm told, work with photographs of the men before they were wounded. They paint either full or half face masks made from lightweight metal. I'm told the masks are very life-like and you can hardly tell they're artificial. It allows these unfortunates some kind of life; otherwise they would never leave their homes or places of residence. They'd be too frightened and depressed to show people their faces."

"The poor cunts," muttered Robb. He gave Donna a cigarette, then said, "Tonight I'll write to Maciver's mother an' ahl jest say in ma letter that her son Rory is alive and is in either the Netley or the Sidcup hospital."

They were both becoming inebriated, so after more wine Robb became more talkative.

"Tell me Donna, why did ye no' want a commission? With yer knowledge of Urdu ye could have become an officer in one of the Indian regiments, or the Dehra Dun Brigade. They need British officers who can speak the lingo. Most of the British officers in the sepoy regiments can nay, but ah suppose ye didn't want to leave yer comrades, eh Donna?"

His friend just shrugged in response to Robb's needling.

Donna, needing air and not being a particularly talkative man at the best of times, simply said, "I think it's about time we fucked off from here Jimmy."

After relieving themselves in the primitive public lavatory out in the street they went in search of the town's market. The town markets were usually the liveliest places. Apart from stalls selling all kinds of farm produce, they attracted gypsy fortune-tellers, organ grinders and performing dogs and there was usually a little fat man selling nude postcards. Corporal Robb bought half a dozen eggs and, predictably, Donna purchased French bread from the patisserie stall. Tiring of the noise and bustle of the market, and ignoring a couple of fat prostitutes giving them the eye, the two headed back towards the main road.

As they passed a row of cottages, they came upon a stocky middle-aged French man beating up a woman who was apparently his wife. The man punched the woman until she fell down. However, the domestic argument carried on, with the man punching the woman and the woman begging for mercy. The woman's pleading was too much for Donna, who, as the man shaped to strike her again, caught the man's arm and shoved him away, causing him to stumble and fall. The reaction he got from the woman being beaten up wasn't one of gratitude. Instead, while her husband was picking himself up, she vanished into the cottage and re-appeared a minute later with a broom and proceeded to attack Donna with it, much to the amusement of corporal Robb. "That should teach ye aboot women," he said as they beat a hasty retreat.

That night Corporal Robb wrote to Rory Maciver's mother but didn't say anything about the gravity of her son's wounds. Perhaps, he hoped as he wrote, the lad's wounds were not as severe as the hospital sister had said. Robb reasoned his letter would take three or four days to reach Scotland. The army postal service was very efficient. Mail from the front was collected and sent first to the central collection centre in London, then re-directed to every part of the British Isles.

Two days later the battalion marched at night from billets in Vieille Chapelle with the 1st/39th Garhwals and relieved the 1st Leicester Regiment in trenches near Neuve Chapelle. The position the Seaforths occupied was near the junction of the Estaires and La Bassee Roads, called by the British, Port Arthur. By daylight Donna noticed that these positions were the same, more or less, that the Highlanders had held before attacking Neuve Chapelle the previous March.

Trench life in the daylight hours involved sniping, retaliatory shelling and trench repair. The hours of darkness were mainly quiet, with the men 'stood-to' or engaged in patrols into no-man's-land.

Although it was now summer, with long hours of daylight there was still the problem of waterlogged trenches and feet that were hardly ever dry. The Germans' elevated positions were less affected by the low-lying water table that drained through the British positions. More British and Indian soldiers were casualties of the brutal winter conditions than of the enemy's bullets.

Donna's malaise had returned since going back into the line. The first signs of trench fever were a chronic cough, a pale skin and weakness, the cough often developing into pneumonia or pleurisy. Donna had the symptoms but the M.O.'s treatment was always the same – give the patient two big white pills and tell them to report sick once out of the line.

In early September Donna received a letter from Tizzie saying that another cousin of theirs, John Kershaw, who lived in Gorton Street near the school, had joined the army. She also said that the Wiener's grocery shop had had its windows broken despite a notice displayed in the window saying that they were naturalised British subjects. Tizzie gave him more bad news about a train crash in Gretna Green where 250 people had died. The casualties were mostly soldiers returning from leave.

A week later, after being relieved into billets at the La Gorque camp, it was noticeable that in the mornings the temperature dropped and there was a thick mist before the sun rose. It was obvious from the changing colours of the trees that autumn had already arrived and in a couple of months the countryside would be white with frost.

Donna's weak condition had hardly changed and he wrote to his sister saying how he dreaded the cold that froze the very marrow. He also added that he doubted whether he would survive another French winter unless he could get unlimited supplies of Gurkha rum. This last line was meant as a joke, but he honestly didn't think his body could last another winter in France. The battalion's strength was now less than half, due mostly to the mauling it had endured since the previous October.

Now, having been promised an extended rest period, it was clear this wasn't to be the case. After a couple of days' rest and delousing, the remnants of the battalion practised bayonet drill, thrusting to the throat and soft vulnerable parts of the body, as well as imitation bomb throwing. The billets at the La Gorque Camp were in woodland off the Kings Road, a road that, despite the hastily filled-in potholes, was continually choked with columns of British, French and Indian soldiers, together with transports of ammunition, guns and horses, and had been for weeks. The over-zealous military police didn't help, always demanding authorisation, which only added to the congestion. The troops of cavalry were hardly able to move. These vast numbers of men and equipment were all going the same way – south.

It was obvious to Donna and the rest that a big offensive was about to begin. But where? The answer came a week later when the Seaforths were back near their old positions facing the Germans at a crossroads at Port Arthur. At first light came the constant rumble of field guns a couple of miles distant. It came from the mining village of Loos, with its high pithead winding gear and slagheaps. The land sloped around the ruined miners' houses, causing any rain to drain and gather in pools at the lower terrain.

October was cold and it brought the rain. It rained nearly every day. After ten days the battalion was relieved at midnight but found it almost impossible to march to their billets at La Gorque because of the many horse and motorised ambulances filled with wounded coming from Loos.

At La Gorque the camp orderlies, as well as preparing hot water for the baths, had made fires for the huts. There had been rumours that the battalion would not see another winter in France. This was finally confirmed by Sergeant Cooper, which cheered Donna up no end. It was the answer to a prayer. The move couldn't come soon enough for the Englishman.

After the usual hot baths and clean up, the armoury sergeant overhauled both battalion machine guns, whilst as usual, out of the line each soldier was responsible for his "best friend" (his rifle). At La Gorque 'A' Company received 25 reinforcements. The efforts of Sergeant Mullins and Lance Corporal Conroy, the company cooks, were much appreciated. There seemed to be plenty of meat, potatoes and tasty stew, until it was realised that the battalion was under-strength and had drawn rations for a full complement of men. Before going back in the trenches they had an open-air church service.

In driving rain, the depleted ranks took over the trenches from the 2nd Leicesters in front of the Rue du Bois about half a mile from the village of Neuve Chapelle. The Rue du Bois had once been a wood of elm and poplar trees by the roadside. Now the trees were stunted and splintered. The constant rain caused the water level in the trenches to rise steadily. Attempts to drain the water by digging channels off the communicating trenches had little effect as long as the rain continued. It didn't take long before the duckboards were awash.

At 5.30 in the morning the Germans sent over a heavy bombardment on 'A' Company's trenches using small minen werfers. 'A' Company retaliated to these trench mortars by throwing bombs and rapid rifle fire. The bombardment by the Germans petered out to silence, but was replaced by shouts of 'Bastard tommies, nicht gute bastards' from the enemy trenches, answered with interest almost immediately from the 1st Seaforths.

October was wet and cold and the days short. By 4.30 in the afternoon it was quite dark, and from the enemy's sap trenches came the glow and smell of wood fires across no-man's-land. Sometimes at this time of the day the Germans sent over what the British called their "evening serenade", three or four shells just to let the British know they were still in residence. The Royal Artillery, dug in behind the front line, often replied with their own "musical interlude".

The First Indian Army, including the Dehra Dun Brigade, the 7th Meerat Division, the 1st Seaforth Highlanders and half a battalion of the 1st Leicester regiment, had landed in France over a year ago. Donna felt bitter returning to trenches in farmland around Neuve Chapelle. He felt that way because going into the line and returning to billets in La Gorque, the battalion had to pass acres of wooden crosses off the Armentières road. Donna knew Campbell and others from 'A' Company would be buried there. Eight months ago, during the battle for Neuve Chapelle, brave British and Indian soldiers from the Indian 1st Army, together with other British regiments, had overrun the German lines and chased the enemy back over two and a half miles to Aubers. Now, to be occupying more or less the same trenches with hardly any gains was, to the Manchester man, a betrayal of some of the finest men who had ever lived. Donna remembered that after the battle of Neuve Chapelle he saw rows and rows of corpses laid side by side, some minus body parts such as heads, arms and legs, and thought at the time of the heavy price they had paid. Now it was as if these wooden crosses and Indian headstones were watching as men marched past in columns of four.

To add to this presence, the wind moaned as it swirled about the graves in a kind of sorrowful lament.

Donna respected his own regiment's officers, with one or two exceptions, but he had no regard for the British High Command. On the battlefield he'd witnessed and took part in hopeless situations that had no chance of success. Nevertheless, men had gone to their certain deaths in no-man's-land against overwhelming odds and with inadequate artillery support just to appease General Joffre and his French staff, who believed the sacrifice of British soldiers would relieve pressure on their own men. However, he condemned Field Marshall Haig most of all for toadying to Joffre, knowing that seven out of every ten of his soldiers would be casualties.

On 2nd November the battalion marched from billets and relieved the 2nd Leicesters in front of the Rue du Bois. Because of traffic on the road the changeover took until 9.30am. The trenches at the Rue du Bois contained one and a half feet of water, which was continually rising.

During the quiet periods, men not 'stood-to' either slept or worked, repairing and improving the trench and deepening the dugouts. Soldiers usually gave these dugouts names of brothels or posh hotels. However, life in the trenches day after day, month after month, was a matter of survival, not only from a bullet or a shell but also from the climate. For some ordinary soldiers the relentless shelling caused mental breakdowns, later to be diagnosed as 'Shell Shock'. The High Command initially considered this as malingering, although officers with the same condition were dealt with more sympathetically, as evidenced by the treatment of the war poets Siegfried Sassoon and Wilfred Owen.

Donna was content in the knowledge that if he managed to keep his head down and stay alive, it would be the last time for him in the trenches of France. Seven days later the Seaforth Highlanders returned to billets to mobilise and prepare to leave the stricken land. The 19th Dehra Dun Brigade and 7th Meerat Division of the 1st Indian Army would leave with them.

At Le Touret Camp, weapons, clothing and equipment was inspected, transport overhauled, and horses and mules re-shod and loaded with supplies for four days. At 6.00am on the morning of 23rd November, the battalion paraded in light rain on the pot-holed road en route for Liller Railway Station nine miles away in Pas de Calais. As the columns moved forward and their ammunition boots slogged the cobbles, there was no talk, no banter. Loaded transports drawn by mules and horses nodded in unison like fairground dobbie horses as the battalion marched north west.

At 8.45am the column arrived at Liller Station, where a train stood bellowing clouds of steam. Written on the straw-strewn trucks in chalk were the words in French, '20 hommes ou 8 chevaux'. The trucks smelt of horse dung, leather and oil. Having got the battalion's transport wagons secured to the flat transporters, the rations for the journey were issued to each truck. Hot tea was to be made during the convenience stops. But the march from the billets at Le Touret had depleted almost all of Donna's strength. He barely made the last half mile. Declining a game of cards, he gazed for a while at the French countryside as it slid past, then fell asleep.

Hours later, as the slow train now travelling south drew to a stop at Arras Station, Donna waited on the platform for his turn for rations but found that the boisterous Kelly had not only eaten his own but Donna's food also. Hunger made the Manchester man furious. Though weak and debilitated, he hit Kelly on the point of the big man's chin. The right-hander knocked the Scotsman flat on his back and hurt Donna's own hand in process.

Donna didn't go hungry that night, though. Some of the other soldiers in the truck gave him part of their rations of bread, cheese and jam. It was cold travelling through the French countryside at night, but once the upper split doors were closed it was quite warm from the heat of the men inside.

Donna didn't trust Kelly not to try something to even up the score if he thought Donna was asleep. But it was an offence to eat another man's rations and the big man had no real complaint. As the train clanked and swayed through the crisp night his eyes were heavy; he closed them just for an instant. He opened them with a start to find it was daylight, but he felt much better.

Two days later, at 7.00pm, the train finally crawled into Marseilles docks. Lined up at the quayside was a flotilla of transport ships. At 9.15pm the 1st Battalion Seaforth Highlanders began to board His Majesty's transport ship Lake Manitoba. To save space, improvised bulkhead racks and hammocks were slung above and below the decks.

The men were issued with pith helmets and spine pads. Other tropical equipment would be distributed once the troopship was under way. Donna's weakness was beginning to subside, which he put down to the sea air. He knew he would have to face Kelly again. He'd heard from members of other regiments how bad blood had been resolved during an action, where one or the other protagonist had finished up with a bullet in the back. Better to face him now. The following day Donna waited for Kelly to go on deck. Then, making sure Kelly had his back to the ship's rail, he confronted him. If Kelly proved too much for the Manchester man to handle, Donna's plan was to push the bastard over the ship's side.

"How are you feeling today?" asked Donna in a measured, casual voice.

"Ye shouldna 'av' hit me," said Kelly, sullenly, rubbing a bruise on his chin with his thumb.

"You shouldn't have eaten my rations."

"Ah'v' a brother in 'D' Company who's bigga than me and he'll deal wi' ye when ah tell him."

Donna nodded by way of a reply, then moved away. He didn't think he'd have any further trouble from the big fellow.

Below decks Lieutenant Colonel Wright and his aide were going over manifests and battalion strengths. The regiment had arrived from India the previous October with 23 officers and 873 other ranks. Now, on the eve of departure, they discovered only three officers and 226 men had survived from the original complement.

After three days of re-supplying, the Lake Manitoba was ready to sail. At 12.45am on Sunday 28th November 1915, two tugs nudged her to the harbour mouth. At 1.00am the H.M.T. Lake Manitoba, with all lights blacked out, sailed for Toulon harbour, where she joined other ships of the convoy. With a French destroyer as escort, the line of transports set forth. The battalion's destination was Mesopotamia.

Postscript

On 8th January 1916, in the battalion's first action against the Turks, Donna's great friend Corporal James Robb was shot in the throat at Sheikh Saad. Despite Donna's efforts to staunch the bleeding, he died in his arms. In France the same year, his cousin John Foggaty was killed in action and received the Military Medal posthumously. The following year, his brother Richard died holding up a Turkish advance by throwing Mills bombs and killing 40 of the enemy. He was recommended by his sergeant for the Victoria Cross, but this was refused and Richard, a corporal, was awarded the Military Medal posthumously instead. Donna's mother died soon after Richard was killed.

Donna survived the Great War, although the years of privation and hardship had taken a heavy toll on his health, so much so that after the war he spent a year in Parkfield Military Hospital in Manchester.

On his release from hospital, in a period of high unemployment, he went back to Collyhurst and married Margaret Stringer. They lived at 5 Bebbington Street, which ran at right angles to the River Irk. The house, like all the other dwellings in the area, was infested with vermin. In 1920, after passing a written examination and lowering his age by two years, Donna managed to get a job as a postman.

In 1940, at the beginning of World War Two, he volunteered for the army, but his application was rejected.

He and his wife had nine children. In 1954 he retired from the Post Office and in 1971 died a widower, aged 79, still carrying in his body the bullet he received in action at Aubers Ridge.

'Little Apples Will Grow Again' is a true story. James Donna was my father. I have used the name Donna and changed the names of one or two others for convenience. In his ten years' service as a soldier the only objects my father kept were his brother Richard's Military Medal and the sporran belonging to James Robb (10091, enlisted Elgin 1906). When my father died the medal and the sporran became revered objects in my family's possessions and were passed on to the next person for safe-keeping when that member of the family died.

My uncle Richard's Military Medal and Corporal Robb's sporran have been in my keeping for over 20 years now, but if by chance any of Corporal James Robb's descendants happen to read my narrative and wish to claim the sporran, I would be happy to return it to its ain folk.

I am sure my father would have agreed to this.

Ramon Towers, 2009

Glossary

Assalam Alaikum	Hello
Alaikum Salam	Return greeting of hello
Baawarchi	Cook
Bandook	Rifle
British 18/28-pounder artilery	Size of shell fired by the British
Char wallah	Tea man/boy
Chapatti	Wholemeal bread
Dhobi wallah	Laundry man
Dulali	Mad/ crazy
Estaminet	Liquor bar
French 75s	75 millimetre shell fired by French artillery
Gunfire tea	Tea minus milk and sugar
Jack Johnsons	Huge German high velocity shell emitting much black smoke.
Khuds	Hills
Kunda' ha'fiz	Goodbye
Oberleutnant	Lieutenant
Minen werfer	German trench mortar
Mistry wallah	Watch maker
Muscleman	Member of Indian hill tribe
Pankah wallah	Fan man
Pour les pauvre	For the poor
Patisserie	Cake/bread shop
R.I.M.S.	Royal Indian Marine Ship
Stabsunteroffizier	Corporal
Salient	Bulge in the trench line that juts out nearer the enemy.
Sassenach	English person
Sepoy	Indian soldier
Sigri	Fire/ stove
S.I.W.	Self-inflicted wound
Whizz bangs	German artillery shells